PN Review 240

VOLUME 44   NUMBER 4   MARCH–APRIL 2018

ON THE COVER
Hannah Bagshaw, 'Pink Half' (acrylic on paper, 59 x 44.5 cm),
2016, hannahbagshaw.com
Curator: Valgerður Þóroddsdóttir.

Editorial

In *PNR* 240 we print the first *PN Review* Prize-winning poems (Poetry and Translation), along with the commended poems. The range and quality of work we received confirms that there is a place for such prizes, allowing one poem and one translation by each participating poet, and affirming that translation can be a primary poetic activity.

We also include a supplement celebrating our long-standing contributor Peter Scupham, on the occasion of his eighty-fifth birthday, pen in hand, inventing and reinventing his work. He has elevated the art of the poetry envelope, popular since the publication of Emily Dickinson's, to a new level with his variegated satirical approach. His annotated book lists (he is a bookseller, too) bring the descriptive bibliographic catalogue into the realm of diary, memoir and high comedy. His mastery of traditional form frees him to experiment and invent 'the selves we have become', as he says in 'A Birthday Triptych', the poem he contributed, with a fine proleptic instinct, to *Poetry Nation 1* (1973). His most recent *PNR* contribution is a review welcoming a first collection by Alex Wong (*PNR* 235, 2017). Over half his adult life he has been with us at *PN Review*, at the heart of things. Among his contributions was a series of seventeen 'Shelf Lives', reminding readers of work by poets who had not (and some still have not) received their due for the pleasure they give and the resources they add to poetry. Connections and continuities: he writes for readers willing to be alive to past and future as well as the present.

Poetry is not 'a broad church'. It is not a place of relativities but of stable values, even when times and genres change. The art of reading poetry, too, develops. Reading can require effort, study. The rewards are considerable.

I have been manoeuvring my way around the elephant in the room, the subject of the letters in this issue of *PN Review*: Hollie McNish, one of the writers discussed in 'The Cult of the Noble Amateur' by Rebecca Watts in *PN Review* 239. Jack Baker's letter is succinct and merits a place in the editorial to this issue.

Rebecca Watts's detractors are attempting to turn an argument about critical integrity into an argument about identity. Hence the predictable jibes – in blogs, tweets, and Facebook posts – that Watts is white, and 'middle class', and went to Cambridge. These charges are calculated not merely to prejudice, but to preclude, critical discussion. They force those damned as 'elitist' to advance their case in the face of scurrilous insinuation: as Watts herself did, with admirable patience, on Radio 4's *Front Row*.

A familiar schism: aesthetics versus ethics. But might it be time to engage the populists on their own terms? What, precisely, is virtuous in the claim that the art is a transparent extension of the artist, or in the related assumption that the most valuable service of literature is to flatter our class-bound, race-bound or time-bound assumptions? The champions of Rupi Kaur and Hollie McNish are perfectly free to wish their poetry 'accessible' – a term usefully glossed by Jonathan

Meades as 'comprehensible to morons' – but they also lay claim to be defending a moral good. This delusion should not go unchallenged.

PNR 239 was published in mid-December. In mid-January the social and national media suddenly responded, as if choreographed to do so. Hollie McNish, already the subject of several features in the *Guardian*, a BBC writer and presenter, author of four books (the last from Picador), responded on-line.[1] *The World At One* (BBC Radio 4), the *Guardian*, the *Telegraph*, the *Times Literary Supplement* and the *Bookseller* sprang to attention. What seemed to be at issue was that a young critic had drawn attention to the *quality* of poetry the media were celebrating. Only *Front Row* (BBC 4) invited a response from the upstart critic.

McNish's reputation is rooted in the social media. Her wounded response was bound to land *PNR* in a bed of barbed tweets, short sharp messages with which even those of us not at home with Twitter have grown familiar from the current White House's practice. McNish took Watts's article, reprinted it in full, peppered with her objections and injuries. Her disingenuous, piecemeal response avoided the issues raised (of cultural appropriation, for example), and finessed her own educational background to make her seem more like her devoted readers.

Criticism of her work she takes personally because she writes about herself. She explains of one piece: 'It's interesting when someone guesses your intentions for a poem. In reality, this poem was the least thought through of the entire collection and was written as a commission for a TV series about a detective which I wrote to a piece of music in about ten minutes. I decided to include it at the last minute because it felt right for how I felt placed between two poems – one about the death of my grandma and one about the death of a friend. But yes, maybe it is also a crap poem but I am still interested in our obsession with murder mysteries and the likes.'

The controversy has demonstrated how 'the establishment' (media, commercial publishers, the book trade) accepts and privileges performance and social media poetry as 'democratic', 'accessible' and on the whole preferable to 'dusty old books', a phrase repeated almost as often as 'a broad church'. The Picador editor, who once lectured against such writing, has had a road to Damascus experience. The trade media applaud poetry that puts money in tills. The poets and their advocates can no longer claim to be counter-cultural outsiders: they have taken the palace and command the traditional media high ground as well as the social media, Twitter and Instagram. They want to take control of critical discourse. There is no arguing with facts: in 2015, McNish's YouTube videos notched up 4.1 million views. Her collaborations with Kate Tempest and George the Poet were popular.

---

1 (www.holliepoetry.com/2018/01/21/pn-review/)

BBC Radio 4 *Woman's Hour* broadcast a seven-part radio documentary series hosted by McNish entitled *Becoming a Mother: A Hot Cup of Tea with Hollie McNish*.

Twitter and Facebook responses, however, differed radically. On Twitter, name-calling. On Facebook, discussion, even-handed, and respect for dusty old books, for criticism and evaluation. A reader, disappointed with bad work whose apotheosis in the marketplace crowds out other kinds of writing and devalues (for new readers) the art itself, might be thought to have a responsibility to speak out. In 1975 Octavio Paz, under considerable polit-ical pressure to conform to the nostrums of the day, described what as editor of his magazine *Plural* he believed his task to be. 'We wanted to reintroduce – against monologue and clamouring, those twin aberrations – the rational word, the critical word, which is always two-sided because it implies a questioner. We know of course that criticism cannot, by itself, produce good literature. That is not, in any case, its mission. On the other hand, we know that it alone can create that space – physical, intellectual, moral – in which a literature can evolve.'

News & Notes

Medellín · The annual Medellín Poetry Festival, now in its twenty-eighth year and one of the most popular and celebrated gatherings of its kind in the world, may be in peril of collapse. It has long been dependent on the Colombian Ministry of Culture. The Festival organisers have been advised that their grant for the year ($260,000,000 or about £65,000) will not be awarded because they failed to complete the application forms correctly or completely (a technical issue, the Ministry's website insists), but also perhaps because, with the understandable hubris that can characterise popular and successful operations who grow impatient with the bureaucracies that provide them with funding, it never crossed their minds that rejection was possible. The Ministry said that the application omitted the 'social impact' assessment, even though the Ministry itself carried out an impact study last July which showed that, each year, the Festival has a direct impact on 45,000 people, and an indirect impact world wide. It is a matter of record that, in its early years, it helped change the culture of Medellín in the wake of the Pablo Escobar cartel years. The organisers suspect the Ministry of unspecified chicanery. They vowed to fight on. Discussions are in progress even as this issue of *PN Review* goes to press. Fernando Rendón, the long-time festival director, recalled that the event has over time brought more than one thousand six hundred poets from one hundred and seventy countries to his country, providing enormous, enthusiastic and informed audiences. The show, he insists, will go on.

Man Booker · More than thirty publishers signed a letter asking the Man Booker Prize organisers to reconsider their 2014 decision to allow American authors to be submitted. Their concern about a 'homogenised literary future' was borne out by last year's shortlist. There is also the issue that the great American prizes are not open to Anglophone authors from other nations. Some poetry publishers were wondering whether a similar case should be made for the major British poetry awards. The Booker letter declares: 'The rule change, which presumably had the intention of making the prize more global, has in fact made it less so, by allowing the dominance of Anglo-American writers at the expense of others; and risks turning the prize, which was once a brilliant mechanism for bringing the world's English-language writers to the attention of the world's biggest English-language market, into one that is no longer serving the readers in that market...'

Helen Dunmore · Helen Dunmore's final poetry collection before her death *Inside The Wave* (Bloodaxe) received the Costa Poetry Award and the major Costa Prize. Poet, novelist and children's writer, Dunmore lived and died in Bristol. She was sixty four when she died of cancer last year. The Costa judges called the book, 'an astonishing set of poems' and 'a final, great achievement', praising her 'spare, eloquent lyricism' which explores the 'underworld and the human, living world'.

Paul Muldoon · Paul Muldoon has been awarded the Queen's Gold Medal for Poetry 2017. He won the Pulitzer Prize for Poetry in 2003.

Richard Murphy · *Mary O'Malley writes:* The poet Richard Murphy has died in Sri Lanka at the age of ninety. He belonged to that great Anglo-Irish poetic tradition exemplified by Yeats. He spoke beautifully, and wrote in 'a voice that hungers for authority and yearns to make people and things, which are sure to vanish, last in verbal granite'.

'I wanted to write about the sea', he told me, 'so I bought a boat'. The boat was a Galway hooker, and when she was repaired he began running a small business carrying passengers to Inis Boffin, earning his living on 'the ribald face of a mad mistress', as he wrote in his first collection. *Sailing to an Island*, published by Faber in 1963, included the celebrated poems 'The Philosopher and the Birds' and 'The Cleggan Disaster'.

His long poem 'The Battle Of Aughrim' was commissioned by the BBC and first broadcast in 1963. Among the readers were C. Day Lewis and Ted Hughes.

The music was composed by Sean O Riada. Its structure was an influence on the long poetic sequences of Montague and Heaney and it is among the finest long poems in English of the past century. Out of the tension of his Irish-English ancestry and the competing voices of his personal history, Murphy crafted a poem that satisfied his own ambition, 'to build a poem that will be beyond repair'.

Like many of the Anglo-Irish, Richard was obsessed with houses and renovation, an activity he turned into poetry in the sonnet sequence 'The Price of Stone', in which he ventriloquised fifty buildings, including an Oxford College, an industrial school and a monk's cell on High Island.

He parted company with Faber after the then editor refused to include the sequence 'The God Who Eats Corn' in what became *New Selected Poems*, and moved to Bloodaxe in 1989 for the publication of 'The Mirror Wall'. Lilliput Press has published a selection of his poems from 1952–1912.

Bobi Jones · *Meic Stephens writes:* Bobi Jones died in Aberystwyth on 22 November, aged 88. He was by far the most prolific of all Welsh writers in the twentieth century. Poet, short story writer, novelist, literary critic, scholar and polemicist, he published a long shelf of books that reflected his passionate nature, his erudition in the fields of linguistic and literary theory, and his religious belief, which was profoundly Calvinistic and Evangelical.

His collected poems were published in three substantial volumes, two of which had the title *Canu Arnaf* ('Singing about myself'). His distinctive voice could be heard from the start: his work struck a note of insolent innocence, spurning common usage and creating a cascade of fresh, often incongruous images – God in trousers – that baffled some readers. In an early poem he announced, *'Angau, rwyt ti'n fy ofni fi'* ('Death, you're afraid of me'). His poems are a celebration of 'a new Adam' who has discovered love, the Welsh language and the natural world all at once. He enjoyed his reputation as an *enfant terrible* who upset many an applecart, thereby offending some of the staider figures in the literary establishment.

His later work is mostly concerned with love for his wife and family, his country and people, but it also refers to the years he spent in Africa, Canada and Mexico. In the anti-epic poem *Hunllef Arthur* ('Arthur's dream'), which at twenty-one thousand lines has the distinction of being one of the longest poems in the Welsh language, he explores the mythologies of Wales with reference to its contemporary state. Making no concession to popular taste, which he scorned, Bobi stretched the reader unfamiliar with modern trends in ways many have found daunting.

Almost as if one name was not enough to contain his prodigious talent, he also wrote prose as Robert Maynard Jones, especially works of linguistic theory and literary criticism. While Professor of Welsh at the University College of Wales, Aberystwyth, he published some two dozen works of literary history and fiction which are among the most erudite, not to say difficult, in the language. This prodigious energy, thought by some to be hyperactive but said by the writer to be 'the least I can do in the circumstances', showed no sign of abating. A selection of his poems was translated by Joseph P. Clancy in 1987. In his last years, beset by ill health and nothing daunted by the poor sales of his books, he published whole collections of new poems and essays on the world wide web. His devotion to the poet's craft and vocation was exemplary.

Landeg White · *Peter Pegnall writes:* Landeg White (1940–2017) was composed of apparent contradictions: an audacious scholar, a restrained hedonist, a rational romantic, nomadic home-builder. He could be fascinating; he could be interminable. These qualities emerge as fully in his work as they do in his life, as anyone unfortunate enough not to have known him will find in *Living in the Delta: New and Collected Poems* (Parthian 2015).

He is likely to best known for his translation of Camões's great epic, *The Lusiads* (Oxford 2001), a formidable task, pursued and delivered with love: he maintains a more or less seamless ottava rima throughout the journey, at times achieving a luscious sensuality, at others rumbustious aggression. The buccaneer protagonist sets off with warning voices haunting his departure and returns to a very insecure native land. One of his very fine, reflective lyric poems touches with proper modesty on parallels between translator and anti-hero:

I'm still wondering about Camões, having
myself (to compare great things with small)
been seduced overseas by visions of home
as a place where matters were better organised
and returned to the grim reality. Thatcher
was not unlike Sebastian...
   (Poetry of Verandas.)

He arrived in England from Zambia in 1979, to direct the Centre for Southern African Studies at the University of York; he was joined there by his lifelong friend, Jack Mapanje, whose release from prison in Malawi Landeg had largely masterminded and effected. To witness the two together in recent years was rather like observing semi-retired thoroughbreds, still capable of more than a canter in politics, poetry and fine Douro wines.

Fidelity to people and places was a central aspect of the man's way of life, he fully recognised the importance of trust and humility, the negligible place of ego in professional and personal life. Take, for example, this beautiful, brief, ars poetica:

[...] my job's to find
a style so transparent you don't
hear any voice of mine shouting
Look at Me, just the depths gleaming
without a ripple to refract the art.

But he could also be stubborn, defiant. In the brilliantly titled 'When Paul Celan Met Heidegger' he cuts to the chase with lethal accuracy:

I write in praise of the canine hybrid
that claims its space by hoisting
a leg, no matter who planted the lamppost.

Impossible to write of Landeg without marking his devotion to his sons, John and Martin, and, above all, to his beloved wife Alice. She was sometimes an amused, dissenting voice, at others utterly supportive. They were so close in mind, spirit and body that these lines are almost too painful to read. But they remain. It is high time for real recognition of his work in these islands:

and my heart kicks at the thought of the message
that must one day far too early come

about her to me or about me to her
in no pidgin I will understand or signs
in any way bearable.
    ('Just fine')

Sarah Maguire · The poet Sarah Maguire died of cancer in November 2017 at the age of sixty. She was also a translator. She trained as a gardener, and her work was inspired by this discipline, about which she knew as a practitioner and a student. Her four collections of poetry were *Spilt Milk* (1991), *The Invisible Mender* (1997), *The Florist's at Midnight* (2001) and *The Pomegranates of Kandahar* (2007). She travelled to Palestine and Yemen and became a noted translator of Darwish, Zaqtan and others. She founded (2004) and directed the Poetry Translation Centre. Her own poems were translated into Arabic by Saadi Yousef and published there, a rare accolade for a British (woman) writer. In a moving obituary in the *Guardian*, Kate Clanchy noted: 'Establishing the PTC took tenacity, vision and great generosity of time. Sarah proved herself equally generous, as she coped with characteristic frankness with her final illness, in letting go.'

Nicanor Parra · After Pablo Neruda, Nicanor Parra (born in 1914) was Chile's great modern poet. His earlier poems and 'anti-poems' have been familiar to English readers since the mid-1960s (they were first published in the mid-1950s, and his first book in 1938) when his work became available in translation. He told the *New York Times* in 1964, 'When there is humor, irony, sarcasm, when the author is making fun of himself and so of humanity, then the author is not singing but telling a story — that is an anti-poem.' There was something refreshing about the work's corrective scale, its humour and unpretentious tone, after the large, sometimes excessive gestures of his friend Neruda. Anti-poetry became a kind of movement and spread well beyond Chile. Given his, and Neruda's politics, it was a tribute and an irony that his death was announced by Michelle Bachelet, President of Chile.

Parra trained as a mathematician and physicist (pursuing his studies in the United States and Oxford). His day job for many years was teaching theoretical physics at the University of Chile. His approach to the language of poetry was initially lateral, through slang, cliché and imitated speech. There was a strong democratic bias in his diction and his prosody, and insistence on staying close to the voices he heard. This was accompanied by a lack of interest in his own mere subjectivity. The poems can be deeply moving, but more by their language and what they reveal of the world than by calculation and rhetorical design. Poems should talk first and sing, if they must, later.

Other deaths reported include:
- At eighty-five, the great Israeli novelist and writer Aharon Appelfeld (Gabriel Josipovici will contribute a memoir to *PN Review*.)
- At seventy-nine, Keorapetse Kgositsile, the South African poet and activist whose work linked his country's struggle with the Black Arts Movement in the United States
- At ninety, the leading Urdu poet Rasa Chughtai
- At ninety-four, the Israeli 'national poet', journalist and film-maker Haim Gouri
- At ninety-four, the Salvadorean/Nicaraguan writer Claribel Alegría, recipient last year of the Queen Sofia Award for Poetry, the major Latin American poetry prize
- At eighty-nine, Yu Guangzhong, the Chinese/Taiwanese poet exiled in his teens when his family went into exile in 1949, and never quite at home in exile: 'China is me I am China' he wrote in 1966; 'Nostalgia is a coastline, a shallow strait. / I, on this side, / The mainland, on the other.'

Votes for Women! · A century ago women secured the right to vote at thirty, and ninety years ago to vote at the same age as men. In Ireland, the struggle for equality continues. The issue is cultural, less a question of entitlement than of fairness. Equality does not mean parity but it does mean resistance to inbuilt prejudices which are buttressed by institutions and by special pleading. The recent issue of the exclusion of women from the National Theatre recalls the concerns surrounding the *Field Day Anthology*. And now they surround the *Cambridge Companion to Irish Poets* edited by (the poet) Professor Gerald Dawe of Trinity College, Dublin.

The book has given rise to a movement called FIRED! Irish Women Poets and the Canon, which is setting out 'to redress the gender imbalance in Irish poetry'. The imbalance is less in the poetry than in its critical perception and reception, its representation in the media, at festivals, in publishing, in critical consideration, and the failure to represent women *as critics*. The Cambridge volume has just four female contributors out of thirty essayists. Only four women poets are seriously considered – Eiléan Ní Chuilleanáin, Eavan Boland, Medbh McGuckian and Nuala Ní Dhomhnaill – and twenty six male writers from the seventeenth- to the twenty-first centuries.

This insistence that women be included as critics and as authors, to assess and be assessed, in the wider sphere is not a question of special pleading. It is a demand that the changes secured in the political sphere be reflected in the cultural sphere. As such it seems unexceptionable and commendable. Exceptional women critics working in the area of poetry, and not only or exclusively on women's writing, are working throughout the Anglophone world. 'For women who write professionally,' the report says, 'comes the realisation that omission on such an academic level remains a fact of life.'

This magazine is at fault. It has itself been criticised for publishing fewer female than male poets and critics, a balance we continually try to redress through commissioning new work and encouraging new writers to submit, and the record is clearly improving. The long-desired outcome, which in our view must be achieved without 'quotas', and which might in time result in some issues carrying a majority of women contributors, is still a way off, but the quest continues. The quest in particular is for writers who have critical and creative integrity and who do not deploy special pleading, not wanting to be patronised or in their writing to patronise others.

Letters

NATALIE TELIER *writes* • I am writing to you about the recent review of the work of Hollie McNish by Rebecca Watts in your journal. I am a long-term fan of *PN Review* and usually love the incisive writing, excellent selection of poetry and its promotion of diversity. On this occasion, however, I was extremely perturbed. The debate about the validity of a range of poetries – and how poetry should be defined – is both necessary and important. I applaud the courage of tackling this difficult topic in print. There were two areas, however, that caused me concern. The first was the use of the term 'pathological'. This is a term with a very specific meaning: to (mis-)apply it to a poet in this way diminishes the work of all in the mental health profession and all those who battle with genuine pathologies – either their own or within the family. Let us not forget also that the question of the correct application of the term 'pathology' has taken on huge resonance in respect to its use for – arguably – the world's most important leader. It is not a term to be used lightly, nor is a comparison with said leader. The second area of concern was the description of the poet's readers as the 'uneducated class'. Quite apart from the fact that I do not believe the readers of a particular poet should be under review (surely it is more useful to engage with the text?), this is the kind of class commentary that displays an equal level of prejudice as overt racism or misogyny. I do not believe any of these belong in a poetry review.

WILL HARRIS *writes* • I'm a fellow of The Complete Works, an Arts Council-funded programme that has sought to develop the writing of poets from BAME (Black, Asian, Minority Ethnic) backgrounds. Why did it choose to foreground poets of colour? Because ten years ago fewer than one percent of poets published by major presses were from minority ethnic backgrounds, despite at least fourteen percent of the population being non-white. Even now, the work of these poets is massively under-represented in prize shortlists, reviews and amongst reviewers themselves (as highlighted by the research of Dave Coates). So is it really true, as Rebecca Watts suggests in her recent article in *PN Review*, that the media is 'terrified of being seen to criticise the output of anyone it imagines is speaking on behalf of a group traditionally under-represented in the arts'? Given that silence is the usual response, the terror seems to be Watts's own.

When I started writing – against a literary background as white as a ski slope – a big problem was just imagining myself as a writer. Watts quotes T. S. Eliot: 'the people which ceases to care for its literary inheritance becomes barbaric'. But 'the people' that care too much for their literary inheritance – or their version of it – can come to treat anything outside of it as 'barbaric'. I remember that feeling of being on the outside and knowing that, if I wanted entry, I would have to speak like an insider. This was where craft came in. Craft, according to Watts, is about 'technical and intellectual accomplishments'. It's all too clear, though, that technique and intellect can't be separated from their political and social contexts. A

culture predicated on exclusion will create an exclusionary literary culture. For a long time, and this article continues the trend, craft has acted as the bulwark – the beautiful excuse – for dismissing work by socially marginal voices. Behind its technical veneer lies an implicit threat: adapt to the rules of 'literary inheritance' or face exclusion.

There is an irony to this line of argument. Watts cites Sylvia Plath (all of her approving examples, I should add, are white), who Harold Bloom once attacked for her guileless and over-emotional verse, saying: 'Poetry relies upon trope and not upon sincerity'. Sound familiar? Then, as now, the espousal of craft grants entry, while 'sincerity' or honesty (Watts's preferred term) bars the way. Perhaps this has something to do with the nature of those experiences being written about? I don't know if the work of Hollie McNish and Kate Tempest – whose work Watts takes issue with – will be read alongside that of Sylvia Plath in fifty years' time, but I know that the opposition between honesty and craft is false. Worse than that, it's in bad faith. It converts one person's taste into a moral or technical fault on the part of the accused.

As with so many defences of inheritance and tradition, Watts's essay also strikes a constantly fearful note. Peeking through the crenels of Fortress Craft, she seems scared at the prospect of it being overrun by youths with funny accents who'll tear up the Shakespeare and Eliot. More terrifyingly, she suggests that they may already be inside, scribbling on the tablecloths and stealing all the awards. Why is no one among the 'middle-aged, middle-class' reviewing guard saying anything? I don't think it's because they're terrified; I think it's because this is a fiction. Literature doesn't need to be seen in Bloomian terms, as an arena for agonistic confrontation. Art doesn't need to be defined by exclusion. Our language isn't a prize diadem, and our role to 'safeguard' it. Whatever the case, poems will go on being made and spoken in ways exceeding any one definition of craft. And as society changes – hopefully for the better – so too will poetry. In the meantime, those who hold onto a singular idea of craft will only have succeeded in buttressing themselves against the world and the possibility of changing it.

MARILYN HACKER *writes* • There has always been one-dimensional 'popular' poetry, just as there are trashy thrillers and saccharine or titillating romances. No one thinks these latter endanger the next Toni Morrison or Salman Rushdie. Admittedly the bad popular poets used to have to know how to use meter and rhyme... but there was Rod McKuen and, what was her name, Jewel? I haven't yet read Holly McNish, so I can't venture a critical opinion.

U. A. (Ursula) Fanthorpe had a poem called 'Patience Strong', which was the unlikely pseudonym of the author of 'inspirational verse' in a local (Gloucestershire) newspaper... in the persona of a hospital nurse (Fanthorpe worked in a hospital) who is told by a male patient how much strength and courage he gets from reading said newspaper verse. She, the nurse, is not going to question his judgment in this situation, even as she thinks about Wordsworth and Blake.

If Picador makes enough money out of a popular, or even populist book – caveat, not populist in the sense of racist, misogynist, or bellicose rabble-rousing! but that isn't the question here – to publish two good and possibly difficult, erudite or experimental books by other poets, so much the better.

There are people coming out of the spoken word scene who are fine poets by anyone's definition, like the fantastic Patience Agbabe. Patricia Smith in the US got started there too. They both have a formal expertise, a virtuoso use of both demotic and elevated language, and a sociopolitical acuteness to which any poet might aspire. Which the young woman writing the angry essay must know.

I'd recommend readers having a look at the American poet and critic Kazim Ali's reaction to the similar phenomenon of Rupi Kaur on the US Poetry Foundation site.

ANDREW BISWELL *writes* • I read the Rebecca Watts article with great admiration and assent when the magazine was published last year. It struck me then, and still strikes me now, as a fair-minded piece which makes its case strongly and persuasively.

I am unimpressed by the self-pitying response from Hollie McNish on her blog. As Alice Goodman pointed out yesterday, poets have been getting bad reviews for thousands of years, and it's inevitable that not everyone will be delighted by what they write. It saddens me to think that younger poets expect a never-ending stream of admiration, or feel that their work is beyond criticism.

As McNish does not write the kind of poetry likely to appeal to readers of *PN Review*, she should not be surprised when a reputable poetry journal articulates clear judgements about the nature and quality of her work.

I will look forward to hearing more from Rebecca Watts in future numbers of *PN Review*. Our culture of reception badly needs critical voices like hers.

Tongueless Whispering

TW: Sexual Violence

VAHNI CAPILDEO

This essay, whether or not printed in *PN Review*, arrives late: late in the inbox of the editors; long after many of the events to which it refers. It is the shadow of another essay, the one I wished to write. I wished to write a detailed analysis of the poet Martin Carter's 'Listening to the Land', a lyric famous in the Caribbean since its appearance in *The Hill of Fire Glows Red* (1951) but lesser known elsewhere. Carter begins with a reminiscence, using the first instant of address to create a past shared with the addressee, and unknown to the reader.

That night when I left you on the bridge

The reader therefore is suspended: waiting to coalesce with the addressee, if the poem proceeds to recreate the past; accepting a floating and partial state, partaking of 'I', 'you', and neither, if the poem decides to get over the past and concentrate on creating the present.

Two other pronouns, however, have been invading my mind: the 'me' of the #MeToo, which accumulates reports and stories of sexual violence; and a highly sociable 'he'. Yes, I have been raped, on more than one occasion (by persons known to me, successful credible straightforward-looking white professionals, whom I may meet or with whom I or my colleagues are likely to work; so far as I know, they are unacquainted with one other; they were in my life at different times), and molested by others. This type of incursion (I shall not say 'experience') began as early as I can remember, and I do not expect it to stop, I mostly determine to retrain myself, with or more likely without appropriate support, to act and react appropriately, or less inappropriately, within the cultures of violence in which we (I appropriate and deploy this pronoun here without shame) live and failingly love.

Did you find that difficult to read? Badly written? The quibbling, the repetitions, are deliberate. What happened; what is this; not 'who is speaking', but how to locate the voice?

I bent down
Kneeling on my knee
and pressed my ear to listen to the land.

The guidelines on the Rape Crisis England and Wales website, regarding how to support a rape or sexual abuse survivor, start with: '*Listen*: Listen, and show that you are listening, to what she or he has to say, even if it's difficult for you to hear. You might have a lot of questions but try not to interrupt.'[1] These are interesting times of devalued language, reminiscent of Mordred's communications in T. H. White's *The Once and Future King*. The adjective 'controversial' appears in reports about speakers who are proven liars dealing in emotion at the expense of reason, and the word 'refugee' seldom moves people to search for ways to *offer* sanctuary. Who has not met with this modish conversation-killer: 'He's a friend'? I have no idea what the motivation is of the novelist, academic, poet, and others whom I have heard pre-emptively deploying that phrase. Without attaching blame, I wonder if they themselves are so precarious that they cannot envisage surviving an upset to the emotional and social structure of their world. Ironically, despite having imaginations formed by the long-established literary trope of 'woman' or 'beloved' as cluster of elemental and/or geographical variables (delete as appropriate, O my cornsilk-haired, stars-and-moon, mango-breasted, oceanic America/Ireland/India/Caribbean), how many fellows (of any gender) in our 'creative industries' might prefer to go on a psychogeographic walk, or a guilt-inducing historical tour of blood-enriched sites, while preferring not to listen to something nasty about their 'friend'? Personal upset is bound to occur during structural change.

The bridge which structures the way into Martin Carter's poem is not simply a physical detail, though it would be good to know whether there was a particular bridge or type of bridge which the poet had in mind, if only to imagine Caribbean poetic geographies less insufficiently (why are we are all still playing catch-up with the Lake District?). If he/I/you has left someone on a bridge, is it because they were accompanying us, but cannot or do not wish to follow? Is the bridge an intersection, suggestive of movement and division, as the poet either returns or enters somewhere that the other does not belong or dare not traverse? Is the bridge a pause, a meeting-point, a location representing compromise, where two speakers have been together in so far as they can, and perhaps only there, but always were going different, if not separate, ways – uptown and downtown, married and single, colonial and revolutionary, or whichever overarching paradigm grabs, claims and limits the souls who long towards each other? Is it a bridge between worlds? In practice, not only in the Caribbean but in societies that represent themselves as secular, there are numerous 'spiritualities' which change the understanding of action and place. Sometimes we trespass, or intentionally cross, into realms that are more than ordinarily meaningful. Sometimes an ordinary-looking interaction is also ceremonial. We cry in the cemetery but not in the office. We lie down and alter our brainwaves in the yoga studio. In saying goodbye, we bless, curse, dismiss, acknowledge, appreciate, liberate. In a workshop discussion, two participants from Martin Carter's country were able to identify intensified or irreconcilable details in the rest of the poem which convinced them that place, here, needs to be read symbolically, beyond documentary record.

In that workshop, trying to go beyond picturing and to feel the events in the sparse yet dense lyric, I actually tested Martin Carter's words by enacting what I thought I had read. Kneeling down, I pressed my ear to the floor. Some of the participants thought that the posture itself was next to impossible, therefore a stylised act of attentiveness and obedience. We needed to know. I did find it uncomfortable enough not to be an obvious thing to imagine doing. Nearly a year later, I realised that with the words flat on a page before us, reading poetry at tables rather than outdoors, unconsciously we had been thinking of kneeling on a level surface. Of course, if the land has a gradient, it is possible to go to meet it, as it comes to meet you.

Dickinson's 'Tell all the truth but tell it slant' sounds like a luxury directive. If you and your listener are not on common ground, whether in regard to a #MeToo narrative or a postcolonial (?) political (?) pastoral (?) text, everything gets at you, gets to you, misses you, like a fun-house done for serious. You meet on a slippery footing, like the mossy steps of a university building where my friend fell, clutched the railing installed for support, and broke her arm.

> I bent down
> listening to the land
> but all I heard was tongueless whispering.

The phrase 'tongueless whispering' becomes a refrain in 'Listening to the Land'. This essay is in a state of distraction. I could further have harrowed up my editors, not only by delivering it late, but by disrupting the 'field' of the page. I need visible erasures. I need strikethroughs,

defacements, semi-transparent warring and jarring skewed and superimposed text. I want multiple columns and overactive footnotes. Impractical criticism, this essay desires nothing but engagement with Martin Carter's words, yet requires space where memoir can be dumped. #MeToo is reverberating in my body, and I cannot make my mind not mind, yet my job is to write about poetry, and my calling is to write poems.

A final note, on 'trigger warnings' and 'safe space'. Warnings go out, for example, when there is ice on the road, or a traffic 'incident'. How many warnings for hazardous physical circumstances have you encountered, issued or observed (consciously or by rote) in the last month? The warnings inform us what kind of care to take as we proceed. They are not prohibitions. It is perhaps necessary to state that warnings are not prohibitions, as I write in a country where an 'advisory' referendum is being treated as binding. I think with joy and admiration about Martin Carter, but cannot reach towards doing the writing he deserves; I write with my ears whining with tinnitus, migrainous floaters in front of my eyes, and a packet of kidney-destroying painkillers at the ready, recently having been 'triggered' by hearing a friend praise the performance of a known serial abuser. Any fool, even of the dangerous-silencer variety, should know that a well-thought-out trigger warning enables audiences to make the adjustments they need in order to listen. Our bodies are already loud to our minds.

A good sample of Martin Carter's writing may be found in *University of Hunger: Collected Poems & Selected Prose* (Bloodaxe, 2006).

There is no conclusion.

NOTES

1   www.rapecrisis.org.uk/supportingasurvivor.php

Letter from Wales

Sam Adams

I cannot deny I spend a lot of time nostalgically looking back. It is, all things considered, a pleasant infirmity of age. I have thought a great deal recently of Roland Mathias's skill and judgement, and values system, as a reviewer – and of course of the clarity and trenchancy of his prose thus employed. In his time as editor, the quarterly Anglo-Welsh Review grew in size and importance as the journal of record for all creative and scholarly work from and about Wales. Roland's ambition in this direction was boundless. He played the magazine like an accordion, expanding it to accommodate all he wanted to stuff in. My first article on Thomas Jeffery Llywelyn Prichard, written at his suggestion, occupied forty pages of *AWR* No. 52, some fifteen thousand words, but didn't appear disproportionate in an issue that ran to two hundred and sixty-six pages.

The reviews section in that same number extended over a hundred pages. Roland took the word 'review' in the magazine's title seriously. Reviews commonly filled almost half of the elastic allocation of pages, and to serve this policy he recruited reviewers far and wide. He was himself, however, by far his most frequent contributor. I once took the trouble to turn the pages in number after number and count the reviews that appeared over his name: one hundred and twenty-four, the majority lengthy, all deeply considered. (I did not bother to add the shorter, though never cursory, notes on other magazines, tracts, pamphlets, spoken word recordings.) While he was editor, no creative work with a claim to be Anglo-Welsh or, these days, 'Welsh writing in English', passed unnoticed, and very few concerning the history and topography of Wales. In addition to reviews, from time to time he published long articles in the magazine. He was the first critic to give serious in-depth consideration to writers of distinction, including Dylan Thomas, Dannie Abse, Alun Lewis and Emyr Humphreys.

At much the same time as Roland Mathias was constantly adding to his prodigious output of critical studies in one form or another, Meic Stephens was placing a similar emphasis on reviewing in *Poetry Wales*. He was equally convinced that literary criticism was an essential adjunct to the 'second flowering' of Welsh writing in English he sensed emerging during the 1960s. Articles on individual poets became a regular feature of the magazine and, between 1972 and 1974, a series of special numbers appeared, on the poetry of David Jones, R. S. Thomas, Dylan Thomas and Alun Lewis among others.

Were these the good old days of trouble-free magazine publication, when an editor could set a course confident that subscriptions, sales – and Arts Council subsidy – would keep the vessel afloat? Not really. At least once a year Roland's editorials would announce the imminent demise of *AWR,* and Christopher Davies, then publisher of *Poetry Wales*, regularly pleaded with the editor to bring out more 'specials', because they sold far better than ordinary numbers. There were constant concerns, but nothing like today's pressures from falling subscriptions, the politics of austerity and concomitant squeezed arts grant regimes, and the tsunami of digital media. To be on-line is now obligatory and our current magazines, the *New Welsh Review*, *Planet* and *Poetry Wales*, have a screen presence that, for all I know, may be attracting a readership far greater than they enjoyed in the past. But in their print editions they do not, cannot, given the constraints under which they struggle to hold on, allow reviews and articles the space they formerly received. The reviews I read in current numbers are well-informed and discriminating; there are increasing numbers of able reviewers for editors to call on, but there is not the scope to give due attention to all the books that merit critical assessment. We look enviously over the border at the *London Review of Books* and wonder if something similar in format and ambition could survive here, not as a fortnightly, but if only twice or three times a year, to review the books and the literary and political state of Wales.

Remarkably, something of the sort already exists, serving Welsh-language books and cultural interests. *O'r Pedwar Gwynt* (From the Four Winds), is an entirely Welsh-language magazine of similar format to *LRB* and about forty-four pages, appearing three times a year at £4.95 per issue. An independent journal published in partnership with Bangor University, it invites us to 'see the world through books'. The latest (Christmas 2017) number has pages given to analysis, for example of the Catalonia referendum, and Welsh culture and the social media; an interview with Emyr Humphreys, one of the most important twentieth century English novelists; new writing including a short story and an extract from a novel; and reviews. In the course of a year it reviews all books of literary merit from Welsh-language publishers. Whether this would be a feasible aim in the field of Welsh writing in English we cannot know, unless the attempt is made.

The need for clear-sighted critical assessment of the political state of Wales has never been greater, but where does one find it? The *Western Mail* still claims to be the 'National Newspaper of Wales', but in common with most print media its circulation has shrunk and it is only occasionally readers find in it a distinctive voice speaking on behalf of Wales that rises above news and 'interest' features that you would find in any newspaper. A few such occasions have occurred recently, two on successive days in the middle of November. In the first, Patrick McGuinness, having moved to north Wales in 2000, gave his perception of the supine posture of Wales politically in the context of Brexit. He writes as one whose vision is clear by virtue of having long experience of other countries and concludes, 'If Wales doesn't stand up to be counted the rest of the world will have forgotten Wales ever existed.' The following day the paper carried an account of the Raymond Williams Lecture, given this year at the Red House, Merthyr Tydfil, by the astonishingly gifted actor Michael Sheen, who has declared an interest in political activism to oppose the widespread rise of anti-democratic forces. I missed the occasion but was glad to be able to catch up with it on *You Tube*. It is worth viewing – a presentation to make any politician deeply envious, thoroughly absorbing, thought-provoking, delivered without a single miss-step or cough or sip of water. Sheen developed the lecture from *Who Speaks for Wales?* a collection of Raymond Williams's writing about Welsh culture, literature, history and politics edited by Daniel Williams (UWP, 2003), a book to turn to again at this time. Shortly after these two items appeared, in his weekly column for the *Western Mail's* weekend magazine, Lefi Gruffudd, publisher at Y Lolfa Cyf., whose books regularly win Wales Book of the Year prizes, introduced his thoughts on Michael Sheen's lecture with the observation, *'Does dim angen edrych yn bell i weld sut wlad gymhleth, ansicr, hunanddinistriol yw'r Gymru bresennol.'* (You don't need to look far to see what sort of confused, uncertain, self-destructive country Wales is at present.') It is chastening and disquieting to see how bright minds are turning at this juncture in our long history.

El Galeón

MOYA CANNON

'The Infinite Bookshop', my guide, the gracious journalist, calls it – a converted cinema on a square in the old part of Montevideo, capital of Uruguay. On the entrance level, where giddy children and young spruced-up lovers used once to queue for movie tickets, the walls are lined with fine, leather-bound volumes. We are warmly greeted by the bookseller Roberto Cataldo. He is genial, stocky, with longish grey hair. The slim, slightly worried-looking woman at the desk might be his wife. Having admired the neatly arrayed antiquarian books, we are led down an angled staircase to the next floor where the books, mainly cloth-bound hardbacks and paperbacks, are a little less ordered. There are also odd pieces of old photographic and cinema ephemera at the bottom of the stairs. Here we are shown a first edition of Onetti, one of Uruguay's great writers. Cataldo also has first editions of Jorge Luis Borges, a letter from the Peruvian poet Caesar Vallejo, a manuscript poem by the Spanish film director Luis Buñuel and a poster for the Football World Cup from 1930.

We are led down a little further and we look into the cinema proper – the inside-out galleon, the structure of the cinema virtually intact, the blank screen sagging, the back and side galleries lined, not with film-goers impatiently waiting for the hum and flicker that would promise to transport them to worlds of glamour and daring, but with silent bookcase after bookcase, each over-filled with books, the floors in front of them virtually impassable due to stacks of books and sheaves of paper. Far below us the parterre is empty of seats but completely covered with a jumble of upended cardboard boxes, with more books, sheaves of paper and rolled-up documents piled beside them.

We descend again and are guided all the way to the back of the cinema, to a space behind the screen where, again, bookcases jostle for space. There are several neatly bound series editions of European classics in translation, Dickens, Flaubert, Gide. The bookseller laments the floods of a recent winter when so much of his stock was destroyed or damaged. He unlocks a door and we descend a metal staircase, bringing us down to the fifth storey, where, through the darkness, we glimpse the black water of a built-over stream silently making its way to the nearby southern Atlantic.

Then back up again to the musty treasures of European literature behind the movie screen on the lower floor – hard to believe that in all of this literary jetsam, each individual book may once have been a cherished treasure or, as the Polish poet put it, 'a new shining chestnut', a joy to its author, a wager to its publisher, an adventure to its reader. Much of it is work 'translated' in both senses of the word. As we Europeans conquered the world we brought our founding myths and our literature with us as part of the ballast of conquest.

I wonder what my grandfather, a young Monaghan man of twenty-two, who had trained as a grocer, brought with him in his trunk when he sailed to Central America in 1902 – possibly the volume of Robert Burns, now on a shelf beside me, which a young nurse had given him when he lay critically ill in a Belfast hospital, or a volume of Irish patriotic verse which he was to leaf through during the seven years he spent managing a coffee plantation in Guatemala – verse which he would recite years later in his farm kitchen in east Co. Tyrone. His favourite recitation was an exile's lament, 'Dawn on the White Hills of Ireland', and another favourite may have been a verse which his daughter, my ninety-year-old mother, abruptly dredged up from obscurity and through a haze of Alzheimer's disease on her last St Patrick's Day on this earth:

Oh, how she ploughed the ocean that good ship Castle Down
the day we hung our colours out, the harp without the crown!

So many ships, imaginary and real, so much muddled cultural ballast listing in the hold. And among them, Shakespeare's storm-blighted ships and the raft pushed off one of them, carrying Miranda, her father, Prospero, and his chest of books of magic, the raft which was to wash ashore on Caliban's island, Caliban who first welcomed Prospero as a guest:

And then I loved thee
And showed thee all the qualities o' th' isle,
The fresh springs, brine pits, barren place and fertile

and who was then tricked, enslaved and brutalised by Prospero – so much cruelty justified in the name of European civility and prosperity. And in the *Santa Maria*, *Niña* and *Pinta* what books were stowed? In the cabin of stout Cortes's galleon? Among the sea-charts and star-charts there were Bibles surely, with their doctrine of peace and love, a doctrine to be enlisted soon in the service of plunder and genocide.

And long before that, there were Homer's fleets of narrow ships, massing at Aulis, the captains' eyes turned east and fixed on Troy – ships which possibly carried rudimentary maps but no books because stories and myths were still sung or chanted, held together with rhythm and rhetoric, as were the epics and the myths of the Charrúa, Chaná and Guaraní, the native people of what is now Uruguay, who were virtually eradicated two centuries ago, their songs and stories almost as obscure as the black waters flowing through the basement of El Galeón.

And before that, again – how little we know of interior human life before the birth of books, before clay tablets, vellum manuscripts, papyrus scrolls, oracle bones – those many thousands of years of human life and intelligence of which only wisps of evidence survive. Humanity is old and literacy is young, barely four thousand years old. Before that, almost all we know of human hopes and longings is surmise. Of our distant ancestors, we know little more of their inner lives than that they lamented their dead, turned towards the life-nourishing light and worshipped the arbitrary elemental powers which threatened and sustained them.

But when human intelligence made the enormous leap into abstraction, into literacy, a rush light was lit. By its glow we can read the carved inscriptions on turtle shells or ox scapulae that tell us of the genealogy of the Shang dynasty of China and of hopes for good crops and successful military adventures; cuneiform script on clay cylinders that gives the rations allocated to the imprisoned king of Judah during his captivity in Babylon; hieroglyphics that give us the autobiographies of the great and good of Egypt and guidance into their country of the dead. For the Egyptians, writing was 'The Language of the Gods'.

For many, perhaps most, early peoples, writing, the preserve of a learned elite of druids, priests and scribes, was magic itself. For us, literacy is a listing galleon in which we travel, weighed down with laptops, Kindles, mobile phones, novels, slim volumes of verse, newspapers, with power and responsibility, the sails of imagination furled or set.

Letter from Austin: Duckbomb

JOHN CLEGG

In Luke Bilberry's bookshop, on 12th Street in Austin, Texas, there's a small shrine to Christopher Middleton, on a low shelf, so you have to kneel to see it. There's the programme from Middleton's Austin memorial service, with a photo I'd never seen before, looking like a publicity still for an Outlaw Country tour – his beard slick, shirt unbuttoned two buttons further than mine (and mine was already open one more button than I'd wear in London, a concession to the ludicrous November heat), gazing moodily at a point just to the left of the photographer. Propped alongside are the last few books Luke bought from Middleton's library in 2014: Hans Arp first editions, a two-volume catalogue of a Surrealist exhibition, a history of German expressionist poetry with its spine badly broken. Luke is a lovely man, with the bookseller's skill of giving the customer enough silence to browse and enough conversation to feel unselfconscious. While I'm looking through his poetry section, he steps into the back room and phones various friends of Middleton to organise meetings for me.

The sun hasn't set, but the thought is definitely beginning to cross its mind. I wander down 12th Street to Jeffrey's, where Middleton spent a few evenings every week after his retirement. Everyone I talk to about Jeffrey's describes a golden age when it was a friendly neighbourhood bar, and bemoans its 2013 refurb, but I like it immensely. The one bartender who would have remembered Middleton retired in September – I'm taken to see the bartender's massive portrait hanging in the dining room, and on my return I'm given a red wine on the house for no clear reason. I order oysters and another red wine. I pinch some monogrammed serviettes.

On my way home I peel off down a side-street to see the two-room apartment where Middleton lived for the last thirty years of his life. I have a photo of his writing desk in that apartment, taken (I would guess) in the early 1990s, and it suddenly feels important to orient the exterior to the interior. There's a poem, 'The Anti-Basilisk', which watches and inhabits an anole lizard climbing up the insect screen on the inside of his window. I decide that the poem had been written in real time, as the lizard moved, and that I should know whether he was watching the lizard on the insect screen on the window in front of his writing desk – and so only had to look up to see it – or whether it was, instead, climbing the insect screen on the window to the right, so he had to keep turning his head. I spent a long while looking at his flat, and looking at the photo, until I made up my mind. (It was the window to the right of his desk. I have a proof of this which is too large for the margin.) I head home, the two glasses of Jeffrey's red weighing me down rather. At the end of his road is one of Austin's 'moonlight towers', the height of an electricity pylon, with a halo of spotlights at the top, an 1890s alternative to street lighting. It didn't catch on because it doesn't work. I decide it was very restrained of him never to have put one in a poem.

The next morning I visit Bradley Hutchinson at his typefoundry in East Austin. He'd been hired as a printer by Tom Taylor, a rare book dealer who'd printed Middleton's *Razzmatazz* in the 1970s, and eventually he'd made Taylor an offer for the equipment and set up on his own. For the next couple of decades, he printed Middleton's very short-run pamphlets: *The Swallow Diver*, *The Six*, *The Redbird Hexagon*, *A Keeper of the Reliquary* and more, a new pamphlet every two years or so, editions of twenty or thirty or fifty copies. His business was called Digital Letterpress, but he'd retained the equipment for setting type in hot metal, and Middleton was one of his last clients to insist on it. Hutchinson would wake up one morning with a premonition that Middleton would visit; around lunchtime, he'd drive up in his white Honda Civic, park out *there* – Hutchinson gestured to the parking space – walk up grinning in shirt and tie and Bermuda shorts and spread his papers out right over *here*. They'd spend hours discussing fonts and paper and title-page motifs. Some of the pamphlets carried the name of a made-up press: Middleton came up with the name in a dream, envisaging three partners, 'Duck, Bomb, and Bêtise': Hutchinson by mistake set it as 'Duckbomb & Bêtise', which they both agreed was an improvement.

As I walk back to campus, Hilary Clinton's motorcade tears past. She's in town to sign copies of *What Hap-*

pened?, her account of the 2016 campaign, at a bookshop called Book People. The queue for returns stretches around the block. My Airbnb, otherwise very well-appointed, doesn't have a table, so in the evening I spread out on the floor with pizza and books – Sheridan Le Fanu ghost stories – and a laptop stand I've jury-rigged from

a clothes-horse. It strikes me suddenly that Middleton *did* write about the moonlight towers, in a poem called 'Anguish' from *The Balcony Tree*. I make a note of that, eat another slice of pizza, and then make a note so I don't forget about the white Honda Civic.

These Trivial Distinctions

FRANK KUPPNER

Dragged in, rather against my will, to an obviously hopeless churchy jumble sale, by one of the eleven or twelve most intriguing people in the entire world – albeit an autonomous agent at present firmly in the grip of a no doubt transient passion (for what, my dear Tristanne, is not transient?) for exotic fabrics – I find to my astonishment that there is indeed something hidden deep within one of these weary, much-buffeted cardboard boxes that I am suddenly eager to buy. Yes. A small book called, I confess, *Sayings of the Saints* – collected by Annie Matheson (Eveleigh Nash, never heard of them, 1908). Not an area I am very likely to do any further research in now, I should guess – (and for the general health of one's heart, head, health and habit, one surely ought not to go about reading only those glorious views which one already agrees with?) – but, more than anything else, this little book takes me instantly back to the world, physical and spiritual, of my ever more precariously-sited grandmother – my mother's mother. Can it really, already, be over fifty years ago that I used to visit her in a neat little not quite poverty-stricken flat just round the corner from more or less hereabouts? (Yes, my lovely (if somewhat non-existent) children. Yes; it certainly can.)

No amount of cold probability theorising and mere absence of actual evidence could quite dispel the irrational feeling that gripped me as soon as I first set eyes on this small book: the sense that my grandmother (an extraordinarily distant person now, given how close she was to me in space and time) – that she might once even have been the owner of this same rare, wisdom-crammed treasure. It simply had that sort of *fated* look about it. Not a quality easy to define, I dare say; but a real one (or very nearly a real one) for all that.

(If not, then at the very least she'll have been the friend or neighbour of either W. Leishman or G.F. Thorne, the second of whom gifted this venerable Catholic chrestomathy to the first on that closing pre-disaster Christmas of 1913 – when my father was already an eighteen-month-old utter irrelevance, repeatedly falling over in the north-eastern wilds of Wilhelmine Germany. (At the *very very* least, she'll have passed (one of) them in the street.) (Yes. Leishman, more likely.) (W. for William, a dead certainty, surely?) (Well... not Wulfilas at any rate.) (Or Wenceslas?) (Hmm. No. No: probably not.))

And, as an unlooked-for bonus, even the predictably heavy drizzle of pious inanity, sanctimony and triteness which makes up most of the content lifted spectacularly once at least. For, right there among so many ecstatic, ecclesiastical bores and bigots telling us with psychiatrically-interesting over-confidence precisely what the Unfathomable Will of the Inscrutable Almighty is, or was, back comes St Teresa of Avila (born 1515; died 1582, just about the time when a clueless lad called something like Shaxberd is getting himself inappropriately involved with an older woman) – back comes St Teresa (who has already put in a very strong claim for a place high among the holy medal-winners) to, as it were, redeem herself with a magnificent late submission to this incense-scented field.

For it's only then, approaching the end of the book, that we are given her (to say the least) remarkable observation: 'Now, I think it is for the Soul's good to abandon itself into the arms of God altogether; if He will take it to Heaven, let it go; if to Hell, no matter, as it is going thither with its sovereign good.'

What? What was that? 'If to Hell, no matter.' Culpable ignorance, perhaps; but, barring one or two suchlike incendiary flickers in the Old Testament, I don't remember meeting anything much like this before. True, in politer circles Hell is rather being phased out these days – but all the same: *there's* a text to base a sermon on indeed! (Or a *meditation* at least.) Yes. So much, evidently, for the Beatific Vision of Paradise – for the ineffable glory which, for instance, Mr Dante put himself to such immense trouble to (completely) (and, need one add, inevitably) fail to describe. Yes. Can't quite see this being stressed – or, indeed, even mentioned – during one of the school Religious Study periods. God forbid, no! Might give the lively little sex maniacs *quite* the wrong idea.

Of course, if Hell exists and if God, whatever he is, is indeed everywhere, then all but the most theologically limber and nimble of tread are instantly driven hard up against the bitter and unlovely conclusion that God must be present in Hell too. (Or is there perhaps some real place where the Omnipresent *isn't*?) Much as, if he made and sustains in existence *absolutely everything*, as we were forever being taught at school – (and would they lie to us?) – then he must have made and be actively sustaining everything evil too. This is as starkly unavoidable as the conclusion that eleven plus twelve equals twenty-three – though it's usually thought more prudent to suggest that, in effect, in this unique case (let us offer a charitable simplification) two plus two just *can't* equal four, in some transcendent and mysterious way which lies far beyond our essentially limited human understanding. For of course we are all pretty much limitlessly limited – particularly those of us who seem to delight in asking questions which are neither helpful, untedious nor welcome. (But, fortunately, here at least our emotions may be relied on – (unlike those of our wretched, nay-saying adversaries, whether they deserve a hint of human sympathy or not) – to point us infallibly, or almost infallibly, in the right direction. (Which is no doubt *just as well*.))

Calligraphies VI

MARILYN HACKER

After disaster
(again) in her small skylit
sublet, N. simmers

lentils while she reads a long
book about Ibn Arabi.

In prison they made
chess pieces out of stale bread.
She taught the women

to play. Their first champion was
an apolitical thief.

*

Political grief,
apolitical despair,
or it's vice versa –

either way, insomnia.
Rapping on the neighbours' door,

three in the morning –
no, it's seven, and still dark.
One of the roommates

next door home from a night I'm
too tired out to imagine.

*

Imagine language
after opaque years
become transparent...

since the hour needs witnesses
who can construct a sentence.

Which was my country?
A schism in the nation,
slogans on banners

while a compromised future
slouches towards investiture.

*

Towards light again, when
wet snow is falling on the
January sales.

The chestnut stairs gleam, but
I'm short of breath, knees give way.

My ideal reader
doesn't read English, and I've
stalled in her language

– or his – while he/she stares at
an impassable border.

*

Bored or despairing
or enduring a headache,
and humid winter.

A book I loved; a reproach:
You read like a three-year-old.

The masters dying,
their festive midnight children
blown out like fireworks.

A constriction in the chest.
An explosion in the street.

*

One Hundredth Street sun-
lit on election morning :
another country

that seemed possible again.
I went to the Baptist Church

to vote – lines, laughter,
scowls, polyglot commotion,
then, fresh air. That night

I read Hannah Arendt till
bad news muddied late daybreak.

*

Bad news for heroes
chain-smoking across borders,
not out of danger.

She smoked outside the café –
it drizzled as we read her

piece for an-Nahar;
rolled cigarettes at demos
between her speeches.

She writes in the ward bed with
a chemo port in her chest.

*

Not a port city
but the river is always
lumbering through it

on its muddy way elsewhere,
banks erased often by rain.

We crossed a bridge in
a shurba of languages.
History trundled

beneath, gravel on a barge,
ground down to its origins .

*

Ground beef sautéed with
onions and tomatoes, then
add frozen okra

N. was so pleased that we found
at the Syrian grocer's

near Faidherbe. Why no
okra in Indian food
in France, we wondered?

Bindhi, bamiyaa. A pot of
white rice swells on the burner.

*

Swells and then explodes,
'like a raisin in the sun',
our impatience, and

others'. Five years ago, in
some café, after some demo,

the Algerian,
Zinab, told the Syrian,
Aïcha, you'll have

what we had, ten black years of
slaughter. And Aïcha wept.

*

Did not cry when I
fell on my face, scraped my chin
and turned my ankle,

or when the midnight and the
morning emails announced death –

a younger man, an
older woman, Berkeley and
Brooklyn, unanswered

letters from two coasts. I took
two pills for my aching face.

*

The two young women
come up the stairs with parcels,
their conversation

punctuated by laughter.
The old woman is coughing

in her apartment.
One of them opens the door.
They can't, she can't know

their white nights' precipices,
her dictionaries' questions.

In Conversation with Sasha Dugdale

Jamie Osborn

[This conversation took place around the time that Sasha Dugdale was finishing her latest book, *Joy*, and was preparing to hand over as editor of *Modern Poetry in Translation*. It was conducted (via email) between northern Spain, Sussex, Brussels and a flight to Moscow.]

Joy starts with a dark stage and a woman speaking. She's Catherine Blake, wife of William. As the poem develops, memory and care and creation are layered together, and I think there's an anxiety here that reflects the multiple, uncertain-yet-definite voices of the poem. When Catherine clutches at her body through her clothes, I can't help feeling that what she is doing anxiously touching at layers of recollection and trying to get a grip on the words searing through her. Maybe one way for the reader to get such a grip is to ask: who's speaking here?

I was primarily interested in Blake, but found it impossible to write about him directly. His own work is filled with a sort of clarity that needs no explication or dramatic footnoting. However, during my reading and research I found myself increasingly wondering about Catherine, his wife and helpmate. Blake burnt extremely bright and I wondered what living in proximity to that brightness would do to a person. Catherine spent many hours every day working with him in the cottage industry of engraving. She learnt all the considerable skills of an engraver, she worked in difficult conditions, handling the acids, pigments and plates, living daily with the chemical stench of the industry and its privations – and she worked alongside a man whose visionary art and fervent purpose may not have been open to her, a man who appeared to choose poverty and near destitution to fame and wealth. Even if we accept that William was the inspiration and the driving force, Catherine's part in his art is significant. She was his apprentice, assistant, model, lover and carer for nearly half a century. Blake and Catherine worked so closely together and in such intimate partnership, that her erasure from the 'mythology' of Blake seemed worth redressing and her own sense of self in the face of such a powerful artistic ego worth considering.

But of course the poem is also concerned with living with artistic creation, and a sort of creation that is bound up with principle and ethics, and it is concerned also with grief, and the still unthinkable grief of losing a partner. In order to properly grieve you need to have known joy. Without the deep joy Blake and his wife clearly shared there would not be such a deep sense of loss.

The wonder of that brightness is something the reader must share with Catherine, and with the poet perhaps. But are there different kinds of brightness, in the poem and out of it? The way you describe Catherine above is touching and clear, a biographer's illumination. That's the kind of light that, in the poem might pick out the clothes Catherine clutches at. But there's also a heaving, fitful burning that shines through in her words.

I couldn't write a biography from the outside in, I knew I couldn't do that for Blake, but I realised I couldn't do that for Catherine either, because the idea of biographical 'objectification' is a troubling one for me. I can talk around it but in fact the idea of writing about another person as if you knew them intimately (as if you even knew your own self that well!) is hard for me. I can almost feel them speaking back, as sometimes happens when I translate and presume too much – interestingly it is the same 'ethical' dilemma I feel about translating, something to do with the risk of eclipsing the speaker with your own body. So, in a sense, Catherine Blake's appeal was that she existed, but nothing much is known about her: a palpable shape, a life, but one I could sneak in and inhabit from the inside. So I wasn't remotely interested in her clothes, or what she looks like as she speaks. However I couldn't start to write until I felt my research made me safe, gave me a sense of her life which was ungainsayable. Then I could stop thinking about it and start thinking about an inner life. I was expressing something myself, I was expressing an anxiety about memory and the impossibility of recalling a life of experiences, and also the desperate isolation we feel when we are in proximity to a powerful voice. So she is haunted by my anxieties.

The abundant and complex and not always easy range of voices in Joy *is something to take great care with. I'm also thinking of 'care' in the senses of curating and of looking after, which I can't help thinking may be one of the most difficult tasks for a poet. Might one might see a similarity to the work of an editor, or of a translator? Do you think of your roles, as writer, editor, translator, as positions of 'caring' or of 'caring for' something? Or is 'care' entirely the wrong word; is it, in fact, a kind of joy?*

I am finding these questions very hard to answer because they probe into something I am almost not ready to acknowledge. The voices in *Joy* are all my own. But increasingly they are filtered through a net of anxiety. It is a difficult position to write from because the anxiety threatens to stifle the voice. I'd say that *Joy* marks a change in my work because I have struggled with being a predominantly lyric poet for a long while, but the work I do in editing, some small acts of activism and in being part of an international network of writers means that it is very hard to write without anxiety, with the probing intellect switched off. Writing now means negotiating a new relationship between consciousness and 'inspiration', or whatever we call the darkness that poems emerge from. There is more 'care' and more mortality, more love for my loved ones and for the republic of letters which I increasingly believe in over all other structures of government. There is also more understanding, less optimism – more honesty, perhaps. I treasure honesty almost more than anything in the poetry I read now. But honesty now takes me to visions and places I don't want to see or know and I find that a frightening prospect for my future writing. Still, honesty is tempered by love, and perhaps that is the 'joy' or 'care' you are speaking of.

It's interesting that you mention a change in your work. Do you think it is a positive change, even if the reasons for it may be worrying? If by 'the probing intellect' you mean a kind of thought that is both provoked by and insists on the urgency of activism, no matter how small, and of supporting an international network of writers, then that should be a good thing. In the end, it is about honesty, and what you say about that strikes me as more inclusive and more modest and more difficult than many of the well-known comments (Shelley, Auden) about what poetry achieves or does.

I think honesty is a good thing in art, but a hard thing, because it is strange and seems unnatural. We have become so used to artifice and repeated and enjoyable tropes that it is easy for a relatively skilled writer who has regard for what others might say or think, to write a pastiche of what a real thought should be (facility is a terrible thing, and yet a writer mostly has it: it is the ease she first enjoyed when she came to writing and then spent a lifetime trying to discard). And in fact the deal between reality and artifice is the one we are all negotiating, so it is easy to cheat on our own selves. To add to that complication, honesty mostly isn't intellectual, but felt truth. I think the most honest writing is where the instinct writes and the intellect refrains from moderation and shaping. As a more lyric poet I have always been drawn to shaping devices and forms but now I have a sense that I must write differently. If not now, then when?

You are quite right about poetics. I feel very strongly that Keats is important in his poetics, but Auden and Shelley are less vital to me. When I read now about poetry I try to pick a fight in my head with the text, because I want to be able to assert my own poetics rather than being deferential, I want my poetics to be proofed by contact with the views of other poets. I have to work hard to assert myself because I am crippled by deferential silence and nagging doubt. I like and embrace the poetics of women poets like Louise Glück, because I understand where they have come from, but I have to arm myself doubly against them, because they are so recognisable and could easily subsume me.

A while ago I was devastated to learn that I wasn't a man. It was while I was reading Keats's letters. I was enjoying them so much, I kept imagining myself talking to Keats, and then something dropped from my eyes and I saw that it would not be possible to be Keats's friend and chat to him about poetics. The best (the closest) relationship I could hope for was to be his, or any other poet's, muse. I don't want to be anyone's muse because the muse is silent. For a long while it didn't bother me, but it bothers me terribly now, not least because I am complicit, I carry within myself the negative photographic image of a muse, mother, daughter, lover, wife. I am easy to silence, I don't put up resistance. So you could say that writing Catherine Blake was a form of redress, an acknowledgement of silence, a slow assumption of equality. By the end of the monologue she understands her importance, she sees the angel.

Your poem 'Cutting Apples' describes thoughts as soldiers assailing 'absence, which so hates to be considered / It throws the thoughts back out like thieves / And bolts the door behind them.' Absence is the core of the poem (and some might say the same goes for translation, though I am not sure about that, personally). The way your writing speaks to loss or to absence is both worldly and almost dreamlike; can you explain that? And can editorial work speak similarly?

Some of the poems in *Joy* are concerned with loss of faith and the oncoming of grief. I don't mean that in a literal and religious way: I didn't write them as a conscious attempt to deal with these emotions, in fact I mostly only realise the truth of the poem when it is on the page. 'Cutting Apples' was a case in point. I hadn't written anything for a long while so I was genuinely writing down the experience of peeling and cutting up a mound of apples for the sake of writing something plainly and without effect, and the rest of the poem sprouted unbidden from this exercise. Writing can't grapple with absence, nothing can, it is the absolute zero, the vacuum where nothing exists, but it can take on our own struggle to comprehend it and 'Cutting Apples' is a sort of 'real-time' grappling with absence. Editorial work is different, because it is more intellectually active, and all about caring for the existing work of another, tending it – although perhaps what you imply is right: this care is in itself a way of negotiating the void.

When I talked about Joy *to a friend of mine he insisted that we never actually feel absence in itself - like you say, it's the absolute zero – but what we experience, rather, is the strangely continued presence of someone or something no longer there. Making sense of that may require a repetitive, half-mindless, half-careful process, an unwilled practice. Do you think that's true? And do you think the practice of 'tending' may be the opposite of 'cutting', or are they on one level the same?*

Yes, I think grief and absence are best expressed by numb repetition, which is why the villanelle is such a beautiful vessel for grief. I don't think we are consoled by our own expressions of grief in poetry: other people may be. This is because when we write or compose we are not grieving the absence, we are actively and positive building a structure for others to grieve in. In that poem ('Cutting Apples'), although the imagery is of violence, of cutting, and the bloody battle between thought and absence, the violence is positive somehow: it is a vital sign, although the fight is essentially pointless and inequal, the narrative slips, it can't get a foothold, it is losing.

MPT *maybe takes a different approach to 'absence'. In a memorable editorial to* MPT *in the summer of 2015, you wrote of how 'the censor's* ✗✗✗✗✗*' has historically attempted to make itself felt on poetry, and continues to do so. At the same time, you implicitly acknowledge that in our current times in the West we are lucky enough not to* ✗✗✗✗✗*. In an editorial just after Trump's election, you write that we must all decide 'Whether we give up our peaceful lives to be activists, or whether we protest by asserting our right to peaceful lives.' Is it naive to ask if there's a change of emphasis in the later piece? 'It is not possible to write in a vacuum', you say, in the 2016* editorial; what then do we make of the absence that so attracts and repels in Joy and which is, one might feel, a vortex, if not a vacuum?

I think there has been a slow evolution in my own thinking about the world. I work with Russian and Ukrainian writers a great deal, and everything we have experienced over the last year has been experienced by them at a higher level and for much longer: the rise in xenophobia, extremism, a nasty parochial nationalism carried into our countries' political life, a polluted media stream, propaganda, lies. I've watched their responses and learnt from them. I've been made humble by their bravery and acceptance of loss, and how they are ahead of us in their understanding of the writer's role in a politically fraught age. Most of all I have learnt from them that bitterness at what is wrong eats us up and cynicism breaks the heart. That does not mean turning away from activism or protest, but accepting that we must stand for what we believe even if it seems a matter of indifference to others. Times have changed. I am not a lover of conflict or argument, so I need to put my sense of the world into my writing and that dilemma I outlined in the editorial in 2016 is constantly in my mind. Translation is one way in which I can fill the void – it is an act of sympathy for the voice of another.

When I wrote about 'not writing in a vacuum' in the editorial I was referring to the wrong idea that poetry is a pure art, and that there is 'political poetry' and 'non-political poetry'. I was making the point that we all write within our social structures, our national and international histories and it is disingenuous to claim otherwise. However, how to use that awareness when writing? When I write I try to push away all the pressing things. To return to your thoughts about the shift from lyric, I am very occupied by this problem of how to integrate the two parts, the conscious intellectual thought process and the lyric impulse which seems best when (as Keats says) it doesn't 'have a palpable design upon us'. I wonder if the answer is that the enmeshing of these two elements happens at a pre-textual level, and then we write from that new position. I don't want to seem certain or prescriptive about this because I am feeling my way. I am reluctant to say anything about writing poetry which makes it sound any easier than it is.

MPT has responded to those challenges, of loss, of political situations, not only by asserting the right to a peaceful life, but by asserting the right to and the vitality of variety. And the more I read of your own work, the more I come to believe the same applies there. There's a dynamic between a kind of flux or dance and a countervailing insistent-ness within each poem. Is that something you're very conscious of as an editor and as a writer?

MPT has a long tradition of vitality and variety and previous editors Daniel Weissbort, Ted Hughes, David and Helen Constantine were exemplary in their commitment to bringing new poetry into English. That spirit was already there, and it is something I feel strongly about and willingly continued. Joy is a particular collection in that I wrote it over the period when I was editing MPT and I had little time for my own work. As a result I think the collection is a series of 'un-tranquil recollections', rather than a collection which is knit together by theme and a sense of con-

tinuity. I am glad you feel single poems have integrity because more than anything I struggle for integrity. For any linguist integrity of voice and spirit is a difficult concept because we learn language by parroting others, and so we speak with the voices of others, their turns of phrase and successful linguists are uniquely sympathetic in my experience. You could say that all language is learnt in this way – through sympathy – even the mother tongue, but for those who pursue other languages at a high level it is a palpable 'evil', we mistrust our every utterance, know that originality of expression is impossible.

I absolutely agree with you about the value of integrity. And I certainly feel the un-tranquillity of Joy and in a different way of MPT is a necessary and inspiring response to our political times. Might it also be a struggle for a kind of pre-lapsarian language? Your description of language-learning as being at least in part founded on 'evil' is striking, and makes me think of a fallen state.

I am very grateful to you, Jamie! I am anxious about any notions of pre-lapsarian language, because such notions are essentially conservative. I think I was using 'evil' here in the sense of 'necessary evil', and I am not really entirely sure that sympathy and originality of expression are on different sides of the scales. I don't know any other way to learn language and a sense of complicity and 'fallenness' are perhaps inevitable if you live in this flawed world and you are curious about it. But increasingly I see that the only way to remain human in such a world is to maintain that almost naively simple love, solidarity and friendship for those who have touched you and you touch.

Coming back to Joy and a question that probably has to be asked: is it a poem? It's set out as a piece for the stage, complete with stage directions. I find much of your writing as mysterious as it is compelling. For example, Catherine speaks of Satan appearing with 'a round sad face like a waterwheel and seemed tired and full of pity'. Might it help if the audience could see Catherine's own face as she speaks? Or do you insist on the poem being in, as the final stage direction has it, 'darkness'?

Joy is not really dramatic, and I am not a dramatic writer. It takes its shape from language, rather than the dynamic between characters. The imagery owes a great deal to Blake, I was really steeped in the images and the language when I wrote it and when I wrote I mostly had either a particular image in my head, or a generic Blakean image. But Blake's images are interesting because they aren't apart from the thinking and the writing. They are full of a truth, but it isn't the truth of physical appearance, or even individual psychology. Often they look like beautiful cartoons, graphic illustrations, or the sort of pictures a child draws when the essential function is to indicate, rather than describe. And in the longer poems where images are not all illustrated we are required to guess at the visual accompaniment. This is how I imagined this piece and its relationship to image and colour.

Grave Goods

PATRICIA MARY POSTGATE

You may keep my best bow,
And my drinking cup;
My chequer board, my flower-coronet
And my little cosmetic jars.
They will be no use to me at all.

You must put in the grave with me
These three things.
A small pot of seed-corn;
The long time coming will ask a lot
And not give much.
No concessions are made in the struggle for being,
And strength must be drawn from where it may.
Put with me a silver piece, or a copper or two.
Life does not come free, and creation must be paid for.
There is no knowing what the cost will be,
But cost there will be in sending the cell, the atom,
On their transient and perilous journeys.

A handful of soft wool there must be.
A bonus perhaps, when sustenance is only a precaution
And payment perhaps not essential.
But terrible must be the cold of the air-swept plains
Where dead stars hang above dying worlds.
Neither sun nor fire will say
'Come, stretch, rest; here's comfort for the journey'
For comfort is irrelevant, and only what is needed is supplied.
I fear the cold more than starvation or penury.

So drop the silver piece in the little pot with the corn,
Sealed with a tuft of wool and close to my hand.

No. I am not yet satisfied. This is not enough.
Give me my bronze cat for a guide.
It has many times passed through the temporal and the eternal,
And knows the road.
Of all beings cats are the only ones
Which sometimes, for a split second, remember, and say
'This is the meaning'.
Nor will a cat ever refuse companionship
Because the companionship of a cat is neither giving nor taking,
But being.

I wish I need not be buried in a box, but as cats are.
Laid in the ground wrapped in an old cloth
To keep the soil out of their eyes,
And so start out unencumbered and clear-sighted.
But start out I must;
So give me my four things,
Cover the grave against jackals,
And go away.
Because I shall not be there.

Coffee, No Sugar

SAMIRA NEGROUCHE

translated from the French by Marilyn Hacker

The only freedom, the only unqualified state of freedom I've experienced, I attained in poetry, in its tears and in the brightness of a few beings come toward me from three elsewheres, love's brightness multiplying me.

– René Char, 'Praise of a Suspect Woman'

There are pages with no writing on them that go across you in the middle of the night pages no editor waits for that are the road towards an imaginary book you watch moving further away as time passes you would prefer to think it was in your computer's dead memory forever.

*

I like to drink coffee with a cloud of cream not true I like coffee with nothing no sugar I only like the hazy cloud of dawn that I catch out before sleeping it slides in and silently fills the hills' hollow I like that thread of cream I cross from breast to nipple.

*

She served me dubious water in an earth-coloured bowl she said I've written a novel but the floppy disk stopped working she said look at my field of olive trees I've always dreamed of having an orchard I go down the three steps I look into the distance a few weeds burnt by the sun a lemon tree surrounded by concrete like a blind pillar I said your olive orchard is beautiful get another brand of floppy disc.

*

One two I count the drops falling from the sky onto a rag of plastic lying insolently on the balcony three four every thought only worth driving away when nothing comes not desire or sleep out of the corner of my eye I search for a cigarette and I don't even smoke.

*

Rue Didouche Mourad the two men come forward they say we're going to walk right to the end till we become kids again till the twenty-third century I say poets are crazy and just as well these two exist we'll ride camels they say right into the desert while waiting I must translate give substance to the bends and turns borrowed from me.

*

Cats don't need you to whisper in their ears they don't circle round the food bowls they park themselves patiently then exasperatedly on the messy desk they curl up adroitly on their centres of gravity at just the right distance from the radiator you haven't lifted a foot before they know whether you're just fidgety or going out.

*

That hand trembling again as it tentatively presses the banal ballpoint on a crossword puzzle grid the piano stays closed and dusty the poet a timid shadow on a dilapidated armchair facing the extinguished lamp of a sleeping mosque dreams of day that will break without her.

*

I said to write the most ordinary things you must first write your birth about your mother your father about the body women men the rapist the assassins incest and doubt about night's doubt and the desert's hunger books jealousy suspicion sex ruins the sea trees archaeology Greek and pagan gods and about the stars I said all that is almost ordinary before and after writing.

*

Must multiply the word mountain breathless and avid hold back what might resemble blackout vertigo like a verifiable border between mourning and resurrection.

*

Sometimes I think I ought to break loose from all moorings fast take the first boat the first plane the first no matter what but leave arms swinging solitary heart with the feeling that the world is immense I cross the boulevard of the port I hear the boat barking trying to distract me I almost knock down a pedestrian and I say to myself that Algiers is one hell of a whore.

*

I can well believe that the future is bitter now that you need biometric photos with white and crimson background to cross the Mediterranean and an exercise bike to relax the Achilles' tendon while waiting for the green spaces to be aerated by a bissextile rotation and the forests cleared by July's false fires.

*

I'd like to encounter New York's mysteries like Prévert and then the mysteries of Paris and then why not write a lament for my own little demons and my oversized whimsies.

*

Tomorrow is a day no one wants to think of any more so tomorrow crosses the hours and stands at the window without waiting for the moon to set.

*

The painter says to me that books are signs for me they are only insect handwriting in the space of my screen since I divorced Arabic calligraphy I'm afraid that the mountain of books will be transformed into a wave of indecipherable signs.

*

She gives me a writing assignment she says tell everything that happened in one day she says use the present tense and short sentences I say my memory is overflowing too many things happen in a day or not enough how to peel Günter Grass's onion how to push the alarm button get into the day that matters with the words that matter how to stare down the truth of that moment that gives birth to or aborts language.

*

I too would like to know what happened in one day in the present tense relive it all but this day now today I'm really tired.

*

When sleep abandons you it's something like injustice or madness.

*

What makes an encounter likely sometimes those four winds mingling over an eagle's nest and the moment of a love-word nullify the forces of opposition.

Unseasonably Speaking

HORATIO MORPURGO

'I am no agitator. But if you have something on your conscience, write it down. It will do you good. Your friends will be pleased.'
– Letter from Joseph Roth to Stefan Zweig in London, 23 November 1933

LONDON, for Stefan Zweig, was as much of a home as he had anywhere between 1933 and 1939. A blue plaque in Hallam Street, to commemorate his time in the city, was refused in 2012. English Heritage judged it 'best to let this debate play out further'. The Austrian writer's 'London connections did not appear strong enough'. His 'profile has never been as high in Britain as elsewhere' and there existed no 'consensus' here on the merits of his work.

The *London Review of Books* had, two years earlier, printed Michael Hofmann's very spirited assault on Zweig's reputation. Hofmann dismissed him as a spoilt child of fortune, unpardonably middle-brow. Showing how this 'purveyor of *Trivialliteratur*' (best left to 'teenagers of all ages') had been mocked in private by more gifted contemporaries, Hofmann added some memorable invective of his own. He was doubtless unimpressed by the writers, actors, scholars (and England football manager) who spoke up for a plaque. English Heritage was also unmoved. A spectral online trace is all that remains of the idea.

Broadcasting House backs onto Hallam Street and the area has been home to many influential journalists. There *is* a plaque, at the street's northern end, for example, to Ed Morrow. There must be a consensus on Ed Morrow's work but I'll admit I was reduced to googling him. An American reporter from wartime London, he and Zweig, the most widely translated living author in the world at the time, might easily have passed one another in the street. It's unlikely they knew each other. Zweig did give one cagey interview to the BBC while in England – an early experiment in television – but generally he avoided journalists.

Ed Morrow stayed as the bombs fell, on Hallam Street as elsewhere. His eyewitness accounts arguably helped to swing American public opinion behind intervention in Europe. His more highly-strung neighbour had by then already departed for the West Country, before taking ship to New York. Zweig finally settled in Brazil, where he and his wife committed suicide in 1942.

An obscure affair about a blue plaque might hardly seem worth recalling. I wonder, though, five years on, whether the sands have not shifted sufficiently under all our feet that we find ourselves now viewing that failed bid from a different perspective? If we are not to have a plaque, then let us at least not have it for the right reasons. I will argue here that the building on which there should or should not be a plaque was never in Hallam Street anyway.

*

It was to 11 Portland Place that Zweig moved in October 1933. He came to England to work on a biography of Erasmus with which he was having trouble, then stayed on to write several other books. It's true he was, even then, less well known in England than on the Continent and relished the anonymity. He was in need of good libraries and space to think. As he moved in to his new address, he 'had the feeling almost of returning to his beginnings', an unknown in London as he had been when he first set out as a writer in Vienna. Zweig had not visited England since his student days and had just turned fifty. His marriage was in trouble: his first wife was still in Salzburg and his secretary would soon become his second. He had multiple reasons for a spell in England.

He liked the place, too, though his observations of English life have a remote, touristic feel. He formed a close relationship with his London publisher and kept up with a few other émigrés but had no extended circle of friends. He appreciated the respect for privacy. He was at least half-admiring of the English immersion in hobbies, though their sense of exemption from European developments puzzled him.

His books were publicly burnt in Germany from May 1933 and many viewed his move as an abdication, a self-indulgence. He had proved reluctant to identify as a Jewish writer and join in public declarations condemning the Hitler regime on that basis. He had his reasons and we'll come to those, but to his critics, and even at times to his friends, he was a coward, an epicure. That the Nazis, newly arrived in power, must have Austria in their sights was clear to anyone with eyes to see. Zweig, for his part, for now, went on imagining that he could still reach his German readership from this new base.

He moved to Hallam Street in 1936 and took British citizenship in 1939 when his Austrian passport expired. 11 Portland Place was pulled down after the war and its site is now occupied by part of a large modernist block. Gaze up from the pavement at the sheer plate glass: this is emphatically not the Grand Budapest Hotel and it never was. That his 'London connections are not very strong' seems, from this angle, an understatement. You are struck, rather, by how total the erasure has been.

*

But were his critics partly right? Did he not perhaps lack some of that pluck in which an Ed Morrow, say, abounded? Wasn't his time here merely the first phase of an ignominious withdrawal? The book he came here to work on might shed some light. Fellow novelist Joseph Roth wrote to him, when *Erasmus* was published in 1934, calling it 'the noblest book you've ever written', praising its language as 'simple and precise'. He asked if he could quote from it in the book he was writing at the time, *Antichrist*. Thomas Mann told his diary that he was persuaded by its central argument: 'mankind has no use for rational, decent order or tolerance, no yearning for "happiness" at all, but prefers recurrent tragedy and untrammelled destructive adventure.'

If *Erasmus* sounds more like a book about the twentieth century than the sixteenth, that was intentional. 'The only other epoch comparable with [the sixteenth century] is our own', its author wrote. He turned down work in Hollywood because this biography 'mattered more' and told a friend that he had not in twenty years felt his work to be so necessary. Alfred Döblin observed how many writers at this time sought 'consolation in historical parallels'. Zweig was not alone in turning to the past as he tried to come to terms with the present. Brecht and Hauptmann had re-written *The Beggar's Opera* in 1928. Roth himself would publish his novel about Napoleon in 1936.

Was this evasion? Zweig for his part understood only too well the role contemporary mass-communications were playing in Europe's disaster – describing Nazi propaganda in a letter as 'chloroform of the spirit'. In London, Broadcasting House was constantly before him, quite literally: the building had opened only a year before he arrived and stood directly opposite 11 Portland Place. Having, on his own admission, 'no gift for polemics', Zweig felt more comfortable expressing his opposition to current events 'through symbols', in this case through a book about the sixteenth century, or 'Europe's fateful hour' as he called it.

His response emerged slowly. From Italy in 1932, where he had given a lecture about the 'European idea', Zweig wrote to a friend about Mussolini's treatment of the press: 'if the National Socialists come to power [in Germany] it will be a thousand times worse...' he observed. The final paragraph of the same letter begins 'I dream of a book about Erasmus of Rotterdam'. Two years later, *Erasmus* was his first book to appear with a new publisher, after his old one dropped him. It sold well anyway, even in Germany.

Luther's stage presence, his mesmerising power as a preacher and orator, are front and central in his account. They are contrasted with Erasmus's quieter gift, with the fastidious intellect and the relative thinness of attachment to particular places of this 'first conscious European'. For all their differences, both men could see that the Church was in crisis. Erasmus urged reform, counselling against a formal break with Rome, fearful of the conflicts that would ensue. Luther 'won' and the Church split. Europe was plunged into a century and more of savagery.

Zweig later claimed that his Erasmus was a 'veiled self-portrait' and the identification was certainly close. He jokingly described his adventures in search of another flat in London not as his own at all but as those of a 'friend of mine called Erasmus'. As England had been, for Erasmus, 'a country of self-discovery', so Zweig wrote to a friend that he had 'not felt better anywhere for years'. As Zweig spent his days poring over manuscripts at the British Library, so Erasmus, escaped from a Dutch monastery, had revelled in England's 'culture and knowledge'.

After a visit to Italy in 1509, Erasmus returned to his newly adopted homeland with the idea for what would become *In Praise of Folly*, still his best-known work. Dedicated to Thomas More, the book is warmed right through with the fellowship he had found in England. He wrote

it easily, taking just a week to set down his superbly ironic survey of European society and its corruptions.

*

The figure of Folly steps forward and asserts from the outset that she alone deserves the gratitude of humanity for all her busy-ness on our behalf. Describing herself as the 'source and origin of all life', she proclaims the 'benefits of keeping oneself untainted from the contagiousness of wisdom'. Unlike lesser divinities, she has no need of temples: the whole earth is her altar. Neither has she any need of formal worship. Humanity pays her the sincerest compliment of all: imitation.

She counsels only a 'wholesome neglect of thinking' – what could be simpler? Science, logic, philosophy: 'in the first golden age there was no need of these perplexities'. Only liberate yourself from 'the pangs of the labouring mind' and you will be 'troubled with no remorse'. Who needs experts? 'Nothing', Folly declares, with an insight that rings impressively true just now, 'Nothing is more welcome and bewitching than the being deceived.' The book ends with a rousing hymn to the triumph of gibberish. Those affected 'speak many things in an abrupt and incoherent manner... they make an articulate noise without any distinguishable sense or meaning'.

Religion is lacerated all the way from respectable church-goer, to the priest, his bishop and the Pope himself. Secular rulers, the professions, the young, the middle-aged and the old – none is spared. Just as party-goers 'send out for a paid comedian' to 'drive away dullness and solemnity', so, Folly observes, do entire peoples, faced with the most serious questions, listen for preference to mountebanks and buffoons. British readers who cannot spot the pertinence of this should buy another round and not worry too much. Cheers!

Zweig's *Erasmus* was his coded attempt to address a 'moment of mass intoxication'. His appeal to common historical experience was in itself an expression of faith in the European collective, but he saw too, only too clearly, the hopelessness of such an appeal. 'There is a fight to the death between Prussia and European civilisation. Or hadn't you noticed?' snapped his exasperated friend Roth in one letter. But Zweig's Erasmian self-portrait was hardly an uncritical one – as Roth appears not to have 'noticed'. Humanism's failings are checked off with merciless precision. Particularly where they ran up against 'the great battering-ram of German nationalist aspirations'. 'Every word' of Luther's sermons 'was racy, pungent, spiced, like the rye bread, freshly baked, that we find on the German peasant's table.'

Erasmus and his 'supranational ideal', by contrast, were no more rooted in England than anywhere else. He was 'everywhere a visitor, a guest, never assimilating the manners and customs of any specific people'. His world was really, like Zweig's, a tiny circle of the very very gifted. This biography might have been written, as Zweig claimed, 'for the small readership of those who understand half-tones', but it was also an act of self-castigation. It issued a damning verdict upon everything he himself had lived for and been. His Erasmus is a profoundly unrealised figure: 'all his life a passionless man.' Only in his *In Praise of Folly* did he show 'that he knew and secretly fought against his inborn rationality, impartiality, sense of duty, moderation.'

If *Erasmus* was an answer to his critics, it was no vindication. Indeed, a chill of premonition hovers about certain phrases: 'non-partisanship and his way of passing things by with averted eyes placed him outside the pale of the living', Zweig wrote, more eerily accurate in his own case than in that of his subject. He did answer those who accused him of going into 'hiding' in England: 'I won't deny it when you say I'm hiding. If you are unable to impose your own decisions, you should avoid them. You forget... that I state my problem PUBLICLY in my *Erasmus*, where I portray the so-called cowardliness of a conciliatory nature *without* celebrating it...'

But this is from a private letter. Couldn't he have ceded ground to his critics more publicly? Yes, if he had been a different writer from the one he was. If the European collective had not been at the core of who he was. If that collective frame of reference no longer obtained, his world no longer worked. Small wonder, then, that he was reluctant to admit it. He felt that the best thing any writer, Jewish or not, could do under such circumstances was to continue writing good books. That it was also in England that he began writing *The Buried Candelabrum*, based on a legend about the menorah, again suggests that the charge of faint-heartedness had found its mark, even if he reserved the right to answer it in his own way. He also supported a Yiddish theatre group and The House of a Thousand Destinies, a homeless shelter in Whitechapel which he heard about by talking to Jewish refugees on the ferry.

11 Portland Place was the scene of a writer's grim, lonely struggle with himself. Everything that ought to have prepared him for this moment left him instead powerless to react in any way that might influence events. Would he even have wanted the scene of that struggle remembered? Perhaps his spirit felt itself inexplicably lightened, on the other side, as the wrecking ball swung in Portland Place.

It was as the 'man with a book' that Dürer portrayed Erasmus. The Renaissance of the humanists, Zweig argued, was as close as Europe ever came to achieving a 'collective life'. It was through them that Europe 'found its vocation'. That vocation not only implied 'the eclipse of national vanity', but also presented itself as a 'spiritual demand'. Those who work for an 'all-embracing European nation... cannot afford to blink the fact that their work in this cause is perpetually menaced by irrational passion'.

*

There is surely a problem about Zweig's analogy between the sixteenth and twentieth centuries. The crudity of his Luther–Hitler analogy upset reviewers, as did the unsubtle identification with Erasmus. Both Luther and Erasmus, after all, could agree about Europe's central problem: the need to reform the Catholic Church. Upon what exactly were the likes of Adolf Hitler and Stefan Zweig agreed? Is it not wilful to insist upon your cultural *habitus* when it is up against a new reality so completely alien to it? When all about you, others are listening to the radio (and/or logging on to their Twitter feeds)?

Joseph Roth might urge his friend to abandon his shallow humanism but knew there was no point in trying to convert him to his view that 'Germany can still be saved by Christ'. Zweig's Europe, like that of his Renaissance hero, was essentially a humanist dream, created not on any imperial or religious model but 'through gentle convincing'. 'Voluntary adhesion and inner freedom' would be its 'fundamental laws'. 'The instinct of his age' chose Erasmus to speak for this dream. Zweig chose him to speak for it again just as the twentieth-century nightmare took hold.

Joseph Roth's *Antichrist* is addressed to the same historical moment. It interprets the global crisis, of which Hitler's 'accession' was a symptom, as part of a wider unmooring, ultimately religious in nature. Roth's vision is darker and more demonic than Zweig's. It comes across as both a wilder and also truer response to that age of extremes.

But Zweig's response, oblique as it is, has lasted at least as well. It's as if he was gambling on Europe's ultimate survival, whatever its immediate prospects. His faith may have been a secular one but it did not prove shallow. To read his *Erasmus* now is to feel, unmistakably, that original impulse from which the European Union later grew. Idealists, he warned, need to remember that the 'torrent of unreason' can be unloosed at any moment: 'Nearly every generation experiences such a set-back, and it is the duty of each to keep a cool head until the disaster is over and calm is restored.'

However evasive it seemed to some of his contemporaries, much of *Erasmus* feels uncannily addressed to what came 'after'. His speeches on Europe in the early 1930s had emphasised the need to stop teaching history as a résumé of who won which war and why, thereby normalising conflict. The young should be introduced also to the infinitely various ways in which their different countries have worked together. For anyone who grew up in the 1980s, the Erasmus student exchange programme, whereby students in one country could attend universities in other parts of Europe, seemed a natural development of this premise. With hindsight, the Europe in which we grew up was a brave attempt, however flawed, to restore the humanist dream.

*

It is Zweig's dream from which we have been woken with a start: 'I love the poorly educated', bawls Donald Trump, irony-proof as ever. And if his Brexiteer friends don't put it quite like that – having enjoyed, so many of them, Rolls Royce educations – it's not because they don't feel it too. Seventy-three percent of those who left school without qualifications voted Leave, which is a lot of people. Seventy-five percent of those with postgraduate qualifications voted Remain, which is not so many. The English school system being what it is, this was inevitably a class issue. How wise it was to fight a proxy class war over Europe we shall all be discovering very soon now.

The Referendum, in any case, returns us to the central conundrum of Zweig's book. 'Pan-Europa, Cosmopolis, must exist before it can win general allegiance,' but it remains always 'a distant and scarcely visible goal.' Was, is, then, European-ness always an identity which appeals mainly to an educated minority? In humanism, 'there is no room for the passion of hatred' so that a 'panhuman ideal such as Erasmism lacks that elementary attraction which a mettlesome encounter with a foe who lives across a frontier, speaks another language, and holds another creed, invariably exercises.' Something very like the outlines of our 'immigration debate' are clearly visible here.

Remainers have been much criticised for their mealy-mouthed admissions that the EU is flawed. They have been criticised, in other words, for believing in an idea which is difficult to realise. 'An idea which does not take on material shape is not necessarily a conquered idea or a false idea', as Zweig put it. Whether or not it prevails, it continues 'to work as a ferment in subsequent generations...'

What form might this 'ferment' now take? It will, apparently, take the form of a parliamentary vote. It might yet might take the form of another referendum. Meanwhile might we not re-run that discussion about how to commemorate Zweig's time in London, five years on? It doesn't matter whether the end result is a plaque or not, in Hallam Street or Portland Place or anywhere else. If we can manage something recognisable as a discussion, that will be victory enough. Because to have such a discussion would automatically, now, become an exploration of what Europe *means*. The pre-Referendum debate, that purely theatrical exchange of snarl-words, amplified and orchestrated by social media, was also manipulated, it now seems likely, by a foreign power with its own dog in the fight. In no way can it be described as a 'discussion'.

Whereas the whole point here would be the discussion. There would be genuine arguments both ways. Those who have never heard of Erasmus or Zweig or Luther and don't see why they should have would of course be welcome to contribute. So would those who know something about all three but for whatever reason cannot see how they are relevant. Those who, for their part, do rate some or all of them, would have the opportunity to explain why.

And plaque or no plaque, we might all emerge, belatedly, a little the wiser.

BIBLIOGRAPHY

Erasmus, *In Praise of Folly*, Peter Eckler, New York, 1910

Michael Hofmann, *Joseph Roth: A Life in Letters*, Granta, 2012

Oliver Matuschek, *Stefan Zweig: Drei Leben, Eine Biografie*, Fischer, 2006

D. A. Prater, *European of Yesterday,* OUP, 1973

Klemens Renoldner, Rüdiger Görner ed., *Zweigs England*, Schriftenreihe des Stefan Zweig Centre, Salzburg, 2012

Joseph Roth, *Antichrist,* Peter Owen Publishers, 2010

Stefan Zweig, *Erasmus*, Cassell, 1934

Stefan Zweig, *Briefe 1932–1942*, Fischer, 2005

Stefan Zweig, *The Buried Candelabrum*, Phaidon, 1944

Volker Weidemann, *Summer Before the Dark*, Pushkin Press, 2016

Four Poems

ANGELA LEIGHTON

Janáćek's Notes

as he notated his daughter's dying breaths

I time you, dearest, to the last minute now,
hold your departing to a page of notes,
scribble each phrase your breathing makes
in breves, minims, in the pause between
each catch, acciaccatura, of your breath –
its stress and start, then a rest – rest...
I hear its sparing quiet on your chest.

I time you, living, to save your breath,
Olga, Jenufa, in the world's free air
that's large enough to sustain the tune
we make, breathing, still lightly keeping
time for a time till, two against three,
these sudden faint syncopations misalign,
and you're out – on a beat much wider than mine.

I compose you, darling, in this plot of time,
the sigh of oxygen sieved through your lungs,
the wheeze and panic of it flying free
beyond my shaky amanuensis hands
into the open, unaccompanied there –
your solo-silence towering, avant-garde,
while I re-arrange these notes in a graveyard.

Sage

i.m. Eugenio Polgovsky, filmmaker

Consider a garden, walled and riverrun,
hedged to windward, level-lawned,
flowered in sudden cuts of colour –
a tidy wonderland queering the sunshine.

It seems a formal dreamscape on location,
a take on how the mind might slip
from wide shots back to jump-cuts now,
and loop a blue flower to the afternoon's

routine soundtrack of youthful voices –
futures opening beyond these walls
where we two stop, and pick few words,
feeling along the hows and whys –

as if by some rewound reportage,
the chance of something said, not said,
and all the accidents of happenstance,
it might have gone another way.

So words – pot-shots at what's just hidden,
keepsakes, wake-men, bearers, forbears,
memos, memorials, makeshifts, lightweights,
mystery's lighteners, gravity's weights –

so we who remain talk in a garden...
The air seems thin through which you escaped,
breathable, and all to share;
the sun dabbles in shots of paint.

And here's the blue slipper of a flower
turning a shape as clear as day:
salvia, sage, for safe, safe-keeping,
itself the strange salve of a name –

as if we'd ever know for a moment
what makes a life too hard to bear,
too long to stay, and yet might spare
a word for the light-jagged glory of it.

The air is patient with nothing to say.
That blue flower signs, like punctuation,
the place where words break off, and roots
riot darkly across old borders:

salvia, sage – for salvage, saving,
for naming a wish larger than we know,
for wise or salutary – even, finally,
a salutation: so, *Salve, Eugenio.*

Naples Abstract

So close so dark

    you're daily tombed

a cage of crossroads

    acrostics of stone

no elbow room

    in poverty's strips

dirty pickings

    in quadrant alleys

flushing to where

    (Caravaggio's

chiaroscuro

    Gesualdo's

Tenebrae)

    sea's a brushstroke

ultramarine

    sky's a cadence

after quarter tones.

    Art's a settling

murders' scores.

    Blue's a high aim.

Dark's our home.

Toccata for the Pezzentelle

The 'anime pezzentelle' are the unknown dead, whose
bones are gathered in three large caves in Naples, and
who are sometimes tended by the living in return for
favours granted – a practice surviving despite a ban by
the Church.

Cittá cantabile, O Partenope –
siren-singer whose song's a despair
          turned over and over,
a wail from earth's fault-line, fluencies of waves,
a corpse knocking onshore at the start,
          a founding in pain.

Neapolis, Naples – shunned enchantress
whose shudder of hurt, like a pulse in the place,
          thrums its bass line
where ancient underworlds press too close,
and the dreamy dead clutter underfoot
          in charnels and crypts –

like these arranged, efficacious death's-heads,
their wise, wide-eyed, look-alike attention
          lovingly addressed,
polished, wreathed, bedded on silk wraps –
anime pezzentell – soft touch for a petition,
          heavenly pets

cherished for a cure or a lottery win,
held to account in this rough market-trade
          of living and dead.
They might grant a prayer for a shinier pate,
a wish, a grace, for a comfier grave,
          for a coin in pay –

unless it's a wager between old and new:
crossings by ferry instead of by flame,
          Charon, not Mary –
This ragging, streetwise, calculable exchange
touches such depths of desire, and story –
          I might even pay.

Cittá cantabile, Napoli bella –
I come with an old emptiness at heart
          for one lost voice,
and discover the call of an ancient lament
in this cracked earth with its rackety cults
          of death and salvation,

in the tune of a land that still quakes and kills,
and takes us in, with its singing ways,
          to the dead-in-waiting –
where Persephone lurks at a crossroads at night,
Vulcan stokes his volcanic fires,
          Avernus gapes.

So here at the cemetery *delle Fontanelle*
I'd touch to summon, in the play of a name,
          some capped spirit
still shut in its bone-lock of fontanelles,
life stubbornly inhabiting its matter –
          and pause, bereft.

For see, my own dead are nowhere and nothing,
their lives finished, their voices flown –
          except when I catch
in the tune of an oath, the lilt of an outrage,
such singing sadness in this city's own,
          like her audible ghost.

So I reach a hand – toccata for something –
tap for the soul long escaped in story,
          riffle a finger
across the anonymous casque of a skull.
For this, for nothing, I'd touch, petition
          for some lost conversation.

Two Poems

ANTHONY RUDOLF

The Card Players (1966–73)

Mesdames, Messieurs
the empty chair awaits you:
first come, first served

to your left, a trickster
card sharp,
              to your right
a fortune teller

of the past, lying
ahead of you,
like a dream, a store

of menace, bought into
like a Ponzi scheme.
Watch your back,

Balthus invites you
to a game of cards,
Balthus invites you

to share his secret,
become a member
of the painting,

become his double,
hypocrite viewer,
pedlar of illusion.

Iron enters
the soul of the real
at last, as you wake

to the knowledge
like a cab driver
that Balthus,

Count Balthazar
Klossowski de Rola,
holds all the cards

in all the streets,
in all the passageways,
in all the arcades.

Fado for Paula

Plane-trees expire on the avenue
And no dogs bark.

Fado singers embrace in a tavern
And the sea is dying.

I hold you tight and I feel
The beat of your heart.

I give you red wine and a book.
Roses are brought to your senses.

Songs drift over like dunes.
You keep to the shoreline.

'How English I Was'

Adam Kirsch, Jews & the Global Novel

DAVID HERMAN

Adam Kirsch, *The Global Novel: Writing the World in the 21st Century* (New York: Columbia Global Reports), 2016, 105pp
Adam Kirsch, *The People and the Books: 18 Classics of Jewish Literature* (W.W. Norton), 2016, 432pp

OVER THE LAST THIRTY or forty years there has been an interesting revolution in reading habits in this country. Curiously, it has passed almost unnoticed.

In the 1970s I was studying English A Level. The course was made up the usual suspects: two Shakespeare plays, a Chaucer tale, Pope and Coleridge, Jane Austen and *Jane Eyre*. It couldn't have been more English. Then we came to the last set text, *Herzog* by Saul Bellow. One of our two English teachers refused to teach it. 'It's not English', he said and that was that. The other teacher, some years younger, grew a moustache, changed his glasses to something from *Easy Rider* and taught it on his own.

For me it was love at first sight. I had never read any contemporary American fiction or any modern Jewish writing. From the first sentence I was enthralled and have loved Jewish-American literature ever since.

I stayed in touch with most of my teachers. Two things struck me about them. First, how well-read they all were. Second, what they read was English literature not Jewish, not American, not European. I was talking with a former History teacher a few years ago. He told me he had read the whole of Kipling and had devoured much of the English canon. I felt so unread. Then it occurred to me that the writers I have read over the past thirty years were mostly Jewish, American, Russian, central European. Stefan Zweig and Joseph Roth, Patrick Modiano, Grossman and Babel, Bellow, Roth and many of the young Americans. And when I think of the writers I talk about with my friends and contemporaries, these are the kinds of writers we talk about. Not Austen, James or even Dickens. Certainly not Kipling. Conrad, yes. Amis and McEwan, certainly. But generally the books most of us stay up late talking about are by foreign authors.

A year ago, Bryan, the English teacher who refused to teach *Herzog* died. I went to his memorial service at the Grosvenor Chapel in London. He had sung with the Grosvenor Chapel Choir for years. He was an extraordinarily cultured man. He acted with the RSC, sang with this fine choir and read and read. The service was deeply moving.

The opening music was by Elgar. Bryan's words quoted in the programme were telling. 'It wasn't Elgar's violin concerto that tugged me this way and that, it was the Introduction and Allegro for Strings: that was the music that made me understand how English I was – all that windswept restless chasing about and cross-rhythm energy and then the sudden, irresistible melancholy and secret sadness, the knowledge of an immense sadness, but held in a balance with the surging, tumbling energy of the rest.'

Later music included 'Thou art my King, O God' by Thomas Tomkins, *Linden Lea* and *The Vagabond* by Vaughan Williams, 'Agnus Dei' from *Mass for Four Voices* by William Byrd and Dum transisset sabbatum by John Tavener. The readings were 'The Owl' by Edward Thomas, 'a favourite moment from *David Copperfield*', 'Blueberry Picking' by Seamus Heaney, 'A favourite moment from *Much Ado about Nothing* and 'Toad's Song' from *Toad of Toad Hall*, adapted by A.A. Milne.

It was magnificent. I sat enthralled. It spoke of a whole life and, more than that, a whole culture. It was so English. Much of it from that great century of English music and literature from Dickens and Vaughan Williams to Edward Thomas and Elgar.

This selection would have spoken to a whole generation. Bryan was born in County Durham in 1935. He did his national service, studied at Oxford, acted with the Bristol Old Vic and the RSC, was head of English at St. Paul's School for almost twenty years. And yet though I love Dickens and A.A. Milne, and once in the sixth form read out a passage about Edward Thomas in class, I love these European, American and Jewish writers more. They are the books of my life.

And my favourite critics are not Leavis or Kermode but émigrés like George Steiner and Gabriel Josipovici, and, increasingly, Americans like Ruth Franklin and Adam Kirsch. By and large, they write about the writers I read.

'Adam Kirsch,' wrote James Wood, 'is the most exciting, the most serious, and the most courageous young poet-critic in America.' He burst upon the American literary scene at the turn of the century, reviewing for *The New Republic* and the Jewish online literary magazine, *Tablet*. He has since reviewed regularly for *The New York Review of Books*, *The New Yorker* and other publications on both sides of the Atlantic.

Kirsch is a prolific critic. The reviews pour out. His range is tremendous, writing on subjects from Heidegger and Plato to Bellow and William Carlos Williams. He is unapologetically highbrow and unusually for a critic of his generation he writes widely about Jewish literature and religion.

He is a poet and writes passionately about modern poetry. He published his first collection of poems in 2002 and his first book on poetry, *The Wounded Surgeon: Confession and Transformation in Six American Poets*, in 2005. *The Wounded Surgeon* was about post-war American poetry, from Delmore Schwartz and Sylvia Plath to Berryman and Lowell.

Kirsch goes his own way. He was never influenced by the Theory revolution. His writing is free of academic jargon and it is no coincidence that his first book about criticism was a book on Lionel Trilling, *Why Trilling Matters* (2011). It is hard to imagine a title further removed from contemporary academic criticism with its preoccupations with feminism, multi-culturalism and Theory.

Above all, there is his critical intelligence. His reviews are among the most incisive and intelligent critical essays published in recent years. What marks him out is his ability to put a writer in context and explore what is at stake in their work.

He has now brought out two new books. *The Global Novel: Writing the World in the 21st Century*, a slim, hundred-page book of six short essays, and *The People and the Books: 18 Classics of Jewish Literature*, a book of essays about Jewish thought and religion from Deuteronomy to Sholem Aleichem (the one concession to fiction).

The Global Novel starts with Goethe. 'The epoch of world literature is at hand', he wrote. What does this mean? asks Kirsch. Does it mean 'simply an age, like our own, in which many books, especially, the classics, are available for reading? Or did Goethe hope for something more – a truly cosmopolitan literature, in which national origin would have ceased to matter at all?' And does the new world literature reflect the globalisation which is transforming our world, economically, culturally and even the books we read?

Kirsch assesses the state of what he calls 'World Literature' through five essays on individual works by an unlikely group of writers: Orhan Pamuk, Haruki Murakami, Roberto Bolaño, Mohsin Hamid, Chimamanda Ngozi Adichie, Margate Atwood, Michel Houellebecq and Elena Ferrante. Each essay is interesting but the book as a whole raises a number of problems.

First, are close readings of very different novels by very different authors helpful or would it have been better to see what, if anything, defines 'The Global Novel'? For example, what do the feminist dystopian novels of Margaret Attwood have in common with those who have written more about the immigrant experience, 'a new kind of life across borders', a world transformed by the Internet, iPhones and cheap jet travel, the subject of perhaps the best chapter, on Adichie and Mohsin Hamid? These novels are literally worlds apart. This new migrant literature is even very different from Naipaul's *Mr Biswas*. Some of the books Kirsch discusses are local not global at all. Think of Ferrante on Naples or Pamuk on Turkey.

Second, how new is 'The Global Novel'? Older readers might wonder about the complete absence in Kirsch's book of the generation of great post-colonial writers like V.S. Naipaul, Carlos Fuentes, Marquez and Achebe, all born in the late 1920s and early 1930s, whose first works were published in the late 1950s. Or even the next generation of writers like Rushdie, Ben Okri, Ishiguro, Michael Ondaatje and Arundhati Roy who received such acclaim in the 1980s and '90s? By comparison, how 'global' are Kirsch's writers? Houellebecq is French, Ferrante Italian and Atwood white-Canadian. Should Kirsch distinguish more between those who have always lived and written in their home country and those who are migrants, such as Bolaño, born in Chile, who spent the first half of his life in South America, and then moved to Spain in 1977 and spent the rest of his life there?

Third, how useful a term here is globalisation? Does it help us make sense of the shifting centre of gravity of world literature from South America and India to Africa and the Middle East? In the 1970s and '80s so many leading writers were from Central and South America: Fuentes and Marquez, of course, but also G. Cabrera Infante, Vargas Llosa, Isabel Allende, Manuel Puig and Ariel Dorfman. Today, as many come from Africa and the Middle East. What does a vague concept like globalisation tell us about this shift? Kirsch uses it a lot especially in his Introduction, but doesn't ask whether it's a useful term or whether we should fall back on the old Marxist reflection theory of literature, 'The Global Novel' coinciding with or reflecting the age of globalisation.

Fourth, what about the English writers who wrote about empire: from Kipling, Conrad and E.M. Forster to Orwell, Durrell and Paul Scott? Empire played a huge role in English literature for decades and some of the most interesting post-colonial critical writing (Achebe on *Heart of Darkness*, Edward W Said on *Kim*) engaged with this canon. There are no references to Said's classic, *Culture and Imperialism* (1993) or post-colonial critics like Homi K. Bhabha or Gayatri Spivak, who exploded on the scene in the 1980s. One of Kirsch's great virtues as a critic is that he has resisted the academic orthodoxies of our time. He has a distinctive and original voice, but there's no reason why he can't engage with others who have thought about these issues.

However, what is most interesting about Kirsch's book is that here is a work of criticism by one of America's most acclaimed critics which doesn't include a single British or American writer. The canon is shifting. More and more of the fiction many of us are reading are by writers from across the world about their experiences of a fast-changing world of dictators and migrants, not of British writers writing about British characters in India or 'Greeneland'.

The People and the Books is a very different and much more substantial kind of project. Four hundred pages, fourteen essays on Jewish thought from the Old Testament to Spinoza, Moses Mendelssohn and Herzl, finishing, oddly, with Tevye the Dairyman, the one concession to Yiddish. Here, Kirsch is much more on home ground. He directs Columbia's masters programme in Jewish Studies and for years has written widely on Jewish literature and religion for Tabletmag.com. Recently, he has been reading and writing for Tablet about a page of Talmud a day.

The book is subtitled '18 Classics of Jewish Literature', but this is literature in a very wide sense. The book is really about Jewish thought and religion, with chapters on history (Josephus) and philosophy (Maimonides, Spinoza).

Each chapter begins with a particular work, assessing its impact, putting it in biographical and historical context and then exploring particular themes. Put together, these chapters evoke a powerful sense of the importance of the Jewish diaspora. Of course, he writes about the great centres of Jewish thought but he also shows the importance of Jews in Persia, Egypt and Spain. This is a book of celebration, 'a history of books', but Kirsch never underestimates the precariousness of Jewish life in the diaspora or the violence and anti-Jewish hatred over more than two thousand years.

Above all, his focus is on 'the canonical books at the heart of Jewish religion', the Bible and the Talmud, 'the foundation of an unbroken tradition of commentary and codification, which is responsible for some of the greatest monuments of Jewish creativity.' 'In the map of Jewish writing,' he says, 'the law and the commentaries are the central continent.' This is not a book about Jewish poetry or fiction and it is no coincidence that it stops at the beginning of the twentieth century. There is no Paul Celan or Isaac Babel, no Vassily Grossman or Primo Levi. Instead, Kirsch's focus is unblinking. It is on God, the Torah, the Land of Israel and the Jewish people.

I have one central reservation. Kirsch is a literary critic but rarely does he engage with the Bible or indeed any of the writers he discusses as literature. There are a few exceptions. In the essay on Pirkei Avot, 'The Ethics of the Fathers', a collection of sayings and aphorisms written around 250 CE, he describes how Rabbi Yochanan ben Zakkai escapes from Jerusalem. Yochanan asked two of his disciples to build him a coffin and smuggle him past the Jewish guards, who knew that corpses could not remain in the city overnight. 'The most important thing about the story,' Kirsch explains, 'is that it offers a symbolic explanation of what happened to the Jewish faith after the Temple was destroyed.' Just as Yochanan underwent a kind of death in order to live, so Judaism died in Jerusalem but was reborn in Yavneh under the care of the rabbis. This is Kirsch at his best. Thoughtful, clear, free of any kind of jargon.

Or take the chapter on Philo of Alexandria. Kirsch reads Philo's account of the burning bush. Philo insists that Moses did not hear a voice from the bush. 'The meaning of the bush, for Philo, is not audible but visible.' For Philo it is an allegory, 'a rational message in visual form'.

However, in general this is very different from the kind of literary reading that Gabriel Josipovici offers in *The Book of God* (1988) (see the piece by Rabbi Howard Cooper in the November/December issue of *PN Review*), the extraordinary opening chapter of Erich Auerbach's *Mimesis* (1946), comparing the homecoming of Odysseus with the sacrifice of Abraham in Genesis, or the collection of essays, *Midrash and Literature 1986*, edited by Geoffrey Hartman and Sanford Budick. Over the last thirty years, in particular, there has been an explosion of critics reading the Old Testament as literature, as a form of storytelling. The shift from the New Testament to the Old, has been one of the great watersheds in post-war literary criticism. Kirsch doesn't mention this critical work in his notes and doesn't seem interested in it as a way of making sense of these 'Classics of Jewish Literature'. As criticism, many of his readings are curiously old-fashioned.

However, there is also much to admire here. As well as familiar classics (Maimonides, Spinoza, Herzl) there are interesting introductions to less well-known figures: Philo of Alexandria, Benjamin of Tudela and Yehuda Halevi and, above all, Gluckel of Hameln.

The book is full of interesting insights. All those apparently tedious genealogies in the Old Testament are 'a chain of authority', a way of speaking about continuity. And the way Pirkei Avot establishes this sense of continuity 'opposes the notion of Jewish history as a series of ruptures and calamities'. There is nothing here about 'the destruction of the First Temple or the Second; nothing about the exile of the Ten Lost Tribes of Israel, or the Babylonian Exile, or the Diaspora following the Jewish War'. These, Kirsch writes, are political events from the past. Ancient history. 'What matters is the Torah, and the Torah lives in a perpetual present.'

Or take his account of the Itinerary of Benjamin of Tudela in the 1160s. It offers, Kirsch writes, 'a revealing map of the Jewish world in the twelfth century'. From Spain to Iraq, the overwhelming majority, perhaps ninety percent, of Jews lived under Muslim rule. In western Europe there were hardly any Jews in even the biggest cities – '200 Jews in Arles, 500 in Naples.' In the Middle East, by contrast, there are five thousand Jews in Aleppo, seven thousand in Mosul, perhaps forty thousand in Baghdad.

Kirsch offers a clear and fascinating account of the great shift from Temple Judaism to rabbinic Judaism. The rabbis redefined Judaism as 'a religion of text and law' and transformed the Jewish relationship to texts. Jewish history 'became the story not of power, but of ideas and beliefs. And its most important turning points would not be the winning of wars or the building of monuments, but the writing of books.'

At his best here, Kirsch is not offering literary criticism but putting the great turning points of Judaism and Jewish thought in historical context. He identifies the major sinews and arteries with great clarity and offers a rich panoptic view of four thousand years of Judaism.

Put together, these two books are examples of a fascinating trend in literary criticism: the move from English Literature, from Beowulf to Virginia Woolf, to foreign literature in translation, with Jewishness moved from the margins to the centre. This was unthinkable forty years ago. Suddenly, some of our best critics are writing about texts written two thousand years before Shakespeare, many written thousands of miles from Jane Austen's Hampshire. And if we read Kipling or Margaret Atwood, the chances are that we may read them through the eyes of a Palestinian critic like Edward Said or a Jewish-American critic like Adam Kirsch.

This is a revolution in the way we read. Does it reflect the age of globalisation? Or the increasing importance of migration in the last forty years? Or a shift of gravity in literature from the English-speaking world to other countries and cultures, past and present? Are we English as we were, or has Englishness itself changed profoundly? How did Jewishness suddenly become so important in literature and literary criticism? In these two books, Kirsch offers a fascinating introduction to these questions.

Bathe/1

(after Dante)

NED DENNY

Now I put that crude and cruel sea behind me,

trimming the sails to steer my ingenuity
towards calmer waters, and presently I'll sing
of the intermediate realm where the cleansing
without which no one climbs the sky is undergone.
Here poetry's corpse is going to rise again,
for I am yours, slender Muses, soul and body,
so let Calliope stand and accompany
my verse with something of that more than human tone
that made the raucous magpies despair of pardon.
The entire orient now showed a flawless sapphire –
a self-asserting radiance, sweet blue fire
suffusing the serene countenance of the air

as far as the horizon, unutterably clear –
such that once more the simple fact of sight
was a thing to marvel at and cause of delight,
my lids no longer weighed down by that world of pain.
The beautiful planet that makes all creatures pine
for what they've lost was shining like laughter in the east,
Pisces invisible but pursuing fast,
and I turned to the right and towards the other pole;
four stars were set there, stars the aboriginal
inhabitants of earth knew but never seen since,
and the skies seemed to take a conscious joy in their brilliance...
deprived lands of the deep north, now I know

why it is you still wear the clothes of a widow!
As I looked at them they seemed to look *into* me,
a fleeting premonition or a memory
I wrenched my gaze away from to find there had appeared
at some little distance a man whose white-flecked beard
hung on his chest between his long hair's tresses;
the four holy orbs lit his face as dawn kisses
the brow of one sitting in the presence of the sun,
and I knew he was worthy of the reverence a son
should pay his father for the sake of his years.
'Who *are* you,' he said, the venerable feathers
of his sinuous locks swaying as he talked,

'who've swum against the blind tide and seemingly walked
out of the cage of shadows called eternity.
Who aided you in your escape from that valley
bathed in unyielding blackness by fathomless night,
for no one could do it with neither guide nor light,
and have the laws of the abyss been broken
or somehow repealed in the highest court of heaven
to enable a damned soul to land on my coast?'
Now my pale duke spoke, but not without having first
made me kneel and lower my head by means of sounds
and signs and, finally, the pressure of his hands.
'I haven't come for my own sake or come alone,

but in obedience to the entreaties of one
who flitted from the sun for the sake of this man...

I am his hurricane lamp and his companion.
You seem to wish to know how it truly goes with us,
so I must oblige. My charge never saw the gorgeous
wrack of fiery cloud that a dying man sees,
but had progressed so far in his idiocies
that he was close to the point from which no flesh returns;
I was sent to rescue him, the way that burns
being by that stage the sole alternative
to death. Now that he's seen how the evil dead live,
I intend to show him those spirits who are

enduring the purity of your mountain lair.
The story thus far would take an age to tell you,
but suffice to say that a potency and virtue
that flows down into me has quickened our ascent...
here he can hear you speak, and, no less important,
observe the justice of your face with his eyes.
He is one who, like you, knows true freedom is
a thing more precious than bestial existence
and slavish days. He seeks it; you died for it once.
No edict's been transgressed, for this man is alive
and I'm not bound by Minos but one who drifts above
those depths in the circle where Marcia implores –

with a speaking glance – that you consider her yours
in death as in life. Let us pass, for her love's sake,
through your seven bracing regions and I will take
word of your kindness to her – if you'll allow
your name's sacred syllables to be sounded below.'
'Back then,' he said, 'the merest sight of Marcia
gave me no option but to be good to her
however she desired, but now the deathly
stream flows between us and her looks can't bend or touch me...
such is what the new law ordained at my release.
Yet there's no need for these elaborate flatteries,
if what you say is right and a woman from the sky

guides your every move. Go, but make sure you tie
a reed around his waist and wash his mortal face
(when he stands before His ministrant, any trace
of hell's grime that darkens his eyes will ignite
in that radiance reflecting paradise's light).
The reeds you will find on this island's muddy shore,
down there where the white surf's perpetual thunder
would destroy any plant less able to relent;
don't come back this way, for an easier ascent
will be shown by the royal orb that now begins to rise.'
With that he vanished, and I stood and drew close
to my guardian's side. 'Step where I step,' he said,

'and this sloping plain will lead us to the reed bed.'
All-conquering dawn was chasing the predawn wind,
the far sea flickering like a Venetian blind,
as we made or half-guessed our way as a man
who has strayed and doubts he'll ever find his path again.
Soon we came to where the silver encampment
of the dew survives in shade, and with reverent
touch the maestro laid his open palms on the grass;
then, placing his streaming hands on my grief-lined face,
he restored the vital glow that night had concealed.
On reaching the bleak coast which no man ever sailed
and lived to tell the tale, he girdled me with a thin

reed instantly replaced by its identical twin.

Bernard

GABRIEL JOSIPOVICI

'I THINK I'VE FOUND the right translator for you', my French publisher, Pascal Arnaud said. 'His name is Bernard Hoepffner and he's recently translated Burton's *Anatomy of Melancholy*.'

This was in 2010. Pascal had just taken me on. He said he was interested in eventually bringing out all my work in French, but he wanted to start with my 1994 novel, *Moo Pak*, which has the young Jonathan Swift at its heart. Since one of Swift's favourite works was Burton's *Anatomy*, Pascal's suggestion made perfect sense. And Bernard, when I met him (tall, stooped, balding, with large intense eyes behind thick glasses and a large sensual mouth, a ring in his ear, an airman's leather jacket and a rucksack on his back, a sort of hippy Giacometti), turned out to be a fan and translator of another of my much-loved authors, Sir Thomas Browne. I asked him if he knew Borges' story, 'Tlön, Uqbar, Orbis Tertius', which ends with the narrator retiring from a world sliding into totalitarianism to devote himself to a translation of Thomas Browne's *Urne Burial*. 'It was reading that story which made me want to translate Browne', Bernard said, and I knew we would become firm friends.

Since taking me on Pascal has published five of my novels, and Bernard has translated three of them: *Moo Pak*, *Goldberg: Variations*, and *Infinity: The Story of a Moment*, which won the Laure Bataillon Prize in 2016. The Prize is given to the best translation into French, taking into account the quality of the book as well as of the translation, and it is divided into two categories, 'contemporary' and 'classical'. Bernard is one of only two people to have ever won the prize twice, the first time, in the classical category for his Thomas Browne, and the second time for *Infinity*.

At the publication in French of each of my books Pascal has been keen for me to come to France and do readings in various bookshops, mainly in Paris. Bernard, naturally, was also involved. We would both read, talk about the book and answer questions. He was much more than a translator, he was a passionate enthusiast and a brilliant communicator. He somehow always managed to introduce topics for discussion which allowed us to talk about the essence of what the book was trying to do. In talking about books to British audiences I find I have to fight hard to get past the trivia, while in France the problem is oversolemnity and abstraction. Bernard had spent enough time in Britain to know the dangers of both extremes and in our bookshop events he always managed to keep the tone light while not eschewing seriousness and depth. And his translations were so good that my partner Tamar, hearing us both read from *Goldberg: Variations*, was led, on one occasion, to say to me: 'You know, I think it reads better in French than it does in English.' This was not entirely a surprise to me as I had tried to write that book in an English that would feel slightly 'translated', but it did highlight the fact that Bernard managed, in book after book, to appropriate totally the work he was translating and make it a new and living thing.

After these readings we would go out for a meal. He loved women and Tamar enchanted him. 'What a shame,' he exclaimed on one occasion when she couldn't be there, 'I was so looking forward to seeing her. She brings light wherever she goes.'

Pascal also sent us off by train to other cities, and in one or two – Tours and Brussels – we stayed the night. I was on my own with Bernard on the trip to Brussels, and in the train he talked about himself. His father had been an engineer turned wealthy industrialist from Strasbourg, who had fought for the Free French and had firm views on what his children should do with their lives. He wanted his son to become an architect but Bernard baulked at this. At school in Paris's smart XVI *arrondissement*, he had been taught by the fiercely independent Surrealist Julien Gracq, who had famously turned down the Goncourt Prize in 1951 because he felt prizes were incompatible with the vocation of the artist, and who confirmed him in his sense that to live properly you have to find your own way. So, after a year of architectural study, and with national service looming, he decamped to England. This naturally caused a breach with his father and meant that he would be faced with a court-martial and possible prison should he ever return to France.

In London he lodged in Spitalfields and earned his living restoring Far Eastern artefacts. Not that he knew anything about the subject but he would read it up in the local library and improvise. 'It was too easy to make money that way', he told me. 'I was twenty-two and didn't know what to do with my life, I only knew it was not this.' His landlord knew of a cottage overlooking the sea at St. David's Head, in Pembrokeshire, without electricity or running water. 'Just the thing for me', Bernard said. So he upped sticks and went off to Wales. 'They were among the happiest days of my life', he told me on that trip to Brussels. 'Girl-friends would come every now and again and stay for a day or two and we grilled the fish we'd caught and made love overlooking the sea, and then they'd go and I'd be alone with only the sea and the sky for company. I loved it.' But then one of the girls stayed, they married and eventually left Wales and settled in a barren island in the Canaries, where the only water came from the sky and when the rains failed the farmers had to slaughter their cattle. 'I learned how to be a subsistence farmer', he said. 'We made a bare living from the soil and were happy. But when our child came along we discovered there was only one midwife on the island and she almost arrived too late, so we decided to head back to civilisation.'

Through his father's intervention (he had come round to accepting that Bernard would never be the son he had hoped he would be) he was given a conditional pardon by the military authorities and the family settled in Lyon, where Bernard decided to try his hand at translation. After all, he was trilingual, with a father and mother who spoke German as well as French, a French education and an English wife. Soon he was in high demand. In the course of his career he translated classics like Burton and Browne, a lot of Mark Twain, including *Huckleberry Finn* and *Tom Sawyer*, and became the main French translator of Robert Coover, Gilbert Sorrentino and numerous other avant-garde American authors, with many of whom he became friends. He rendered Jacques Roubaud into English. He was involved in the Pléiade *Ulysses* project, translating the Ithaca, Aeolus and Circe chapters. More recently, he tackled my novels and those of Will Self. When he worked on the Burton he did not simply provide a French version, he consulted the Oxford editors of the Clarendon *Anatomy of Melancholy* and produced an annotated, scholarly tome of over a thousand pages. He regularly gave classes and workshops at French universities and at the Arles Centre for Translation At the time of his death a book of his is scheduled for publication with Editions Tristram in the spring of 2018. The title is characteristic: *Portrait du Traducteur en Escroc* (*Portrait of the Translator as Crook or Con-man*) a homage to Melville and Joyce, of course, but also a signal that he, who had done so many different things in his life and eventually found his true vocation in the art of translating, did not take either himself or the practice entirely seriously.

When we had travelled to Tours with him, early on in our acquaintance, he had shown us a photo of the woman he was living with in The Hague, a Croatian translator, the daughter of a famous Croatian author, for whom he had abandoned his second wife. When her stint at the Hague Tribunal came to an end she got a job as a translator at the Croatian Embassy in Brussels and they moved there. Three years ago, though, Bernard sent a circular email saying he had moved back to his house in the wonderfully named town of Dieulefit or God Made It, in the Drome region, south of Lyon. When I wrote to congratulate him he said it wasn't really good news as it signalled that Suzanne had thrown him out. He did not venture to say what had happened, only the bare facts. When we travelled to Brussels to do that reading he was full of foreboding: Suzanne had said she would be there. In the event she popped in beforehand to say she would have a meal with us afterwards but had to be elsewhere during the reading. The owner of the wonderful Ptyx bookshop where the reading was held, who had made his fortune in IT and at thirty-five fulfilled his dream by opening the shop (it would have been a restaurant in England), informed us that he had to take part in an all-night bicycle ride that night, so would not be joining us for dinner. That left me with the two of them, which did not make for a comfortable meal, and I excused myself as soon as I decently could and went back to my room to read.

In the train on the way back to Paris Bernard assured me it had gone well and he was now cured of his infatuation. But it was clear he wasn't. I realised then what a romantic he was. Part of Suzanne's attraction was that they had both decided almost as soon as they met that they were soulmates, and each abandoned a spouse to be with the other after two years of passionate dissimulation. Besides, she was beautiful, exotic, the daughter of a famous writer, and a translator in her own right. Bernard told me how he had first seen her at a translators' conference, how over the years they had exchanged over ten thousand emails – but also that they often quarrelled about how she should bring up her two sons. Later he gave us a book he had had privately printed consisting of those ten thousand emails.

When he came to London he stayed with us. Two years ago we drove down from where we had been holidaying on Lac d'Annecy and spent a few days with him in his house on the edge of Dieulefit, with its hammock on the terrace and the smell of fig leaves everywhere; he told us then that he was in the process of leaving the house to his daughter Chloe, and that eventually it would pass on to her son – the only two people in the world he appeared to love without any reservation. Last September he came to stay with me in Lewes and took part in a day-long celebration of my work organised by kind friends and ex-colleagues. The weather was perfect and we had a memorable walk on the Downs above Lewes. In November we went to Brittany together for the Laure Bataillon Prize and then travelled back to Paris where – the French being the French – more events connected with the prize were planned. We had a free afternoon before us and Bernard offered to show me Delacroix's studio off the Boulevard Saint-Germain. We neither of us found it particularly exciting but it was a chance to stroll through Paris and talk. After the official event we joined the organisers for dinner, but both felt exhausted – it was eleven thirty by then – and walked back to our hotel before the dessert. Bernard was leaving at six the next morning – he was always an early riser, when he stayed in Lewes I would come down to find him, a roll-up as ever between his fingers, reading in the garden – so we said goodbye and I went to bed.

It's not often that you make a friend of that kind after sixty, let alone after seventy. Tamar and I both felt that he had brought something special into our lives. But it didn't seem to me he was altogether well those last years. I felt that the shock of his separation from Suzanne had not been as easy to shake off as he tried to make out. I worried for him. But he was not someone who would confide his innermost feelings even to those close to him – anyway not to me. There would certainly be more women in his life – at seventy he was still attractive and so adored them that they in turn flocked to him. We hoped, though, that he would find someone who would bring a little peace into his life.

The last novel of mine Pascal brought out – *In a Hotel Garden*, published by Carcanet in 1993 – he had given to Vanessa Guignery to translate. 'I owe her', he had told me, though not explained any further. Bernard pretended to be offended: 'But I'm Gabriel's translator!' he jokingly protested – but I felt it was not entirely pretence. Vanessa did a fine job of it but she was teaching in the States when the book appeared in France in April 2017, so I did the bookshop gigs with Pascal. Tamar and I both missed Bernard's warmth and enthusiasm, and his ability to make difficult insights easy to grasp. We got back to England and were down in Lewes when an email from a Jacques Hoepffner appeared on my screen. I had to read it twice to take it in. He was Bernard's brother, he said. Bernard had in all probability drowned off the Welsh coast at St David's Head. His jacket had been recovered and identified but the body had vanished.

We will never know what happened that day in May or why Bernard had gone back to the place that had meant so much to him in his youth. Tamar entertained the fantasy that we would find him many years later in Australia with a gorgeous blonde, but the reality was more prosaic: the body was washed ashore a month later a hundred miles north of the spot where he vanished. Was it suicide or did he slip on the rocks? Was it the kind of romantic death he would have relished or a tragic accident or both? Will Self wrote to me: 'There is such a thing as accidental suicide.' And also voiced what I didn't quite dare admit to myself: 'It's very very sad, but it's kind of annoying too, if you know what I mean.' I did. I had lost a dear friend, someone for whom I had the highest regard, but also someone greatly respected in French intellectual circles whose championing of my work made its reception in France considerably easier than it might otherwise have been. I had hoped to work with him for the rest of my life.

In the pocket of his jacket, quite dry, the police found two hundred and fifty pounds in cash and two photos, one of Suzanne and one of his grandson.

From the Archive

Issue 140, July–August 2001

ROBERT WALSER

From a contribution of twelve 'Microscripts', translated by Christopher Middleton. Fellow contributors to this issue include John Ashberry, Lawrence Sail and Matthew Welton.

from MICROSCRIPTS

I have lived in rooms
where I could hear myself
sniffle with the glooms,
for apparently the rooms
to which I then was fated
would contract and expand
like living creatures, and
inside of them I drowned
or had been suffocated.
          Then again
some rooms gyrated round me
as if in fairystory rings,
galleries and towers, so
high they gave me vertigo.

Literary Review

FOR PEOPLE WHO DEVOUR BOOKS

**Try 3 issues for only £5 +
a free *Literary Review* tote bag***

Sixty-four pages of witty, informative and authoritative reviews each month by leading contemporary writers and thinkers plus free access to our app, website and online archive dating back to 1979. For more information please visit us online at **www.literaryreview.co.uk/3for5**

Three Poems

RACHEL MANN

Lex Orandi

A slow train, I'm carried north to speak
Of mystery, *out* and *in*, *The Divine Vision*.

Windows jolt and I see fields north
Of Northallerton, ridges grassed over,

Echo of strip farmers, so meagre,
Long lines of soil the difference

Between life and death. Further out,
Steam plumes where horizon should be,

That is what electricity looks like
After it's passed on; finally, Durham,

Cathedral towers wrapped in white
(Swaddling? bandages?)

So this is glory, glory-bound!
I might close my eyes or pull down

The blind, but why, oh why?
It's the inner eye that sees,

My carriage companions stare
At table tops, computer screens,

The man opposite mutters,
A Love Supreme, *A Love Supreme*,

His voice raw winter, behold, a cold rain falls!
He knows, he knows what I cannot.

Achilles in Albion

About praise we know so little, Patroclus,
You and I, who taste sour limit of skin,
Pitch and roll, pitch and roll in troopships,

About praise! Praise, Patroclus, avoids rain,
Climate is truth, sick fact, grey on grey;
Whale-road smashes into chalk,

Our beachhead crumbles, I found relics
In the night attack: Brittle stars and snake stones,
Did they ever know praise? Our enemy lurks

In glass towers, I see glow, backlights,
People transact, tap, tap, tap, zeros and ones,
Tap, tap, tap. Near-praise. Not near enough.

Compline

Night, and my offering is due,
I have electronics, touch screens, apps,
My stall is cold, a candle casts white flush

Of death across my hands;
Sacrifice, the ever-sacrifice – Table,
Bread, Wine, flesh, flesh, flesh –

Awaits, deeper in the dark,
Further away than ever before,
O God make speed to save us.

My knees crack on stone, oh prayer,
Holy Ghost! Come! If, and if all things,
Defend us from perils, dangers of night.

I search whitewashed walls for glimpse –
Flick of feather, magic-light, dove –
I look down. Backlit icons await my grasp.

From Glasgow to Granada

EDWIN MORGAN

A Translator's Notebook (6)
edited by James McGonigal

ON 28 SEPTEMBER 1968, in a letter to Robert Tait, his co-editor on a recently-founded cultural journal *Scottish International*, Edwin Morgan referred to a translation from Lorca that he had himself submitted for consideration:

> I can see you don't believe that Lorca really wrote that wee poem! He did though – and perhaps that's why he was murdered too. You know the theory that there are people who attract murder, as there are those that attract accidents, or fires, or cats... For a short poem, it has an extraordinary insight into the 'ultimately perilous' moment, especially as it is not wholly naturalistic. Lorca is one man I would like to know a great deal about.

Here is that wee poem:

MURDER
Two Voices at Dawn in Riverside Drive, New York

How did it –?
– Scratch on the cheek,
– that's all. Claw
– pouncing on a green
– shoot. Pin plunging
– to meet the roots of the scream.
– And the sea stops moving.
– But how – how?
– Like this.
– Get away from me! That way?
– Sure. The heart
– went out alone.
– Oh no, oh god –

The list of holograph poems in the Morgan Papers in Glasgow University Library[1] dates this translation to 24 September 1968. Morgan must have finished it and sent it off immediately to *Scottish International*. The postal service was speedier in those days, and Tait had clearly had time to both read it and reply. On the same busy day as 'Murder', Morgan translated Lorca's 'Sleepless City'. These poems open the Lorca selection in his *Collected Translations* [CT] (Carcanet Press, 1996: 262–7). But the other collected Lorca poems are of a much earlier date, and do not appear on the holograph listing. And mysteriously, even the book in which Morgan had originally hoped to place these earlier translations fails to appear in Hamish Whyte's fascinating bibliography of Morgan's work in *About Edwin Morgan* (Edinburgh University Press, 1990: 140–255). So for me too, Morgan's Lorca is one man I would like to know a great deal about.

The following pages from the Translator's Notebook of the early 1960s are a reconstruction. They follow traces within books that Morgan read and annotated, and chart the sequence of languages he translated. We become aware of the role of chance and personal encounter in the act of translation, of opportunities for publication offered and seized. At the beginning of this decade we find him travelling in imagination from Glasgow to Granada, and then, with a Spanish-American consciousness, into the urban spaces of New York.

Morgan is particularly associated, of course, with Eastern European poetry, both Russian and Hungarian. His translations from Spanish are probably less well-known than his engagement with the Portuguese of the Brazilian Noigandres poets. But although Spanish and Latin-American poets are outnumbered 30:8 by the Russians and Hungarians in *CT*, their sweep in time may surprise us – more than five hundred years of Spanish poetry explored or translated during five different decades of Morgan's life. Within that collection's name index, the five centuries seem to begin in the early sixteenth with Garcilaso de la Vega (1501–1536) and to end with Haroldo de Campos (1929–2003). Yet also to be found within Morgan's uncollected translations are the earlier 'Coplas por la muerte de su padre' of Jorge Manrique (1440–79), cotemporaneous with 'Three Spanish Ballads' (*CT*: 453–5), Morgan's versions of fifteenth-century Spanish romances. And in the 1990s the Latin-American interest was reawakened in still uncollected translations from the work of Cecilia Vicuña (b. 1947), the Chilean poet, film-maker and performance artist. His translations of Vicuña into Scots were published by Alex Finlay, son of Ian Hamilton Finlay, in *PALABRARmas / WURD–WAPPINschaw* (Edinburgh: Morning Star Publications, 1994).

But Lorca was first among the Spanish poets he worked on. Although some of the Spanish poems he came to translate also appear in J.M. Cohen's *The Penguin Book of Spanish Verse* (1956) with its literal prose translations at the foot of each page, it is clear that several of his Lorca translations predate 1956. In fact they hint at Morgan's library searches of some twenty years earlier. His fascination with the poetry and personality of Federico García Lorca is combined with a teenager's view of Andalusia, as glimpsed from a semi-villa in smoky Rutherglen near Glasgow.

Morgan encountered Lorca's work through conversation with a Glasgow University music student, Lex Allan, hired to teach him to play the piano. Morgan's parents were business-people, quite well-off, and they felt that playing the piano would be a good social skill for their bookish son. Lex Allan was about six years older than his pupil (who was then sixteen, in 1936) and very interested in contemporary politics and writing. The Spanish Civil War was being fought, with writers and intellectuals enlisting mainly on the Republican side, and Morgan remembered his tutor saying: 'You know, if you were a couple of years older, you could have been going to Spain, have you thought of that?' This was certainly an intriguing thought for a Lanarkshire schoolboy. There was also a gay undercurrent to the relationship of pupil and teacher, in Lex Allan's slightly effeminate manner ('A bit of a Jessie' was Morgan's father's description, a Scots term for such a man), and also in their discussion of the 1930s literary scene, including gay authors. As Morgan recalled in a late 1980s interview with the poet Christopher Whyte: 'He was quite open about it. Though I remember the first time he talked about all these gay authors, he said at the end of it, "I don't know how we got onto this subject!", joking about it.' Lorca came up in their conversation mainly in his political connections, but the young Morgan got hold of his work shortly afterwards and was quite surprised that 'There seemed little about it that one could identify with writing about being gay or on gay subjects [...]. So I was left wondering a great deal about Lorca, but being very much impressed by him, liking his work a lot.' (*Edwin Morgan: Nothing Not Giving Messages*. Edinburgh University Press, 1990: 152.)

Now where, we might wonder, did the schoolboy get hold of Lorca's poetry? Included in this same anthology of Morgan's interviews and articles is a list of 'Books I Have Read (1927–1940)'. Here we learn that Morgan persuaded his parents to join several different libraries, in addition to those he belonged to, so that he would always have access to his favourite authors. He used a system of symbols to indicate which library a book came from: School, Grant's, Argosy, Art Club, St Vincent. Unfortunately for my purposes, the list is marked 'except poetry', although it does include some verse anthologies, notably Michael Roberts' *The Faber Book of Modern Verse* (1936), which made a powerful impact.

But perhaps the most likely access to Lorca's poetry lay close to the single-sex fee-paying school to which his parents had sent him. The High School of Glasgow was then in Elmbank Street, a couple of hundred yards from the Mitchell Library, the major civic library of Glasgow, open to the public and to generations of high school and university students. Hamish Whyte, Morgan's bibliographer, was a librarian there, and through his influence 'the Mitchell' would come to house Morgan's final collection of thirteen thousand books, 'a poet's working library'. Many of these still contain the annotations or interleaved reviews that help us trace his reactions to them. This is helpful in the case of Lorca.

Morgan's early sense of intrigue about Lorca's republican socialism and orientation led him to translate several of his poems from the 1950s onwards. These were certainly bleak years for Morgan, who had returned from war service in the Middle East in an all-male 'homosocial' army context. In the army, he had been involved in several homosexual affairs, but then returned to Honours level study of English, which had been interrupted by national service. This was followed immediately by work as junior lecturer at Glasgow University. In this industrial city he found little sense of a 'gay community', but rather a number of fairly isolated individuals engaged in covert and transient relationships. The breaking down of inhibitions experienced in a time of war could not be continued in peacetime. This feeling of isolation was reinforced by his relatively slow development as a poet,

or of any readership beyond small magazines. He was now in his thirties.

Lorca's poetry offered something extremely different in its conservative, rural, folkloric detail and 'striking imagery of the Baroque poets', as J.M. Cohen describes it (*The Penguin Book of Spanish Verse*: p. xxiii). This all seems at odds with Morgan's modernising urban vision. Cohen notes that Lorca's 'sole experiment with modern techniques, *Poeta en Nueva York*, was far less successful than his gypsy ballads [...]'.

Perhaps it was the sheer difference from his own early life that drew Morgan to Lorca – but it is interesting that he opens his own translations of the Spanish poet in *CT* with two poems from Lorca's New York: 'Asesinato' ('Murder: Two Voices at Dawn in Riverside Drive, New York') and 'Ciudad sin sueño' ('Sleepless City: Brooklyn Bridge Nocturne'). The first of these perhaps recalls the underworld of threat and sexual violence that Morgan would describe so vividly in 'Glasgow Green' in the early 1960s. The male homosexual world was often a night-time one of risk, in his experience. Their date of translation in September 1968 also places them in the period when he was writing his essay 'Three Views of Brooklyn Bridge' (*Akros* III, 9: Jan 1969, reprinted in his *Essays*: Carcanet Press, 1974: 43–57), to which I will return.

These New York poems of late 1968 are at some remove from the earlier Lorca translations. In Morgan's correspondence there is a letter dated 24 July 1954 from the editor of *Platform* quarterly, Fred Woods, returning some translations: 'not because I don't like them or think them bad, but because I feel Lorca is rather over-translated'. He adds a comment suggesting that such translations might identify his journal with elitist modernism. Morgan had previously approached *London Magazine* with seven Lorca poems in June 1954 without success. Hugh MacDiarmid accepted 'Casida of the Bright Death' for *Voice of Scotland* in February 1955, but seems not to have published it. Morgan tried *Poetry Review* (October 1955), *Partisan Review* (October 1956), and *Sewanee Review* (December 1956) without success. *Spectrum* accepted some in June 1957 but did not publish them. Morgan's listing of poems sent out and returned in the 1950s makes disappointing reading. In *CT* only six of these early poems remain. The other, 'Gacela of the Bitter Root' ('Gacela de la raiz amarga') was re-titled 'Love-Wind'. Perhaps caution or self-censorship caused Morgan to abandon his translation, which seems more explicit in its violent sensuality than other versions of the poem that can be found online:

LOVE-WIND

One root is bitter,
One world of a myriad windows.
Not even the littlest fist
Shivers the door of the water.

Where – where – where are you gone?
One sky, myriads of terraces.
Myriads of bees, angry battles
And one root, and that bitter:

Bitter.

A pain for the sole of the foot.
A pain for the heart of the face.
And pain for the throbbing trunk
Of night raw from the blade.

O Love, my enemy:
Your root in my teeth is bitter!

What spurred Morgan's choice of poems, and which original text did he use? Checking out Morgan's books by or about Lorca in the Mitchell Library, we find one published in Buenos Aires in 1943, *Antología Poetica, 1918–1936, seleccionada por Rafael Alberti*. Here he has ticked three of the casidas that appear in *CT*: 'Casida del llanto' ['Casida of Weeping'], 'Casida de la rosa' ['Casida of the Rose'], and 'Casida de las palomas oscuras' ['Casida of the Dark Doves'] (*CT*: 264-65). The casida is an Arabic poetic form, 'usually on an amorous theme' – and the original publication of these in Lorca's *Diván del Tamarit* (1936) would have drawn Morgan's attention in the early 1950s, since he had first heard that word 'divan' in the Middle East. In Arabic poetry, a 'divan' is a long poem that is a collection of verses, not clearly structured in the European fashion along narrative lines but rather making a virtue of randomness and variety, the mind and senses moving from one experience to another, enjoying the alteration of mood or perspective. Morgan may have been drawn to these poems in the 1950s because he was still missing the Arabic culture that he had experienced in wartime. At one point he even considered rejoining the military, as T. E. Lawrence had done.

Morgan would later write his own collection, *The New Divan*, a hundred-poem sequence based on his experience of living in and closely observing Middle Eastern culture, a long poem on the themes of love and war played out over an ancient landscape of ruins and set within a society of radically different cultural expectations. The sequence was begun in December 1973, and completed over the following year and a half, the final sequence of ten poems being completed in July 1975. Contemporary newsreel footage of the Yom Kippur War of 1973 may have brought his own military experience to mind. But I think that the idea of the 'divan' may have had its roots in that late sequence by Lorca, combined with a boyhood fascination with ancient Middle Eastern history and culture.

We have already seen in this 'Translator's Notebook' series that Morgan had lectured on his translation practice in the 1950s, at Durham, Keele and Bristol universities. His approach involved the idea of a 'flickering web' of pictorial, acoustic and sensuous impressions that the translator picks up from early readings of the text. These provide a first sense of the foreign poem: its 'symmetry or ruggedness', line-length and rhyme, its 'close or open texture, curious or common vocabulary' – all taken in at a more or less impressionistic level, and stored at the back of the mind. Next, the front of the mind would focus on a 'grid of meaning', a sequence or pattern derived from close work with dictionary and grammar, word by word and phrase by phrase. Then Morgan as translator would re-focus the grid of meaning on to the web of impressions: and 'when they coincide, the translator feels he can really see the poem'. In one of those lectures

Morgan likens the procedure to range-finding in military life or piano-tuning in musical life (interesting echoes there of his own early piano lessons which combined thoughts of civil war and Lorca).

But then as the actual translation began something curious happened. There was a search for equivalence across two languages, but not of the words of the foreign language so much as: 'the words of *the poem itself*, which has attained some sort of non-verbal interlinguistic existence in the mind. [...] Without wishing to be mystical, I believe there seems to be some sense [...] in which the poem exists independently of the language of its composition.' ('The Translation of Poetry', *Scottish Review* 2:5, Winter 1976) This essay recapitulates his 1950s thinking. He then goes on to refer to Walter Benjamin's 'The Task of the Translator' (1923): 'It is the task of the translator to release in his own language that pure language which is under the spell of another, to liberate the language imprisoned in a work in his re-creation of that work.'

This almost Platonic view of a pre-existent poem clearly held attractions for someone who had struggled to find his own successful poetic voice, but could discover some self-affirmation as co-author, as it were, in the act of translation. It has resonances with 'that huge Shelleyan poem "which all poets, like the co-operating thoughts of one great mind, have built up since the beginning of the world"'. Morgan employs this quotation from Shelley's *The Defence of Poetry* (1821) in his defence of Hugh MacDiarmid's use of montage from multiple sources and authors (*Hugh MacDiarmid*. Harlow: Longman Group, 1976: 32). But it clearly also endorses his own experience of the translation of poetry.

What does all this mean for his Lorca translations? We can take the 'Casida of the Rose' as an example – not because it is the best but because it is the shortest. Here is a prose version of the poem from the Penguin 1960 collection, *Lorca*, edited by J. L. Gilli (Morgan owned this, but its publication post-dates his translation) and Morgan's own version from *CT*: 264-5, interleaved with the original:

CASIDA DE LA ROSA

The rose did not seek the daybreak: almost eternal on its
   bough, it sought another thing.
The rose did not seek knowledge or shade: boundary of flesh
   and dream, it sought another thing.
The rose did not seek the rose. Motionless in the sky it sought
   another thing.

La rosa
no buscaba la aurora:
casi eternal en su ramo
buscaba otra cosa.

The rose's gaze
was not on the sunrise:
it lay on a timeless tree,
it gazed on another place.

La rosa
no buscaba ni ciencia ni sombra:

confín de carne y sueño,
buscaba otra cosa.

The rose's gaze
was not on sign or on sense:
outpost of flesh and dream.
it gazed on another place.

La rosa
no buscaba la rosa.
Inmóvil por el cielo
buscaba otra cosa.

The rose's gaze
was not upon the rose.
Still with all the sky to seek
it gazed on another place.

We can see Morgan here responding to the pattern of assonance and alliteration in the original – and also focusing on the aspiration or expectation inherent in 'buscar' (a sense perhaps of having searched out the symbolic resonance within its dictionary meanings, to help carry forward in translation the European heritage of the image of the rose). We also may get the impression in stanza two of his having taken up the idea of science ('ciencia'), and of 'sombra' not merely as shade or shadow but as darkness, so as to engage this symbolic rose in the active-and-outward searching movement of the final stanza. Perhaps there is even a glance towards contemporary space exploration by telescope and, soon, by satellite, which interested Morgan greatly. In fact, we may think he has transposed that darkness from the second stanza, where his translated line 'not on sign or sense' catches the alliteration of the original but has the 'darkness/shade' idea merge with the night-time sensuality of its following line, 'outpost of flesh or dream'. The darkness, however, remains implicit in the final stanza's feeling (to me) of space exploration – in tune with Walter Benjamin's and Morgan's idea of the poem being 'out there', somewhere in the universe, awaiting rediscovery in and through the translator's different language.

Morgan was also concerned to discover more value than earlier critics had in Lorca's New York poetry. His essay 'Three Views of Brooklyn Bridge' (*Akros* III, 9, January 1969), running parallel to his translations of the New York poems, reveals a twin-track of critical analysis and creative response typical of the energy of his 1960s career. The essay compares Lorca's response to this striking piece of architectural engineering with those of Hart Crane's 'The Bridge' (1930) and Vladimir Mayakovsky's 'Brooklyn Bridge' (1925), written during the Russian poet's trip to New York. In Crane's poem, the bridge is seen both 'as a universal symbol of union and aspiration (aspiration towards "the other shore") and as a possible symbol of the American consciousness which could be used because it showed a conscious linking of bold vision and untried technology' (*Essays*: 43). Mayakovsky responds to 'the futurism of sheer technology' in America with a desire also to harness it in the interests of humanity. But his 'central vision of the bridge is constructivist rather than suggestional, it reminds him of

his own struggle as an artist, "the struggle for construction instead of style"' (*Essays*: 53).

Lorca's response was different from both of those, Morgan suggests, partly because of the timing of his own visit, in the desperate autumn and winter of 1929–30 when the Wall Street stock market crashed and the Great Depression began. Moreover, Lorca did not speak English and so was doubly isolated from the familiar landscape of Spain and from any real engagement with the crowds in the streets and houses around him. Hence perhaps the anguish and painful excitement of his New York poetry. Morgan reminds us that Lorca had been interested in surrealism and knew both Dali and Buñuel. Now precipitation into an alien environment 'gave his surrealism a use and a meaning: his American poems are not strictly surrealist, but employ some surrealist techniques to convey his nightmarish, almost hallucinatory feelings about American society during the crack-up of 1929–30' (*Essays*: 54). He also notes Lorca's prophetic recognition of the explosive qualities of life that had been denied outlet in the black American experience (as in his poem 'King of Harlem'); and his recognition too of the optimistic tradition of Walt Whitman, whom Lorca brings into his own poetry as a mythic figure to be addressed ('Ode to Walt Whitman').

Morgan's description of Lorca in New York conveys a sense of pity and, partly, of identification with the Spaniard's isolation in the turbulent city. This is reminiscent of his sympathy for the poet and priest Gerard Manley Hopkins, working among the teeming poor of nineteenth-century Liverpool and Glasgow. The identification is also with homoerotic and homosexual elements in both those poets – as also in Whitman – and with the relative isolation entailed in their sexual identity. But Morgan did not share Lorca's sense of dislocation between the rural and urban worlds – he loved cities and their industrial energies, and their crowded streets, and new technologies. That close sense of identification was a key factor in Morgan's approach to the act of translation. There were certain poets such as Montale in Italian, Mayakovsky in Russian, and Sándor Weöres and Attila József in Hungarian, with whom he felt a profound closeness of vision and purpose.

The Lorca of New York half-approaches that closeness, while remaining at a mysterious remove. His earlier casidas were part of the picture, albeit shadowy and liable to vanish from the main path. Perhaps Morgan's sense of identification was more with the decade in which those three poems on Brooklyn Bridge were composed, when he was himself a bright young boy in Rutherglen with a growing awareness of both creativity and constraint. Perhaps like Mayakovsky he was reminded by those earlier poems of 'his own struggle as an artist'. Maybe that is why he was content to allow those early translations to disappear from the scene, until resurrected for *Rites of Passage: Selected Translations* (Carcanet Press, 1976), before vanishing again.

What of the disappearing book, missing from the bibliography? It was *An Anthology of Spanish Poetry from Garcilaso to García Lorca* (Doubleday, 1961). It is to be found in the Mitchell Library. When Morgan was asked in the late 1950s to translate Spanish poets of the sixteenth century for this volume, he already had a deep awareness of Petrarchan poetic tradition and much personal experience of unrequited love to draw upon. The editor was Angél Flores, who taught European languages in Queens College, New York. He had been put in touch with Morgan earlier by Hugh MacDiarmid, as a possible translator of German poetry for an anthology that Flores was editing. He had already completed an *Anthology of French Poetry from Nerval to Valéry in English Translation* and now eagerly wanted to publish similar anthologies German, Spanish and Italian poetry.

The anthology on Spanish poetry was already well in progress, and would be published in the following year. James Wright, Samuel Beckett and Denise Levertov are among the listed translators. Morgan tried to interest Flores in his translations of Lorca as well as of Pablo Neruda and Luis Cernuda, but Lorca had already been allocated and Neruda's royalties were too expensive. So Morgan's Lorca languished again. And the anthology must have been misplaced on the poet's bookshelves or lent to someone, for Hamish Whyte omitted it from his bibliography.

The fifteen books on Lorca in the Mitchell Library's Morgan collection reveal his continued curiosity about the man: they include *Lorca: the gay imagination* (1985), *Sonnets of Dark Love / Sonetos de Amor Oscuro* (1989), and *Poet in New York* (1990). But Morgan's own translations of the casidas, rejected yet again, could perhaps be laid aside until another enterprising editor, also of Hispanic-American ancestry, and probably even more energetic than Flores, incorporated them in *Rites of Passage*, and from there into *Collected Translations*.

NOTE
1 (http://special.lib.gla.ac.uk/manuscripts/search/results_ca.cfm?ID=1510)

EGRESS

NEW OPENINGS IN LITERARY ART

DIANE WILLIAMS KATHRYN SCANLAN ELEY WILLIAMS GORDON LISH DAVID HAYDEN LAURA ELLEN JOYCE GREG MULCAHY KIMBERLY KING PARSONS CHRISTINE SCHUTT SAM LIPSYTE EVAN LAVENDER-SMITH CARRIE COOPERIDER ASHTON POLITANOFF GRANT MAIERHOFER HOB BROUN SCOTT ESPOSITO LILY HACKETT

FICTION · ESSAYS · ART

published by Little Island Press

www.littleislandpress.co.uk/egress

A Visit to Old Hall

JANE STEVENSON

South Burlingham isn't far from Norwich but it's in deep country. Getting there involves navigating smaller and smaller roads into a maze of hedges and big trees, with an occasional stone-built church, the odd overdressed former farmhouse, and once in a while, a working farm. The little Elizabethan house stands back from the road, red brick under a thatched roof, made distinctive by a dramatic three-storey porch adorned with frisky merpersons, and the twin Tudor chimneypots which rise on either side of its pediment like ears. On the other side of a blue-painted farm gate, there is a formal garden with box knots, yew cones and mown grass on either side of a central path. Mature trees nod over the hedge on the left, implying less formal planting behind.

The Old Hall isn't an easy place to bring into focus, because generally, one is so pleased to have got there, sometimes due to the successful achievement of a feat of navigation (unless one has been retrieved by Margaret from somewhere in Norwich), but mostly, because impressions crowd on top of one another and in any case, the main principal memory is always of the conversation, which begins almost at once, and continues more or less without cease during waking hours until the moment of departure. Arabesques of well-formed sentences, in which books, people, recondite facts, objects, and memories flow; one leading to another in intricate and ramifying chains of association. Nothing so vulgar as table talk, subtler and more gnarly, the result of long reflection, striking sparks off whatever it is the visitor brings to the table.

On arrival, one enters a narrow hall made narrower by a big chest and chairs littered with miscellanea; there is a momentary view of dark corridor and steep stairs and walls crowded with pictures, but off to the left is the kitchen. Peter might be found sitting in a chair by the Aga, but the chances are that when he heard the wheels of a car crunching on the gravel, he hauled himself to his feet and shuffled out for a courteous greeting, at which point, the visit gets properly under way. The kitchen is a big, square, room, containing among other things, the aforementioned Aga, lodged in a Tudor fireplace, a long table, two dressers, cupboards tucked into odd corners, and a long Indian wooden bench by the low window, decorated with naïve floral motifs in red on white, and littered with books and papers. Every one of these items is painted, often in several colours, in fact, barely an inch of bare wood is to be seen (the table is covered with an Indian printed cloth). This is the antithesis of minimalist, and the room could only be in England. Upstairs, in more private parts of the house, there are surviving Elizabethan wall paintings with vivid colour and exuberant patterns; these have been used as a cue to the decorative treatment. Beyond the flat colour, there are decorative paintings by Margaret on window embrasures and other surfaces, patterns of flowers and leaves for the most part, and paintings by Mark Hearld are a strong presence. He is also responsible for many of the textiles, prints and paintings of English animals and birds which crop up through the house.

Though Peter's dislike of the Bloomsbury set is hardly news to anyone who has read his catalogues with attention, the Old Hall shares an aesthetic with Charleston; that of multiple small diapered patterns, bold colour, handmade things, and clutter, which runs from the Arts and Crafts movement through the Omega Workshop to Laura Ashley and Emma Bridgewater. In the kitchen of the Old Hall, the colours of walls and furniture are deep and strong, reddish-pink, turquoise, blue, ochre; colours which would be at home in Charleston (though in the Old Hall, the tones tend to be purer). There is pattern everywhere, all the walls are subtly different shades of the basic turquoise and pink, and almost nothing is white, except a large and handsome black and white cockerel, which Mark Hearld painted on the door of one of the cupboards. At most times of the year, there are likely to be brightly coloured flowers on the table, in a vase chosen for colour-contrast; for magenta and shocking pink dahlias, a jug the colour of heather honey; for daffodils, perhaps one glazed in a strong green, or turquoise. All of this detail has to be absorbed in snatches, since it is a background to welcome, solicitous enquiries as to travel, health, and current work in progress, strong tea, and ambient cats. For many years, the principal cat was the large and ceremonious Goodman, named for the secretarial cat in the *Uncle* books. Goodman, alas, is no more, and the current ruler of the house is Burlingham Bertie the Bengal, who looks like a small snow leopard, but is domestic in his habits. He and Peter dispute the chair by the Aga, comfortably.

Food is an important part of the visit. Margaret is not a cook who refers anxiously to recipes. But the style, or flavour, of her cooking is discernibly that of Jane Grigson, or at least, that of her era. Like other aspects of the house's overall style, the food is very English; not in any evident way influenced by the novelties proffered by the Sunday papers' food sections, but attentive to what is local and fresh. Quite a lot of it comes out of the garden. Her treatment of these ingredients often indicates an awareness of the history of English food, as redacted by writers of the fifties and earlier, such as Grigson, Elizabeth David, and Dorothy Hartley. Jam and marmalade are made in season; quinces are grown, and made into quince jelly. Dinner is always an occasion (as is breakfast); an occasion for meeting and talking. Attention is paid, both to the food itself, which is always worth attending to, and to the other people round the table, in a way which was once entirely taken for granted, but is increasingly eroded by the culture of the mobile phone, and less common than it once was.

Though much of any visit will happen in the kitchen, the formality and ceremony of a proper visit causes the company to remove after dinner. We go down the narrow corridor to the Red Room, which is the same size as the kitchen but at the far end of the house, and like the kitchen, has a vast Elizabethan fireplace. In the Red Room, it is open, and has a basket grate to burn logs. The pert Elizabethan merman and mermaid on the porch have evidently encouraged the acquisition of a variety of Far Eastern mermaids, who are hung from the ceiling, and cast handsome and exotic shadows. At right angles to the great fireplace, there are two enormous sofas, facing one another on either side of a narrow table. This is another room with a bookcase of treasures, which certainly includes a variety of large-format illustrated books, including Kathleen Hales' Orlando the Marmalade Cat series, in the original lithographed editions, which find their home here. I'm not sure I have ever seen this room in daylight; lit by lamps, it has a cavernous quality, with half-seen furniture looming bulkily from the shadows.

The house retains an archaic plan, which makes it a place of narrow corridors and strangely related rooms; the room at the centre of the ground floor ('Margaret's Room') is only entered from the Red Room at the end, presumably carved out of an original Great Hall which occupied two-thirds of the house's footprint. Similarly, on the floor above, there are two small rooms which can only be entered via the master bedroom. The disposition of space does not conform to modern notions of privacy. However, the first-floor room which the guest is most likely to enter, the study, is self-contained, and is over the kitchen. Visits to Peter's study tend to happen in the morning. A lovely square room, it is lined to the ceiling with bookcases, the interiors painted a dark pinkish maroon, the shelf edges slaty blue. Most of the furniture is Regency, Japanned black and gold. On the shelves, nineteenth-century calf bindings coexist amiably with the less-uniform products of twentieth-century private presses. Though most of the shelves are crammed with books, some hold favoured treasures. One such is a nineteenth-century tableau in a box, mostly put together from fragments of fluorspar and other decorative minerals, which features a temple frontage and a small doll, and is known to the household as 'Little Bo-Peep in the Vaults of Death'. This assemblage can be related to a strand in English aesthetic life which goes back as far as the 1920s; an admiration for inadvertent surreality in popular culture. As Barbara Jones observed (in *The Unsophisticated Arts*), 'Popular arts have certain constant characteristics. They are complex, unsubtle, often impermanent, they lean to disquiet, the baroque, and sometimes terror.'

The three special ceramics in the next bay along are also in continuum with English aesthetics: two of them are the early nineteenth-century Sunderland pink lustre jugs prized by many twentieth-century aesthetes, and the third is a Persian vase featuring a poetical gentleman playing a long-necked instrument like a sitar. Sunderland ware was embraced by 1920s aesthetes as part of what they enjoyed about Victoriana; the transfers on Sunderland ware are in a continuum with the 'penny plain, twopence coloured' theatre prints which inspired Sacheverell Sitwell and Lord Berners' ballet, *The Triumph of Neptune* (1926). The Persian vase is a more unusual item for an English room; but its boldness and fluent, asymmetric, decoration is perfectly in keeping.

Visits often involve an excursion in the afternoon, possibly including a pub lunch. Norfolk is extraordinarily rich in medieval churches, so the destination tends to be a church crawl; armed with Pevsner or the Shell Guide, the party sets out in search of angel roofs, interesting wall paintings, or curious monuments. All my Old Hall memories are entwined with these church interiors, frequently fascinating, but inevitably cold and grey, forming the strongest contrast with the colour and warmth of the kitchen to which we return.

Additionally, no proper visit would be complete without a tour of the garden, which is enormous, and beautiful. The first impression on coming into Old Hall is of Elizabethan grass and box, but there is a discreet little entry to the garden behind the hedge on the left, which is mostly practical, and consequently organised as a series of narrow beds, with grass walks between. The dahlias, zinnias, roses, and so forth are mostly for cutting, and there are various edibles sharing the beds with the flowers. Though this area of the garden is not a display area, it has considerable charm. There is a sense of essential tidiness; annuals such as marigolds put themselves where they will, but rampant weeds are under control. After the cutting garden, coming round the corner of the house to the principal the garden is a succession of surprises. Its hugeness is only gradually revealed. Near the house, there is a series of compartments, outdoor rooms in the manner made famous by Hidcote Manor, which are seriously gardened with carefully chosen shrubs and roses, and beyond that, there is grass and mature trees. This area is adorned with a variety of architectural salvage and structures which have accumulated over time, including a beautiful lead cupola resting in the grass, a shepherd's hut which has been there since long before they became fashionable, and a very fine, sturdy and well-thought-through tree house, which one can sit in or even sleep in, which was built for the entertainment of the young, though I think it sometimes comes in useful for Margaret's theatrical productions, which have long been a feature of Old Hall life, when a regiment of actors and helpers has to be accommodated by hook or by crook for a week or more.

In many ways, Old Hall is a late bloom of the English devotion to the detailed understanding and appreciation of an old house which starts, perhaps, with the Nicolsons' work on Sissinghurst, and encompasses notable projects such as Lucy Boston's rescue of Hemingford Grey. What the latter has in common with the Old Hall is both a triumph of empathy over limited financial resources, and the quality of dialogue. Through a process of hauling a building back from near dereliction, there has always been an educated, fastidious ear cocked towards what the mute stones were trying to say.

Poems

PETER SCUPHAM

Coronation

One Christmas morning
I heard myself sing
to a steaming kitchen
'I'm as happy as a king

belie-eve-mee',
things going to pot
and everyone doing
the turkey trot.

As happy as Henry
and his court of beeves,
basting his fat
for My Lady Greensleeves,

as the snow-starred baby
in his candled stall,
they say is King
and Lord of all,

as George the Sixth
and his cigarette,
coughing over Margaret
and Lilibet,

whose words will struggle
to be great and good
through Marconi's
fretted wood,

while twists of tissue
go stammering down
uneasy heads
that bear the crown.

Stichomythia

For Anthony Thwaite

They're sticking it out today: sages, poets...
There's Doctor Spooner with his stalking wick,
a host of Marsh-land Georgians with blackthorns

and Mr. Thwaite, his ferrule twisting molehills,
hoping the velvet gentleman has paddled him
a Samian fragment or a clipped denarius,

his feet robust, well-grounded, even at times iambic,
and with Ben Jonson, his 'learned sock' well on,
taking new illumination from old footlights.

We brandish our armaments, or leguments –
my prop for Aged Hippies, Morris-flowered,
dating from the daggers in my femurs –

and set our quarter-staffs at sharp riposte
while Charon watches from his pleasure-boat,
murmuring the name he chose for his dark water.

En Plein Air

A page stares back at the sun's brilliance;
a pen flickers, tugs: a kite's tail
winding a simple message into the blue.
Words tremble in a fluster of ribbons

as a host of small particulars
hovers between visible, invisible:
spume, spindrift from a swollen sea
dragging its rhythms there and back again.

Under a wind iced by clouded water,
the richest lexicon dwindles
to the kiss and sting of sand-grains,
Long, long ago, a bleached face,

jounced over metalled thunders,
stared from a carriage window
where a pother of smoke and smut
ground lost words into ancient light.

Five Portraits of Peter

NEIL POWELL

I

The covering note, dated 2 May 1970, was written in a tiny Cantabrigian script and formal to the point of irony. 'Dear Sir,' it began, 'I enclose a handful of poems for your consideration and the means to return them if you do not care for them.' Then there was a verblessly modest second paragraph: 'Introductory: poems in several magazines, *Listener*, *TLS*, *Priapus*, *Outposts*, *PEN New Poems* etc. A collection shortly appearing in Phoenix Pamphlet Poets. Yours sincerely, Peter Scupham.' He listed the titles of that 'handful': 'For Roger', 'Model', 'Topology of Ruins', 'Dissolution', 'Collector', 'Convulsion'. None is in the imminent pamphlet, *The Small Containers*, nor in his first collection, *The Snowing Globe*; one would resurface in *Prehistories*, two more in *The Hinterland*; of the other three, I've no trace or memory unless (as is possible) he changed their titles. I may have turned them down, but I'm more likely to have explained that the magazine, *Tracks*, was an occasional and fragile thing without an issue presently in preparation.

Undeterred, Peter wrote again in October, enclosing three more poems, and this time I have the carbon copy of my reply: 'Many thanks for sending me three poems: I like these very much. As you know, wherever possible I prefer to publish a group of poems, rather than a single poem, by each author; so I'd like to use all three in the next number of *Tracks*, which will appear probably in February 1971.' Ah yes, 'probably'; or, as Touchstone has it, much virtue in 'if'. *Tracks*, which I'd edited through university, had been quietly propped up by my father (whom I thought of as the Arts Council of Sundridge) for eight numbers; but, now that my MPhil research period was drawing to a close, I had to finish my thesis and get a job. Although Peter looked forward to being in the magazine – and said so on a bright pink postcard of his poem 'Four Fish' – *Tracks* 9 would never appear. I did at least write to him and the other contributors to tell them the dismal news.

But how on earth had Peter even heard of *Tracks*? The answer must be: through his friend John Mole, whose poems had been in numbers seven and eight. I don't think I'd made the connection: both lived in Hertfordshire, but that was a quite heavily populated county, so there was no reason to suppose they'd know each other.

II

Like any number of bookish young men before me, I thought I'd try teaching for a bit, but getting a job was obstructed by a long postal strike in the early spring of 1971: week after week, the Ed Supp became fatter with classifieds advertising posts for which no one could actually apply. When the strike ended, a kind of delirium took over, in the midst of which a school at a place called Kimbolton, of which I'd never heard, summoned me for interview: it was a conventional minor direct grant public school, grandly housed in a castle, and they whimsically liked the idea of a long-haired literary youth who would (in the headmaster's words to me) 'liven things up'. They must have been mad, and so must I, but

I did my best to take them at their word. One sort of enlivening that occurred to me was to invite writers to talk to the sixth-form literary society in the stateliest of our state rooms, the Saloon.

I can't now remember whether it was Peter or John whom I approached first, nor whether I'd by that time noticed that Hitchin and St Albans weren't too far apart on the map and proposed a double-act; but at least I'd noticed that Huntingdonshire, which Kimbolton splendidly insisted on being in, was adjacent to Hertfordshire. When they arrived, we'd have gone for a drink and a bite to eat in the Half Moon, and then a piece of arcane Kimboltonian etiquette intervened. The gravelled approach to the south side of the castle, including the Saloon, was used only by the headmaster, governors and other persons more important than assistant masters and their guests; on the north side, where members of staff parked their cars, one had to enter through a much dowdier basement. I cautiously chose the latter, so we had a longish trek through subterranean corridors before miraculously reaching the staircase with the Pellegrini mural and the Saloon itself. Afterwards, Peter wrote to me: 'I do like your Gormenghast.' It must have been a summer evening, because at the half-way point either John or Peter suggested that we might wander out onto the balcony and the headmasterly territory beyond it; I couldn't refuse, as it was their idea. Anyway, I no longer much cared; I was enjoying myself too much. Peter and John were indeed a double-act: they had boxed-and-coxed at readings before, and now they both charmed and divided their audience. The sixth-formers took sides, which at least suggested that they'd been taking notice; one boy was so firmly committed that he acquired the nickname 'Mole' for the rest of the term.

'By the way,' said Peter to me at some point, 'there's an English job coming up at St Chris, if you'd be interested.' He evidently suspected that Gormenghast wouldn't suit me forever, but I felt I ought to stay there a bit longer. Things might look different in a year or two.

III

Things did. St Christopher School, Letchworth, where Peter taught English, seemed as unlike Kimbolton as possible: progressive, international, vegetarian, with a degree of self-governing pupil-power that appalled most of my colleagues. That was one reason to give it a go. In fact, I'd already visited St Chris with a group of our own sixth-formers as part of a General Studies project: they were interviewing pupils and staff and taking photographs in several schools very unlike their own, another of my so-called 'livening up' ideas. These two schools were chalk and cheese: Kimbolton was very blackboardy and St Chris quite cheesy, in its rennet-free, vegetarian way. When the English post came up again in 1974, I applied.

The day of the interview, early in the summer term, was sunnily benign; all the same, a more sensible man, or one who was having less fun upsetting the Kimboltonian old guard, would have turned the job down. I met Peter for coffee and later had lunch with him and Margaret Steward; in-between there'd been the formal part with the headmaster, Nicholas King Harris, and deputy head, Mary Murray. What Peter and Margaret didn't know (though they probably guessed) was that Nicholas and Mary had offered some friendly yet determined criticism of Peter's teaching style and gently coaxed me into promising that I'd do things in a more orthodox and organised way. I was agreeing to two incompatible versions of the job; I should have said no. But I was persuaded by Peter's lightness of touch: 'It'll be fun', he said. I hoped so.

Teaching English alongside Peter at St Chris was a novel experience. In traditional schools, English departments started with this advantage: most other subjects were so punitively dreary that pupils looked forward to the fizz and creativity of an English lesson. But at St Chris almost everything seemed relaxed and enjoyable; even the chemistry teacher looked like a hippy. Moreover, whereas two of my English department colleagues at Kimbolton had been on the dull side, Peter was an almost impossible act to follow. His motto was 'Keep English sweet'. Quite often, he'd simply read aloud to a class for forty minutes from something that took his fancy, or play one of his many self-invented word games; among these was one of glorious simplicity called 'Repairing the defective dictionary'. He'd open a dictionary, apparently at random, and pretend that two pages had been torn out; the last remaining word before the lacuna and the first word after it were written on the board or at the top and bottom of a grid duplicated on the staff-room Banda (remember those?), and the class had to find as many as possible of the 'missing' words in-between. This worked because it could set off all sorts of discursive hares about why words did or didn't belong, how similar-looking words were related (or not) and so forth. Peter's playfulness sometimes became naughtiness. Once, between periods when we were about to set off to our parallel O-level classes, I confessed to him that I hadn't yet finished the novel we were both teaching and wondered what happened in the end. 'I don't know,' he replied, 'I've never read it.'

But with A level we were more serious and scholarly. After a year or two, we'd adopted the demanding O&C syllabus, teaching way beyond the minimum set texts and finding excuses to add supplementary favourites of our own. At the start of each academic year, Peter and I would haggle over who'd teach what: I usually conceded to him, as long as he agreed to do the Chaucer (which he enjoyed). We set no entrance barrier to the course and yet, to the bafflement of some other departments, for year after year we had no failures. In retrospect, I think this was simply because we both inhabited literature to such an extent that talking and enthusing about it seemed as natural and necessary as breathing – as well as a huge pleasure after some of the other things we'd do in a working day. The English sixth-form at its best is the most intellectually stimulating environment most people will ever experience, so it was no surprise to be told by students who went on to read literature at university that their seminars and tutorials fell short of ours; I remembered feeling much the same myself. A sour colleague once complained to me that Peter and I taught our sixth-forms as if all the students would go on to read English at university. Exactly not, I replied: we teach so that those who won't do that can still have an understanding of great literature.

One of the snags about working at St Chris was that it was almost impossible to leave: not just because you grew addicted to finding out what such a mad institution might get up to next, but because such a very odd place was a highly acquired taste among CV-reading potential employers. So when I tentatively wondered whether it was time I moved on to run a department of my own, Peter simply said: 'Have mine'. He wanted to reduce his teaching load, not least to spend more time on co-directing plays with Margaret, printing Mandeville pamphlets and dealing in rare (or just quirky) books. Together we approached Nicholas who, suffering from a back complaint, was to be found in his house, lying on a sofa disguised as a bed or a bed disguised as a sofa. He listened to the proposal without interest or surprise. 'By all means,' he said, 'but there's no money in it.' There wasn't. I didn't particularly mind and for quite a while we could exploit the fruitful confusion: 'Who's Head of English this week?' someone would ask, distributing unappetising bumf in the staff-room pigeonholes. 'Peter', I'd say. 'Neil', Peter would insist.

Then the place changed, after Nicholas was killed in a cycling accident. There was a new headmaster, Colin Reid, and a managerial bursar and lots of new buildings; this smartening-up was long overdue, if somehow at odds with the old ramshackle St Chris spirit. Staff meetings were held, for unexplained reasons, in the History Room on Mondays; to neutralise one of then, Peter and I decided we'd each write a complete poem during the meeting. I scribbled but he succeeded: his poem was appropriately called 'History', although in print it appears as 'The Sledge Teams'. It may have been during that very meeting that Colin, attempting to coax out Peter's opinion on some uninteresting matter, unwisely resorted to exasperated sarcasm: 'I'd like your view on this, Peter, unless your mind's on higher things.' To which Peter calmly replied: 'I'm afraid it is, Colin.' They'd never get the hang of him.

IV

The Mandeville Press lived in the cellar of Peter and Carola Scupham's house at Taylor's Hill in Hitchin. I was keen to help: I'd done some printing in my schooldays, but I was self-taught and inexpert. Before my first typesetting session with Peter was over, I'd acquired such vital skills as how to use a composing stick properly, and before long I was rediscovering the incomparable satisfactions of typesetting and printing, doing it properly this time. Mandeville's run of hand-set, hand-sewn pamphlets is special and distinctive; I'm lucky enough to own a complete set, as well as the 'Cellar Press' broadsheets and the various series of 'Dragoncards' in their printed envelopes. By instinct, design, or a mixture of both, many of the poets included were the unfashionably excellent – often underrated and sometimes forgotten writers chosen by Peter and John Mole. If there's a house style, it's a loose formalism, civilised but unshowy, clearly exemplified in the press's occasional anthologies, *Spring Collection*, *A Mandeville Fifteen*, *Mandeville's Travellers*, *A Mandeville Bestiary*. I'm glad I was able to introduce into this company two neglected poets whom I'd known at Warwick, Bernard Bergonzi and K. W. Gransden.

When Peter and I worked together on a pamphlet, we were like the First Folio's Compositor A and Compositor

C (John would have been Compositor B), and I could identify C's pages, even now, at a glance: they're slightly more narrowly spaced, with an inclination towards ranging left as opposed to A's decorative centring. From memory, I think that at the outset Mandeville just had a medium-sized table-top press, possibly an Adana, but that Peter soon acquired a much bigger cast-iron treadle machine, although quite how it was conveyed into the Taylor's Hill cellar I can't imagine. There was always a touch of the crazy inventor about him, as the 'spare-part sculpture' on the cover of *The Snowing Globe* suggests; he also drove a cobbled-together car, Morris Oxford at one end and Austin Cambridge at the other, a Mostin Oxbridge, with the registration letters HCE (Humphrey Chimpden Earwicker, Here Comes Everybody). So it was to be expected that he'd somehow rig up an electric motor for the press; I'm almost certain that this was plugged, unearthed, into a ceiling light socket and that its running-speed was regulated by a dimmer-switch on the wall. Can that really be true? If so, it's wonderful that anyone's survived to remember it. It's also wonderful that we still possess hands; for, once the press was going, you had to whip out a sheet of printed paper and replace it with a fresh one before the thing slammed shut on your fingers, and Peter naturally thought it fun to have it running as fast as possible. For the cleaning of inky fingers, he swore by a huge tin of green gunk which removed the ink but left you smelling like an industrial ruin. Yet the pamphlets were quirky and beautiful, hand-sewn by Carola, who sometimes also coloured illustrations in the low-numbered signed ones. Is there anything remotely like Mandeville in existence today? I rather doubt it.

V

Peter and I left St Chris within a couple of years of each other, in the late 1980s: he to rescue a decaying Norfolk manor house with Margaret, I to run a bookshop until I became a full-time writer and editor. It seemed a good idea to have a small second-hand department, stocked by Peter, within the bookshop, although this – like the rest of the enterprise – proved to be more enjoyable than commercially successful. In any case, he was soon permanently installed at Old Hall, which he liked to call 'Mermaid Manor' after the pedimented pair above the front entrance who also supplied the name for his antiquarian and second-hand catalogue business, Mermaid Books. Meanwhile, after four years of bookselling in Baldock, I moved to Suffolk, taking on freelance editorial work for publishers such as Carcanet and Faber (and, for fifteen years, on *PN Review*).

That was my role when Peter's *Collected Poems* (2002) was being prepared. It's a lovely book, I think, and I'm still pleased with the handsome page layout which the typesetter, Grant Shipcott, and I designed for it. But, since this piece has become in some ways a cabinet of curiosities, I'd better mention two strange things about it. The first is that one of the poems appears twice; I shan't spoil the inquisitive reader's detective-work by revealing which one. Although there are several instances of much earlier poems resurfacing in Peter's middle-period collections, this was a straightforward duplication, several books apart; and neither of us, despite carefully going over both copy-text and proofs, queried it. I remember that we collated our proof corrections over a pint and ploughman's in the garden of the Wherry at Geldeston: Peter was more casually relaxed about this process than any author I'd ever worked with, except Charles Sisson (who'd simply add the initials 'CHS' to completely unmarked proofs). The second is that there's a notable instance of a phenomenon that quite often occurred around that time: editorial intervention by scanner. It comes in one of my favourite poems of Peter's, 'The Web', where the scanner has chosen to read the phrase 'lust and hunger turning into green' as 'lust and hunger fuming into green'. Now this I did pick up and naturally I wanted to correct it, but Peter was so delighted – no doubt recalling that compositor's 'improvement' in Auden from 'poets' to 'ports' – that he insisted on retaining it; so there it is. That tiny blemish apart (and I do prefer the earlier and proper version) this is a perfect poem about an imperfect web, torn and 'hung about with rain', and the ghost of a paradox lurking there is one that haunts Peter's work. Here, since I can't imagine a better way to end, is the final quatrain. It's perhaps especially worth noticing the way in which the syntax and simplicity of the last line both slow and quieten, at once rallentando and diminuendo:

Clouds come, clouds go. They never look much wrong.
The fly gets framed, gets trussed. If there's a soul
The web is hung how something wants it hung
And would not be more perfect were it whole.

Peter Scupham in Conversation

It's good to see you looking so spry after all these years. Shall we dive straight in, Peter. When did it all start?

Do sit down, do sit down. Well, there was heavy snow up north on 24 February 1933 – three days before the Reichstag fire, I think it was – and at ten o'clock that evening a Bootle hospital echoed to the cry 'It's a boy!' Being used to being told what's what, I accepted this at the time and...

Cut the cackle. Let's go to childhood. James Reeves wrote: 'It is the child of toil and want / who learns to make the future grow'. Were you a child of toil and want?

No, but a child in a household that had to watch the pennies. My father was a frustrated schoolmaster, a scholarship boy with a double-first from Cambridge teaching C and D streams in Liverpool and Derby; day-release students at Cambridge Tech while assessing prospective students in history for Exhibitions and Scholarships at Emmanuel. My mother was a hard-working and depressive housewife. They did their very best in toughish times. My schooldays mean little. I had amusing nightmares of the Perse School, where I dodged Old Gob, the gowned and mortar-boarded headmaster, hurling tins I seized from a proto-supermarket at him as he came on like a tank. But my childhood was a running-free childhood, and I always had one good friend.

Running free?

In Derby, traipsing suburban streets, helping push salvage carts, collecting shrapnel. The usual. In a Cambridgeshire village, hedging, ditching, picking up bits of the war and putting them down again or hoarding them in the garage. Baiting a bamboo-cane rod with gentles, decked up in a tin hat hurling clods and stones, I still remember the vivid pleasure of knocking out china insulators on a telegraph pole, with a four-square elastic catapult and leather sling. Happy days. No questions asked, but be in at teatime and cut the muddy rind off your boots.

More Just William *than Fotherington-Thomas?*

You say so. But also, to set against the pretty threadbare years, visits and a six-month evacuation to my stately grandparents on my mother's side in Lincolnshire, with a big, gas-lit house, long corridors and a live-in maid. My maternal grandfather was a big man in pyjamas; he owned three draper's shops. That was the house about which I feel, as Geoffrey Grigson felt, writing in his autobiographical *The Crest on the Silver* of his father's vicarage in Cornwall, everything was in the right place for the last time.

You don't sound like a reading child?

Not quite Eliot's small soul curled up with the *Encyclopedia Britannica*, and not that many kisses and toys to grasp at. Books seemed mostly reach-me-downs from my parents'

early years. Some Nesbit, Gene Stratton Porter's *Freckles* and *A Girl of the Limberlost*, the wonderful American *St Nicholas Magazine*, circa 1900 – and odd volumes of Kipling. *Puck of Pook's Hill* and *The Day's Work* I pored over again and again at the age of seven or eight. I was tremendously lucky to have the inexhaustible ten volumes of *The Children's Encyclopedia*, with its breathless amazements – The Wonderful Story of a Nail and so on – Padraic Colum's *Children of Odin,* which was big magic and annihilated the insipid sunlit gods and goddesses of *The Tanglewood Tales*, also de la Mare's anthology *Come Hither*. Later on, smuggled into the Sheldonian in an Oxford scholar's gown, I was delighted to hear Auden talk of his luck in being given that same anthology, with its mysterious and rambling introduction and haunting poems.

And did your schools and parents have much influence in your response to poetry?

Only by accident and happenchance. My father was given, in his lighter moments, to chanting bits and bobs of stuff about the house. I can hear him swinging through Swinburne's *Atalanta in Calydon* chorus, Jean Ingelow's *High Tide on the Coast of Lincolnshire*, or, as they now put it, more accessible stuff: 'I'm looking for the Ogo Pogo, To put him in the Lord Mayor's Show' or 'There's going to be a wedding in the stars, Between Miss Venus and Mr. Mars'. Of such stuff my dreams were made of. As for school, my skin rose and prickled at 'The road was a ribbon of moonlight across the purple moor...', but not at anything else that I can remember. But I loved rhythm, cadence, the waterfalling of words. And I hung around half-understood words – always, says Auden, a good sign for an embryo poet.

If cadence and 'waterfalling words' were part of your make-up, how much did or does music matter to you?

The house was music-free. I knew the signature themes to *Music While You Work, Itma, Much Binding in the Marsh...* sang 'Run, Rabbit, Run' or 'Sierra Sue', admired classic songs with such impressive lines as 'No matter how young a prune may be, it's always full of wrinkles', pirouetted on some stage with a brolly singing Flanagan and Allen's 'Umbrella Song'. My mother had a piano-stool full of Chopin, but early arthritis in her hands meant that I never heard her play. I made do by playing her old 78s over and over again: 'When You and I Were Seventeen', 'In a Quaint Old Normandy Town', 'Romola'...

You were twelve when the war ended. I wonder, reading your poems, whether you ever got it out your system, or even tried to?

I think somewhere Peter Levi talks of the sky, when war broke out, becoming a huge hovering hawk. During the war we were never far from that hovering hawk. In Derby, never very seriously bombed, the Luftwaffe flew over to the Midlands and searchlights and anti-aircraft batteries were all about us, then in Cambridge it was the Americans, the Eighth Air Force and fleets of Flying Fortresses. In Lincolnshire, Bomber County, we were surrounded by bomber bases and the sound of flights out and the

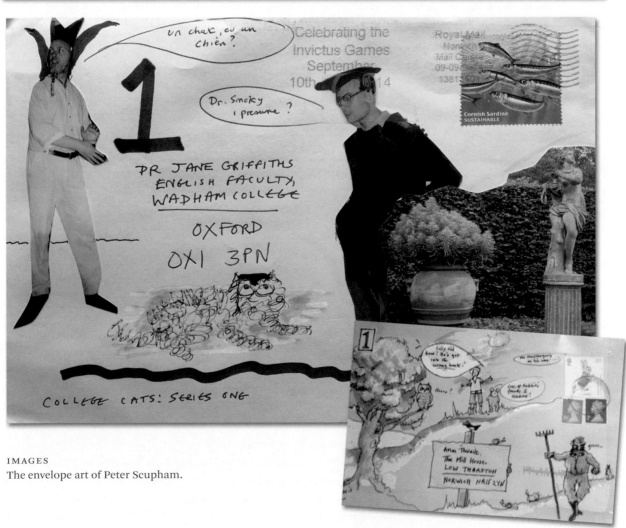

IMAGES

The envelope art of Peter Scupham.

DR. JANE GRIFFITHS,

WADHAM COLLEGE,

PARKS ROAD

OXFORD

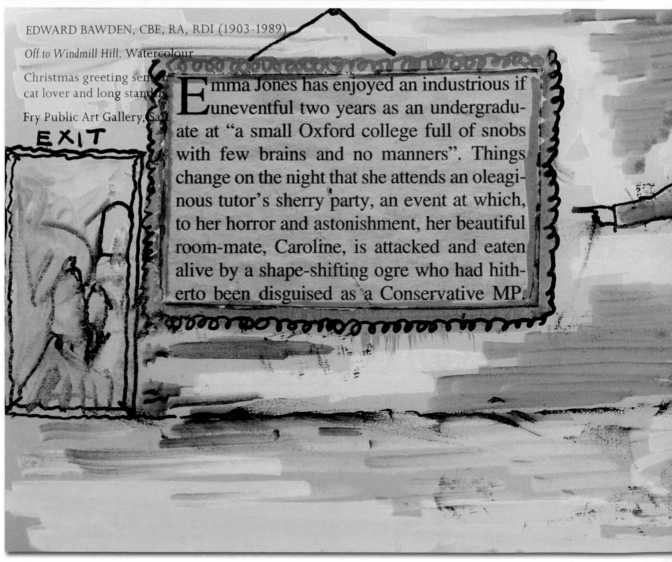

EDWARD BAWDEN, CBE, RA, RDI (1903-1989)

Off to Windmill Hill. Watercolour

Christmas greeting sent to a
cat lover and long standing

Fry Public Art Gallery, Saffron

EXIT

Emma Jones has enjoyed an industrious if uneventful two years as an undergraduate at "a small Oxford college full of snobs with few brains and no manners". Things change on the night that she attends an oleaginous tutor's sherry party, an event at which, to her horror and astonishment, her beautiful room-mate, Caroline, is attacked and eaten alive by a shape-shifting ogre who had hitherto been disguised as a Conservative MP.

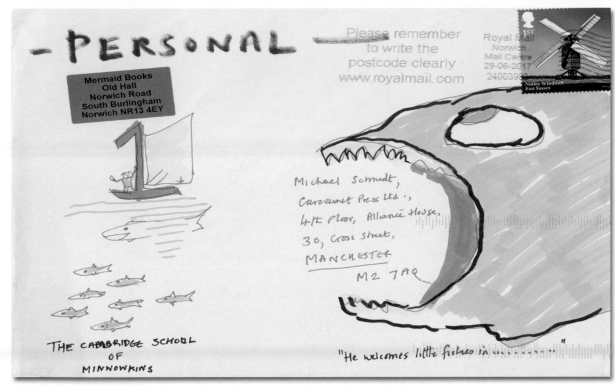

diminished sound of returning planes. I was brought up in a world of black and white, and it has taken me a long time to properly consider the nature of grey. I am still a blackout boy, always haunted by small lights in dark places, the candle that lit me to bed, the evening star, the single firework against the night. And, of course, I am haunted by the cobwebs of 1914–18, the living background to my parents' generation, and my trivial but vivid national service when I was sent on three embarkation leaves for Suez then told to get back to Cambridge and stop bothering them. No, I can't get it out of my system, but it is molten and protean, not fixed. But I can be caught by unreasonable tears at certain images from that period, so vivid, so badly understood.

What about the 'kisses and toys'?

We were not a kissing family. My parents were undemonstrative. They had enough to worry about without kissing. Toys were mostly reach-me-downs. When a child, I played, like a little Edwardian, with my mother's hoops, tops and scooter. My standby was a jumble of Meccano. Now, the importance of Meccano, which made it such a good training for a poet, is that things have to be *built*, and you mustn't do the nuts up too tightly as you go along. You start with easy models, quatrains and tercets and so on. Then you branch out, making your own variations on sonnet-form or ballade. The Nirvana, Prelude or Four Quartets of Meccano was well out of reach. It could be the Eiffel Tower, on a scale of 1:1 built by Clergyman with several Number 10 sets in handsome wooden boxes. The problem with poetry comes when the Lego generation just pushes one clump of verbiage up against another and makes a red and white monster. So, after the Meccano years I spent some time translating French poems by Jammes, Verlaine, Baudelaire et al into formal English verse. Good training, thanks to Meccano. Oh, and I loved the words: trunnions, fishplates, grub screws, pawls and ratchets...

Quite enough about childhood. By the way, when did it stop?

In 1947 my mother came into a little money, my father got a job in the BBC and started on an extraordinary second career which culminated in his role as Controller of Educational Broadcasting, and then Jenny Lee's right-hand man in helping set up the Open University. The cesspit, pushbikes and village school – my sister, who caught TB there, remembers its buckets of straw to piss in – were exchanged for the commuter-belt and a stockbroker's Tudor house with carved faces round the front door. Both parents stopped smoking; the Medici prints metamorphosed into English watercolours; period furniture and parquet glowed with Briwax and Ronuk. So I had two sets of parents, the childhood ones and the adolescence ones.

And somehow you got to Cambridge?

'Never thought he had it in him', said my headmaster. My first wife and I got State Scholarships – a novelty then – and the head gave the school a half-holiday to celebrate. How unjust the world can be.

I believe, knowing you as I do, that you have certain reservations about reading English at Cambridge in the fifties?

I went up in 1954 at the age of twenty-one. Too old. I thought I'd forgotten my history, so changed to English. I'd spent two years in the RAOC training recruits. As they said on my discharge: 'His smart bearing and efficient manner have made him an asset to his unit': I hope that applies to some of my poems. Well, I'd also read a lot of books. So, sampling Dr Leavis, I was not altogether pleased when he held up a small book of Victorian Verse, said, in his inimitable adenoidal way, 'I don't think we need bother with him' and dropped it on the floor to sycophantic laughter. The general air of intellectual murder and mayhem, the internecine warfare, the battle-lines between those who wished to turn literature into a Calvinistic theology and those who didn't – well, it was enough to make one go punting.

And were you writing then?

Had one poem in *Granta*. Didn't try again. Looks OK in my first book a dozen years later. Worked for a bit on a poetry mag, *Delta.* Then got a job teaching in Lincolnshire, rushed about the wolds in a 1934 Austin 7 I painted blue and called 'Little Mr. Bouncer', rang cover on the church bells and had two children. Also wrote poems but didn't do anything with them. I think my first appearance on the World Stage was in 1964 when Anthony Thwaite, a marvellous editor and fine poet, took a poem for *The Listener* at first try. After that the die was cast.

Cats or dogs?

Oh, cats every time. When young I remember sitting on a grass verge while my father offered a half-crown to a small girl who'd been bitten by our Irish Mastiff. And my mother was discomfited in spades when, being asked to say something at a ladylike tea party, I offered '*Dam de dog*'. I can't read aloud without faltering my poem 'Cat's Cradle', for our Timmy, dead these seventy years. Margaret and I live in *a mènagerie à trois* with a snow-spotted Bengal. Are you going to ask me for my favourite colour?

If I must.

Well, I told my grandmother it was red, so I'll stick to it. Actually, it's blue. Play it for the contradictions. That's why my name should, by all reasonable Lincolnshire standards, my father's instructions, and the BBC pronouncing dictionary, be pronounced Scuffam. I answer to the name of Scupham. Sometimes.

I'm glad we got that clear. Now, do you still admire your early admirations?

How can I not? The first book I bought with my own money at about fourteen was Housman's *Collected Poems*. Two or three years after that I was much taken by Robert Graves, which led me to James Reeves and Norman Cameron. Then to the Fugitives, particularly John Crowe Ransom, then Richard Wilbur. Frost, of course, and Marianne Moore. I know there's a strong element of the 'two inches of ivory' about some of these predilections, but so what? 'The strength of the genie comes of his being confined in a bottle', said Wilbur. Make good bottles; hope for genies. And I suppose I've always preferred the church to the cathedral, the hedgerow to the forest, the song to the symphony. Start small, go big. Look at the philosophical mileage Louis MacNeice gets from the Budgie who 'stands at his post on the burning perch' in that last tremendous collection.

Several stateside poets there.

Of course. And think how much grief, pain and loss a well-made box can hold. I'm suddenly thinking of two marvellous poems by Louis Simpson: 'Carentan, O Carentan', his elegiac poem for soldiers in his company ambushed in the Normandy campaign, and 'My Father in the Night Commanding No', where father, mother and the child Simpson were sit motionless and dumb on 'the stage of terror and of love'. Wonderful. I'm proud, too, that when John Mole and I ran our Mandeville Press outfit that we published – and set letter by letter – Anthony Hecht's *A Love for Four Voices*. After discovering Hecht's first book, *The Hard Hours*, I have always thought of him as 'il miglior fabbro', brilliant in his combination of the rough and the swash, the dazzle and the trouble. I think of my own poems as elegiac, palimpsests, evocations, gifts for the dead – and if my boxes are sometimes coffins I can't see why they shouldn't be tied with ribbons and bibbons or glow with painted scenery. No surprise that the first two poems I ever chose to learn by heart – and they are still with me – were Edwin Arlington Robinson's 'For a Dead Lady' and Walter de la Mare's 'Fare Well'. And since I've stressed some American poets, let me put in a very strong word for Cornwall's Charles Causley. There are poems to move the human heart, of which 'Eden Rock' is singularly marvellous. I remember his being guest reader at one of my Arvon courses and being asked how he wrote his poems by an eager student. 'Oh, never ask a poet that question. And never ask yourself. It is a black and secret art, and that is all there is to say about it.' Exit a Creative Writing Masterclass.

You say 'elegiac'. The English vice?

I don't know about a vice. Northern under-the-mountains-with-the-dwarves stuff. Who was it who said the typical sound in the war was 'the patter of rain on an empty stomach'? Goodness, how sad. Isn't there a tribe whose tenses see the past in front of them; the future behind them? I live in an old house, where, with Hardy, I see vanished hands turning the door handles and like David Jones in 'A, a, a Domine Deus' searching for the divine, when I am faced with the world of beautiful interior design and declutterers I find 'the glazed work unrefined and the terrible crystal a stage-paste'. And even the word 'elegiac' isn't quite right. Too much 'gone'. Poems are a continuous and living conversation with people in the next room. But I do like my own line 'Ghosts are a poet's working capital'.

The divine?

Let's just say, with the excellent P. J. Kavanagh, that 'there's something about'.

You seem to put it about that you're some kind of miniaturist, shying away from the big stuff. But you do seem to write an awful lot of sequences.

True. Sequences are important to me. I have always seen my poems as filling in a kind of map. The map, which does not stay stable, is littered with various names, each suggesting a territory which deserves exploration. My books usually home in on one of these territories, allowing for divagation and meanders, or, as Aubrey put it, 'ruins and umbrages'. Some of these territories are: Prehistory, War, The Edwardians – my parents' generation, Darkness... And sequences seem to be a natural way of doing this hacking-through-the-undergrowth work. My favourite sequence, *The Hinterland*, a sequence where the last line of one sonnet is the first line of the next, and the fifteenth sonnet collects all the repeated lines, was once reviewed under the heading 'Crawlies Discouraged: this is the kind of thing that gives poetry a bad name'. But what other name *should* it have? This Hungarian Sonnet Sequence I first discovered in the work of John Fuller, whose brilliantly exact poems I have admired since his first book, *Fairground Music*. The problem with my map is that there are some places marked 'Here be lions' where I lack the courage or idiocy to go.

What kind of courage, what kind of idiocy are you shying away from?

Well, I am uneasy about hijacking other people's lives. Oh, all poets do it, with their green fingers, gunman's fingers. Who said that? Well, Auden's 'In Memory of W. B. Yeats' tells us that poetry makes nothing happen, but exists in 'the valley of its making'. He also says somewhere that if you could write a brilliant poem hating your grandmother, you should do no such thing, as a poem is a moral act. I have known, as we all know, suicides, plunges into drugs, alcoholism... I am uneasy about writing where there is little control and distancing from the immediacy of claws and blood, and am not much in sympathy with the *maudit* American generation; Anne Sexton, Delmore Schwartz, John Berryman... And I found it hard teaching *Ariel* to a sixth form only too anxious to succumb to its enticements. I am well aware that dancing with wolves can produce astonishing things, but not for me. My lack of courage or idiocy – they may be synonyms – prefers the kind of sanity where poetry is not a consuming fire in which one whirls like a vatic dancing dervish. Not quite sure about that image. Of course I have serious limitations! I don't think I could do you a convincing Tom Raworth or Jeremy Prynne, let alone a Sylvia Plath, but if you want a sonnet which is also an acrostic with the first and last letters of each line and contains the names of ten hidden birds, I'm your man.

So, do you inhabit literature or visit it? Can you leave it alone without withdrawal symptoms?

Marianne Moore said that 'there are things that are important beyond all this fiddle'. While one is fiddling, one must make the best tune one can. I dislike the professionalism of poetry, the whole circus of residencies and creative-writing classes. Of course, I don't have the cleanest of hands, having tutored Arvon courses and worked with students on their writing. But I remember more fondly teaching *Tess*, *Lear* or *The Waste Land* to my sixth form, playing word-games and telling ghost stories to a first form. And I have never felt that things around me didn't really exist until they were turned into words; teaching, stroking cats, tumbling up four children, restoring an old house with my wife Margaret, helping her direct Shakespeare in our garden, book-selling, printing... all these things and more are what have made me, and, of course, helped to make the poems, though that was nor the reason for which these other activities came into being. But shall we stop now, or I'll be starting at the beginning again. Make yourself comfortable and we'll have a drink, but no more conversation, my 'affable, familiar ghost'.

Song Cycles

PETER SCUPHAM

1. Summer 1954

i.m. Ray Kinross

Let Saint-Malo put its golden self together
where you came a purler on the tramlines,
ravaged France crawl towards and past us.
Windily we head-butt wounded ghosts
down gritty avenues of dust and poplar,
swung valleys, cluttered by old stone:

Tenteniac, Chinon, Langeais, Saint Mars,
Rigny Ussé, Angers, Orlèans...
In a rowdy bar in a particular nowhere
Michelle's blonde hair teases to smoke,
as she waves back into our futures
becomes kisses on a Carte Postale.

Montsoreau's fishermen can only see
long wands tapering out of time,
floats hovering on crushed silver.
I watch you yawn, feel for a Caporal;
our propped bikes mesh their shadows
to a lean tangle of dark and bright-work

while sun savages our noonday dawdle.
Come on, tighten toe-clips, a quick swig
then, crouched over dropped handlebars,
rough-ride the pavè, bounce and skirr
past staring children, gossip mothers,
your beret jaunty, my jerkin open.

Let name shake into image, image blur,
air loosen its hold on long-lost luggage.
Scout for an auberge, Ray. I'll catch you up –
just half-a-sec to ease this chafe and ache:
head down, unstrapped, and hurt by bright
on the dust road I can see nothing, nothing.

2. A Brilliant Shadow

His voice eager,
the timbre light,
he adds words daily,

defining hillocks,
twists of water,
the lane's corner

where his flung bike,
dazzled in the sun,
scurries into silence

as a vanished summer
conjures it all
to a slow dissolve

and what he is
leans from a window
swung on a far garden,

glances, puzzled,
at a brilliant shadow
leaping off the grass.

Debonair Forms and Feral Terrors

The Poetry of Peter Scupham

ANNE STEVENSON

Ghosts are a poet's working capital.
They hold their hands out from the further shore.
('Prehistories', 1975)

Poetry, although it has long laid claim to values far superior to those of the market place, is really a very competitive field of endeavour, so it is an irony that the games poets play are rarely won in their lifetimes but depend on the assessments of generations that come after them – especially today when standards have been broadened to allow anyone who cares to compete to enter the ring. Given present conditions, I was at a loss as to how to introduce the deep-rooted, surely unique poetry of Peter Scupham until in a serendipitous moment I received from a poet-editor in North Carolina a just published *Selected Poems 1950–1985* of Radcliffe Squires, an American poet whose teaching assistant I was lucky enough to be when a graduate student at the University of Michigan. I have long feared that Squires' poetry, like Scupham's in England, was in danger of being overlooked in the contemporary melee, so it was with a sense of pleased rediscovery that I opened this welcome gift to find in the introduction an apt passage from Squires' 1974 essay, 'The Dark Side of the Moon', first published in the *Sewanee Review*. 'The act of creation', wrote Squires, 'involves really two processes or aspects that are at war with each other but which must nevertheless be made one.' These he identified as a 'feral' voice (Frost's wildness whereof poetry is made), which, in any well- constructed poem, tends to quarrel with the civilising or 'debonair' voice imposed by the poem's form. The latter, in the spirit of the game, seeks to tame the feral voice, endeavouring to hide or bury it in craft. If a poem is to last, argued Squires, it needs to reconcile these opposed voices, which is why its formal trappings are not so much embellishments that sweeten its message as defensive manoeuvres 'against barbarians at the gate'.

Such a marriage of opposites cannot and does not, of course, relate to the great bulk of experimental verse produced in our time, but it does accurately apply to Squires' own poetry, as to Scupham's personal, very English poems. Fortunately, although we may be on the point of entering a computer culture that has little need of books, we can be glad that the present is a great age for books, especially books that collect and republish out-of-print slim volumes from the last century. In the spirit of the times, Carcanet Press, in 2002, published Scupham's *Collected Poems*, a thick volume that brings together all his poems from eleven collections. It was followed in 2011 by a twelfth, *Borrowed Landscapes*. So we now have access to a track over forty years long that leads to the full phenomenon of Peter Scupham the poet – a sensibility, a memory, a mind which, while it is inseparable from all the other roles Peter has played in his lifetime, stands apart from them, too, distanced not only by his powerful imagination and fine craftsmanship, but by his still unexhausted need to find just the right language for a lifetime of feral terrors.

When I first encountered Peter Scupham's poetry – it must have been in 1974 – a collection of my own had just been published by Oxford University Press, and Jon Stallworthy, then poetry editor for the Press, suggested that I might find OUP's recently published *The Snowing Globe*, compatible. Like myself, Peter was a late starting poet. Born in the same year, we had both turned forty in 1973, and both were married, with children. Cambridge was common ground too, as was a background in teaching – though I was an amateur, while Peter... I remember a colleague of his telling me in confidence, 'There are good teachers, there are better teachers, and then there is Peter!' At any rate, I liked Peter's poems – a late Georgian, I suspected, touched by war and the classics like Robert Graves. I must have lived happily with that impression until the appearance of Peter's third Oxford collection, *The Hinterland*, in 1977, when its title sequence changed my mind. 'The Hinterland', is a tour de force of fifteen linked sonnets in which the final pentameter line of each one is repeated as the first line of the sonnet following, the fifteenth sonnet being composed of all fourteen repeated pentameter lines in a rhyming order that clarifies the meaning of the entire sequence. Here is the fifteenth sonnet:

> The summer opens where the days draw in,
> Leaves pressing home their small advantages:
> The rim of summer, when great wars begin.
> But there's a no-man's-land where skull-talk goes,
> A hinterland, to breed new summers in.
> The unfleshed dead, refusing to lie down –
> What inch of sunlight gilds their vanishings,
> Those penitential litanies of stone?
> A silence runs beneath these silences,
> And there our conversations must be held,
> Where blood and stone proclaim their unities
> And all the shadow cross on one high field.
>   Behind the parched leaves glistening in the lane,
>   Diminished thunders, breaking in new rain.

I remember reading 'The Hinterland' with feelings of awe, thinking that despite its perfectly executed pentameters, its author might not be so very Georgian after all. He had done something new with a traditional form, had used a game of connected sonnets to camouflage a war poem that might – had not Eliot already written *The Waste Land* – have been called 'The Burial of the Dead'. As a sequence, the sonnets surely owe more to W. H. Auden, than to Eliot or Graves, although Graves' 1914–18 war was certainly a spur. So was the Second World War, which in later collections Scupham recalled again and again in dream-like scenes from his childhood.

Indeed, beyond the cultivated pale of all Scupham's poems lies a hinterland – personal, historical, universal, sewn thick with the dead – that undermines the smooth surfaces of his rhymed pentameter stanzas with a mysterious 'feral' violence. Viewing the achievement of the *Collected Poems* from the high point of *The Hinterland* reveals contours of what seems not so much linear development as a widening circle of variations on a few salient themes – war and a war-shadowed childhood; the recurring presence of the dead; memory and the distortions memory inflicts on personal experience; the continuous intrusion of history into the present; inevitable losses associated with time's passing and the dying away of past generations. All these preoccupations are set repeatedly among East Anglia's level fields, rural roads and domestic gardens, recalled with loving pain by a sensibility that spins poems out of a range of uniquely personal memories while revealing curiously few facts about the poet's life.

This *Collected Poems* is arranged by book, and without a book of my own to expand into, I can do little in the way of criticism except pay a few poems appreciative visits. To note that these books tend to become more personal, more mysterious, darker and more paradoxical as they proceed is to assert their autobiographical independence and at the same time their instance on occupying imaginative territory uniquely Peter's own. Two collections composed chiefly of dreams and memories followed *The Hinterland* before *Out Late* opened with the superb lyric 'Looking and Finding' that concisely defined the parameters within which Scupham confines his haunted England:

[...] This is where we belong,
Who have inherited
The parish of the dead –

That dark substantial thing
Which hugs itself alone
In rubbed brick, flint, bone,

And speaks with riddling tongue
Of what we were, and are:
Memorial, avatar.

Look in *Out Late*, too, for the sequence based on *A Midsummer Night's Dream* that identifies elements of mystery, mockery and violence in Shakespeare's play and so belies the fairy story or knock-about comedy the play can too lightly be taken to be.

In 1988 *Out Late* was followed by *The Air Show*, a book composed of 'bits and ribbons' of memory from Peter's wartime childhood. The poems are gathered into four sequences that have less to do with actual air-battles and the war's high 'fields of vertigo' than with 'the small animal' himself 'doing a hop-dance over a patch in [his] head', or lying 'head cupped' looking up from the grass, playing his own private game. The title *The Air Show*, like *The Hinterland,* introduces a host of associations – a boy's innocent game of watching planes in a dangerous sky; a visit by the boy as a man to his wartime home where a 'different air' reveals his young self as a ghost; a sequence called 'Good Flying Days' that moves from recollections of kite-flying through the 'Going Out' of Lancasters in 1944 to a parachute 'Not flying, but floating [...] Out, out under the flight path / [...] the ghost of a moth.'

Scupham's most elegiac and (I think) most coherent and moving collection is *Watching the Perseids,* written after the deaths, two years apart, of his parents. Of its two central sequences, 'Young Ghost' traces the last days of his dying mother back to herself as a bride, 'her long hair coursing / down to her shoulders', photographed after her wedding by her husband's box camera. The shutter clicks and her face, banished forever to a small silver frame, is saved there, or made 'safe from growing with what is growing'. To anyone who has watched over a dying parent, the entire sequence must be painfully affecting, although it eschews sentimentality by making peace between Squires' warring voices that Scupham unites with apparently effortless skill, as in the lively villanelle, 'Dancing Shoes':

At Time's *Excuse me* – how could you refuse?
How long since you wore out your dancing shoes?

A second sequence recreates the poet's father dying fully in character, taking part in little scenes of witty exchange between himself and his attendant son – perverse and hilarious in the spirit of Shakespeare's Mechanicals meeting to rehearse by moonlight in *A Midsummer Night's Dream*. Surprisingly, the only despairing lines in *The Perseids* are to be found in a truly horrific sequence, 'The Christmas Midnight' – eighteen sonnets placed as a coda to 'The Young Ghost' and recording the poet's feelings on his last nightmare drive to his mother's nursing home. Although their references are vague, it is impossible to miss that these frightening sonnets just skirt an impulse to suicide, making all the more beautiful the controlled lines of the title poem, 'Watching the Perseids: Remembering the Dead'. And so this collection that confronts actual, not imaginary death, climaxes in an evocation of the annual August miracle of shooting stars, meteors 'riding softly down: / Hair-streak moths, brushing with faint wings / This audience of stars with sharp young faces '. These heavenly apparitions that really have nothing to do with life become symbols of what we must all suffer to leave life, 'the comet's tail we must all pass through / Dreamed out into a trail of Jack O'Lanterns, / A shattered windscreen on the road to nowhere', retaining an image from that nightmare Christmas drive to be a sign that

We wait for last words, ease the rites of passage,
The cold night hung in chains about our questions,
Our black ark swinging lightly to its mooring.

The potency of that final line must have handed Peter a title for his next book, *The Ark*, which proved to be the last OUP produced for him before that publishing house disgraced itself by banishing its poets. How that 'black ark swinging lightly to its mooring' became, in this new book, a metaphor for the thinking brain carried from birth to death in the human skull is the conundrum Peter Scupham now set himself to illustrate in the most difficult to approach of all his books. *The Ark* asks unanswerable questions relating to life and death that were raised but brushed aside in the close emotional atmosphere of *Watching the Perseids*, and is altogether more abstract and unsettling than its predecessor. Of the four sequences that fill its pages, 'The Accident' looks to be an experiment in storytelling whose foreign tone and manner owes characteristics to modern Europeans (Milan Kundera? Alain Robbe-Grillet?). 'Annunciations' is a fantasy based chiefly on Italian paintings; 'Nacht und Nebel', also with

European references, is a particularly dark meditation on death, dedicated to George Szirtes. Only 'A Habitat' takes us home to the fertile ground of Peter's local imagination, celebrating in eleven chapters the long life of Old Hall, the Elizabethan manor house that with Margaret Seward he rescued from boarded up decay in the 1990s and turned into the teeming centre of his later life. Two more collections followed *The Ark*, both well populated with ghosts but freed (at least partially) by the passing of time from the heavy perplexities associated with the actual dead. *Night Watch* (Anvil Press, 1999) brings back Scupham's parents on holiday from the Underworld, both looking well and in a quipping, merry frame of mind. Other poems return, with ironic twists, to the poet's days as a National Serviceman. In a brilliant satire on military pomp, the dead in Arras receive a centenary embassy of 'bearers, kin and one survivor', joining forces with the dead to endure 'yet more spit and polishing'. They meet to honour two dead 'metal dog-tagged fusiliers', but persist in punishing a third for losing his name; he 'must be sentenced to the usual reprimand – "A Soldier of the Great War, Known unto God"' – even though he is known well enough to 'Privates King and Anderson'. The wit is vintage Scupham, and it lightens both his most recent collections, which together recall, mostly with equanimity and amusement, a world fast becoming ghostly in the memories of all his (and my) generation.

Enough. There is more praise to offer Peter Scupham on his eighty-fifth birthday, and doubtless more poems to come from him, but, short of writing a thesis, I must give way to shortage of space. Get hold of *Borrowed Landscapes* once you have a copy of *Collected Poems* by your bedside, and read for yourself the poems of one of England's bound-to-be classic poets of the future. To finish with a flourish, it seems right to sign off with a rhyme. 'A Merry-go-round for Megan' was probably written for a granddaughter but surely it's for all of us. Find it on page forty-three of *Borrowed Landscapes*:

If you start from here,
you could end up there,
on a roundabout
with a dragon and a star
and a wide-eyes owl
and a three-wheeled car.
always in the middle
wherever you may be,
the riddle in the middle
of the place called ME.
[...]
if you start from there,
you could end up here,
with a mouse and a cat
and a fancy that,
with a dog and a frog
and a velvet hat,
always in the middle
wherever you may be,
the riddle in the middle
of the place called ME!

Genius of Activity

ROBERT WELLS

Peter once told me that he has never begun a poem without finishing it. My thoughts soon turn to this remark, a salutary one for me, when I think of him. With Peter, there is always activity – and the activity always has a result. When invited to write about some aspect of his activity for this birthday celebration, I find myself puzzled. Which is it to be? It must be the poetry, first of all. But each of Peter's doings, each with its result, is an aspect of the genius of activity which rules in him indivisibly and shows itself with the same deft accuracy and practical spirit in whatever he sets his hand to. Whatever task, I was going to say. But task is too heavy a word. Peter makes heavy things seem light – the writing of a formal ode, the assembling of a book catalogue, an open-air dramatic production, the restoration of an ancient house. His gravity allows for play and delights in it. He distrusts the vatic, and indeed any sign of undue literary self-importance. But if amid the gossip and banter of casual conversation you stop and ask for Peter's settled view of some matter, he will pause briefly, and then with a Johnsonian directness and finality he will give it in plain and perfect sentences.

Peter's poetry began, amid the press of family life and his professional life as a teacher, as one among a dozen pursuits – one that had been kept rather in reserve because of the value he placed on it – and that, once released, came swiftly to embrace and dominate, as it also drew upon, the rest, reaching to discover the full extent of its range, with Peter racing to keep up with and somehow outflank this imperious claim upon him. His first two books, *The Small Containers* and *The Snowing Globe*, appeared in the same year, 1972. The books that, along with these, make up his *Collected Poems* (2002), each of them a full sheaf in itself, have followed one another for the most part at intervals of no more than two or three years. Somewhere between *Prehistories* (1975) and *The Hinterland* (1977) a vocation comes powerfully into its own, which it must have been ruinous to resist. With each deep excursion into the *Collected Poems* (the latest just before writing this) it seems to me that I, too, am only now beginning to catch up. I still find poems or parts of poems which I had somehow previously passed by or not taken in. On this last occasion it was the spacious symmetries of his 'Natura' sequence which captivated me – a dreamed landscape-garden design for some never-built or long-vanished palace.

Anyone with an aspiration to poetry can begin a poem. A first line comes and the fingers tap as they count. To shape and revise a poem, to fill it in, to bring it or patch it up to a conclusion, is – as we know to our cost – another matter. Here the resources of memory, wit and ingenuity, lore and learning, come into play, and the ability to access these as needed. For Peter this access always seems to be quick, and the resources endlessly various. The handy words are there, and if not the missing piece of the puzzle, then a patch will have to do, and may do as well or better. His poems wear their patches with pride, as indistinguishable from felicities. Some of the most enjoyable and best of his poems seem at first to consist entirely of patches – coats of many colours, almost constituting a genre, among others, in his work. Patch or felicity – which is which? You can hardly tell, and hardly need to. Yet amid the variety as beneath it, and always present, sometimes very barely and strikingly revealed, like the Johnsonian judgements amid the conversation, run plain-speaking and a drive toward clarity. Similarly, the busy and hopeful and multiform activity may slow (as in his fine unrhymed sonnet with this first line) to 'They go about some job, as the rain falls', and to words that are smooth only because 'worked bare and to the bone'.

Finished works as they are, Peter's poems remain active within themselves, restive, not yet stilled – reminding me sometimes of a lively class whose teacher has been called for a few minutes into the corridor. The class know he is there, not far away, but with his presence at one remove a stir runs through the room, a ripple or series of ripples, a subdued babel, the first tremors of a disorder held in check by the knowledge that at any moment he may walk in again. This restiveness or restlessness is a part of Peter's subject. Time and again he tries to catch it by showing it in movement in his poems. Once you notice it, you find it everywhere.

The Spring wind blows the window grey and white,
Stripping the hangings, pouring out the rooms.
There are the dados, and the beaded moulding,
The gather-ye-roses on the children's wall.
Doors shake on their jambs: the spine of the house
Thrills as the sprung wood quivers, and goes still...

There is also and everywhere in his poems the movement of the past within the present, the two intermixed in a continuous traffic at once ghostly and substantial. Again, which is which, and which takes precedence? Is it that revenants visit us here, or is it we who are the ghosts there as we visit or revisit the past? The wordplay and habit of punning in Peter's poetry, where one half of the pun can seem to be floating adrift, and which can be distracting, becomes much less so when understood as an expression of this continuing activity, this intuition of simultaneity. Accumulation and compacting are a part of his method. Fresh colours have their place beside faded ones, Primavera but also the pressed flower, the theatrical performance but also the elaborate stage-set cast adrift when the performance is over. The poetry will always outrun our attention. There will be more than we can take in.

Peter is a collector, of poems first of all (which he collects chiefly by writing them, that anodyne phrase 'a collection of poems' being restored in his case to a very literal sense), of books, of curiosities, of fine often-overlooked things which he has an eye for – a sympathetic eye, because all these things reach out to him, and his instinct is to help, to rescue, to find a home for (his own or another's). The damaged folio will have its covers reattached and burnished up, its missing leaf or leaves restored either in photocopy or immaculate handwriting. The wrecked manor house, boarded up and reduced to a stable, will be made habitable, and more than habitable, a refuge for the Graces – surrounded again by garden, its history recovered, so far as it may be, and continued. 'The pain of all things loose, discarnate', some lost thing intuited out in the fields, or here in the room, will be given its voice and place again in the poem. So the activity of the past, with its abandoned or neglected results, becomes serviceable again and a part of our present doings. The essential thing about Peter's collections and his instinct in collecting is that they are not fixed, they are more a matter of sharing and passing on than they are of possession. Possession is temporary. They remain in movement, just as his poems do. And while Peter has been writing his own poems, he has also, as proprietor with John Mole of the Mandeville Press, printed and published the poetry of others. Two notable Mandeville productions that I turn to are E. J. Scovell's *Listening to Collared Doves* (a wonderful poet, and so quiet a presence that she always has to be rediscovered), and Michael Riviere's *Selected Poems* (which includes 'Oflag Night Piece', one of the best poems to come out of the Second World War, and 'Late in the Day', a sequence about old age, hardest of subjects, which I don't think has been bettered).

All of which brings me (as most visits to England have brought me and my family over thirty years) to Old Hall, the 'cock-eyed house, beset by open fields' which I have just mentioned. I should thank Peter, and Margaret Steward, for their keeping open house to us – to all of us who, coming and going, have met there and shared in the occasions of the house and its hospitality. Old Hall is not on the way to somewhere else. Hard to find as it can prove among the Norfolk lanes, and with Reedham Ferry, trailing its chains, to cross, it is, or we think of it as, a hidden centre to which we are drawn. What draws us, we might describe, with all allowance for difference in scale and the vanished fuss of patronage and rank (which Peter would have no truck with at all), as a Penshurst feeling, alive still or brought alive again.

Peter's Mermaid Book catalogues, too, as well as providing a further education, jokes good and bad, and incorrigible commentary, give the sense of belonging to a secret community. The literary enthusiasms which had seemed to isolate us draw us together. As readers of Oldham or Barnes, Sisson or Grigson, Kilvert or Jules Renard (to name a few among the Mermaid irregulars), we discover that we are, after all, not alone. A parcel from Mermaid, neatly and sturdily made up and with a richly eclectic content to be unwrapped, arrives rather like one of Peter's poems and bringing something of the same pleasure. Peter, as Enchanter of the Castle, turns out (*pace* indolent James Thomson) to be one and the same as the Knight of Arts and Industry. But it should be added that, as bookish tempter, he is not without a Mephophelean gleam in his eye.

The restoration of Old Hall has meant great labour on the part of Peter and Margaret, but thanks to them it is, for us – its guests, its audiences and participants at the Poetry Days and performances of Shakespeare – a given, there to enjoy and to enjoy remembering. Old Hall keeps changing. The Mermaid bookroom shifts about. Or you look for the bathroom and find yourself in the pantry. A tree-house appears in the wood (where Peter goes to read), or a shepherd's house in the field, or a new garden has been 'cut where a garden grew'. What has not changed is the presence of Peter and Margaret, and the undiscouraged activity which sustains the house, as it continues to sustain Peter's poetry.

The other day I asked my daughter, now grown-up, what she recalled of Peter and of our visits to Old Hall. This is what she came back with, instantly remembered, over the dinner table. Of Old Hall: 'An enchantment, a magical place: mermaids, peacocks, cats, white doves, Mark Hearld's painting of the Tree of Life. A kitchen with other rooms built round it – you do get lost in that house.

We don't know what happens in the library. Where do I sit where a cat isn't? Which garden to have tea?' Of Peter: 'He has a good laugh, is a children's book character, a story-teller, has a story which fits everybody, puts his hands behind his back, is not *chichis*, is never embarrassed, is permanently non-PC (in a positive way), drives a little topless sports-car, conducts conversations from the ingle-nook...'. She remembers him telling her and her brother, 'Oh, just go and look for the peacock feathers', and adds, 'We'd go back with peacock feathers. Picking up peacock feathers was pretty good. It doesn't happen all that often.'

Celebrating Eighty-Five at Eighty-Seven Plus

ANTHONY THWAITE

I have had a fellow-feeling with Peter Scupham from the beginning – and by that I mean my accepting for publication 'The Children and the House' in 1964, when I was literary editor of the *Listener*. Peter has more than once acknowledged this as the start of his 'career' as a poet. I went on publishing him, in the *Listener*, then the *New Statesman*, then *Encounter*. And then there was the moment in 1977 when our new books (my *A Portion for Foxes* and Peter's *The Hinterland*) were reviewed together in the *Observer* by Craig Raine, superciliously and patronisingly. It's something to be glued together as objects of Craig Raine's scornful facetiousness.

Much more recently, in 2016, Peter and I found ourselves more fully represented than any other poets in Kevin Gardner's anthology *Building Jerusalem: Elegies on Parish Churches*. Since according to Peter I had some years ago balefully warned him to 'keep out of graveyards for a while', this representation might seem just. I find Peter's frequent elegiac note congenial, and also his delight in 'things' – by which I mean not just portable objects but buildings, and in particular the marvellous house in which he and Margaret live, Old Hall, South Burlingham, a sixteenth- and seventeenth-century building in Norfolk (about half an hour's drive from us) which they saved from becoming a ruin (though he likes ruins too). Its large garden has been the setting for the Shakespeare plays the Scuphams have put on for several years, as well as the annual 'poetry picnics': these aren't the endurance tests (or only intermittently) that the words might suggest. In fact I think there's a principled lightness of touch to almost everything Peter does. His poems have always been shapely, well-woven, witty, tenderly observant. He should be much better known than he is.

Transactions & Touchstones

Peter Scupham's Sequences

LAWRENCE SAIL

For Peter Scupham the sequence has long been an instrument of choice on which to sound his central preoccupations – childhood, the two World Wars, the natural world, and English literature and history: subjects seen variously through the prisms of family, autobiography and an acute sensibility finely attuned to detail and atmosphere. Every one of his collections contains one or more sequences, with the rule-proving exception of his very first collection, *The Small Containers* (1972), whose very title might be thought to militate against the sequence's expansionist nature. But from *The Snowing Globe* (also 1972) onwards, sequences are a consistent feature of the work, and it could be argued that an apogee of a kind is reached in *The Air Show* (1988), with the whole collection set in what the opening poem describes simply as 'the land of was'.

In a number of instances the sequences complement one another, or one starts by continuing a narrative that was the ending of another. Thus 'Playtime in a Cold City' with its subtitle, 'Emmanuel College, Cambridge. 1954-1957' (in *Borrowed Landscapes,* 2011) takes up where 'Conscriptions: National Service 1952–4' (*Winter Quarters,* 1987) left off; and 'Conscriptions' is itself shadowed by 'The Northern Line', with its sub-title 'End of Leave, 1950s', published in *Night Watch,* twelve years later. Also in *Winter Quarters,* 'Notes from a War Diary (HJB 1918-19)', which draws on his father-in-law's experience of the war, finds a sequel in 'A Civil War' (*Borrowed Landscapes*). Some of the sequences have in common a dominant formal structure, notably the title poem of the 1977 collection *The Hinterland* (an intricately linked sequence of fifteen sonnets, in which each successive sonnet begins by repeating the last line of the one before, with the final one made up of all of these repeated lines, in order), or 'Natura', in the next book (*Summer Palaces,* 1980) – much freer in structure but still rounding to a repetition of the opening line, 'A few glint beads, prisms of shaken life.' In *Out Late* (1986), the sequence closely based on *A Midsummer Night's Dream* finds a delightful companion piece, theatrical in a different way, in the brilliant parodies of poets in 'The Poets Call on the Goddess Echo'.

But an overview can reach only so far: to appreciate fully the nature of Scupham's achievements in his sequences requires a more detailed consideration. From those above, by no means a complete list, I've selected two, in the hope of illustrating at least some of the sequences' characteristics.

For intimacy and inter-connection, Scupham has never

surpassed the poems about his parents, published soon after their death three Christmases apart. 'Young Ghost', written in memory of his mother Dorothy, and 'Dying', about his father John, form the heart of *Watching the Perseids* (1990). It's the first of these two sequences I want to consider. 'Young Ghost' gives us sixteen poems, none longer than thirty lines, six of fewer than twenty. Nearly all of them rhyme, the exceptions being numbers eight and sixteen (the symmetry is no surprise), with the natural impetus of rhyme towards closure juxtaposed to the raw openness of grief, as is clear from the opening poem, 'Arriving'. On his journey to his mother, the poet finds the car radio offering 'dance-tunes shaken / Out of the past's throat', and sees himself in a place

Where something fragile as blur on the warm windscreen
Hangs to old furniture, the once, the might-have-been
Of things.

Unease and dislocation are to the fore; his destination is 'the wrong place', even if it 'gathers the ghosts of love into its own right dream'. In a later poem in the sequence, 'It is time to die in a house which was never home'.

'Young Ghost' – the implications of the title, with its sense of pathos, unreadiness, the untimeliness of grief, are developed in poems notable for their tenderness, which circle round remembered incidents and details of his mother's life. And that 'blur' in the opening poem recurs: the blurring caused by tears, perhaps, but also the dissolution of the clear boundaries separating past and present. A response to a garden is seen as an indifference expressed 'In blurs of white, or green and brown'; Christmas cards are 'blurred with angels and unpacked memories'; the ending of one poem asserts that 'Beyond shine and blur / Her mother's coffin-trestles wait for her'. Scupham refers in a number of his poems to his mother's love of dancing: here, in 'Dancing shoes', an excellent villanelle in which the dance is seen as representative of his parents' love and of time itself, 'The records end in blur and monotone'. One constituent of this blurring is the uncertainty of grief, the poet's attempts to come to terms while at the same time remaining resistant to the reductive fixities of what is left – 'I watch you turning into memory'. Throughout, there is the attempt to capture in some way the fluidity of the moment, before it is too late. In 'Christmas 1987' the setting is '[...] this molten place, where a silver photograph-frame / Runs like mercury...'; in the same poem, he evokes his mother 'With hat over dark hair, the white dress poured into shade'. In 'At the Gate', the context is 'the dissolving landscape'; in '1946', 'She fears cancer, being dissolved from us all /Into a nothing...'; and 'The Finished Life' sets the residue of what is left beneath 'an unfocused sky'. What gives the sequence its particular emotional charge is that the solvent here is love, explicitly acknowledged more than once, and appearing in various guises, from the evidence provided by an old Kodak, to his parents dancing together, to the echo of Dante expressed as 'Our share in that love which steadies the sky from falling, / And lights the stars' ('The Stair').

Though the poems encompass the external processes of death, from the diminishment of the body as it dwindles before 'That plain and simple hugeness: being dead', to the rituals of saying goodbye ('I pass the baked meats, and the funeral tea'), the true centre of the sequence is the interplay between love and loss, as the poet finds himself 'With double sight / Angling the dark for the truth of yesterday's ghost'. 'The Christmas Midnight', the poem placed immediately after the sequence, puts it perfectly:

I hold her far away, as far as God;
I wear her closely as a second skin.

This not a report of grief, a grief observed, but its evolution and enactment, set against the stasis of death in a series of musical movements, and given urgency by the knowledge that too soon will come the moment when 'She floats away light as ash in its tiny casket', an image repeated at the start of 'The Finished Life' – the life which 'floats away / In rest and syncopation': and it is no coincidence that in this sustained threnody it is not the past, but the present tense that is deployed for two-thirds of the poems.

The contrast with 'Dying', the sequence of nine poems in memory of Scupham's father, is instructive. In 'Young Ghost' the poet explores the nature of grief and of his relationship with his mother; in 'Dying' he is above all listening, recording, reporting. True, there is a comparable sense of symmetry at work, with the first, fifth and ninth poems all headed with specific dates, while the groups of three poems between them all take as their heading something said by his father. And it's also the case that here too is the depiction and defining of a crucial relationship: but in looser patterns, with no rhyme, and little of the lyrical tenderness so evident in 'Young Ghost'. Here love is expressed more in the guise of a challenging duologue, as well as a hallowing of his father's words, whose authority seems enhanced by their use as titles.

The eleven poems which make up 'The Northern Line' (published in *Night Watch*, 1999) carry the sub-title 'End of Leave, 1950s', and so relate to Scupham's other poems about his experience of National Service. On one level the sequence is indeed an account of a train journey, as the titles of the poems describe, starting with 'Boarding' and calling en route at, amongst other places, St Pancras, the Underground and Waterloo, before reaching 'Terminus'. As you might expect, given the army context, the faring individual is held within the iron casing of structures and routines, in a National Serviceman's humble version of Vigny's *Servitude et Grandeur Militaires*; in Scupham's case, subject to the demands of the R.A.O.C., whose Latin motto is quoted several times: *sua tela tonanti* ('to the thunderer his weapons'). In the poems you catch now and then the distinctive yelping bark of an R.S.M., and the sequence works perfectly well on this level, with Scupham as cipher number 22651134, on his way to rejoin his unit. But this isn't even half the story.

There are in fact two journeys here: the literal journey is exactly overlaid with, as it were, an extended train of thought which runs the length and breadth of the neural network, laden with allusions, quotations, synaptic connections, junctions and couplings, through landscapes bright with references to literature, art and history as well as the poet's own story.

The passengers transported on this substantial ghost train, along with the reader, include Baudelaire (especially his poems 'A une mendiante rousse' and, aptly, 'L'Invitation au Voyage'), Lewis Carroll ('Jabberwocky' and, from Alice's train journey, also in *Adventures through the Looking-Glass*, the splendid advice: 'Never mind what they all say, my dear,/but take a return ticket every time the train stops'), Chesterton ('The Invisible Man'), Coleridge's ancient mariner, Dante (with a play on 'nel mezzo del cammin'), Dickens (with particular reference to the story 'Mugby Junction'), Joe Miller (his jest book of 1739), Spender ('The black statement of pistons'), Tennyson (his 1889 poem 'Merlin and the Gleam'), Thomas Lovell Beddoes and Edward Thomas ('Adlestrop', of course). In an adjacent carriage, as you might imagine, are the artists he conjures – Duchamp, Gertler, Magritte, Henry Moore, Paul Nash (whose *Totes Meer* is the front cover of *The Air Show*), in another the musicians and singers – Sidney Bechet, Claude Luter, Elvis Presley, Vera Lynn.

The songs that feature in the sequence would require a significant amount of space, enough to accommodate 'We'll meet again', 'Muß i' denn' (from which Elvis evolved 'Wooden Heart'), 'Pack up your troubles', 'It's a long, long way to Tipperary', 'Your King and Country want you', Pete Seeger's 'Where have all the flowers gone?', a John Keble hymn ('The voice that breathed o'er Eden') and Matthew Locke's 'Up and down this world goes round, down'.

There is also room for *Love's Labour's Lost* ('You, that way; we, this way'), as well as *Brief Encounter* and Celia Johnson (Anna Neagle, voted the most popular star in Britain in 1949, is another passenger): even, via the old joke of '*c'est magnifique, mais ce n'est pas la gare*', the charge of the Light Brigade. Among other travellers are the Reverend Awdry (with his own push-me pull-you trains), Eccles, Bluebottle, Moriarty, Orpheus and Mithras.

History has its say, too: here are Dulles, Eisenhower, Stalin, Molotov, Churchill and Eden; the route passes by Vimy Ridge and Neuve Chapelle; and the history of childhood comes in mentions of 'the Hornby loco' and Harbutt's plasticine. Also present is the grim association of railway tracks with murderous extinction, 'The lament of the birches at Birkenau, /and half a century's epitaph: *Arbeit Macht Frei*.'

You might well think all this would add up to the kind of gross over-crowding familiar to Southern Rail commuters, or an untidy agglomeration of *disjecta membra*, the locution used in the final poem in connection with engine parts. The wonder is that everything seems perfectly in place, with sitting room for all and no jostling. That it is so says a great deal for Scupham's deftness and wit, as well as his lightness of touch: for the reader, it is both the evocation of a historical moment, a particular journey in a particular life, but also simply highly enjoyable, a kind of headlong combination of quiz, riddle and memory test. Taken together, the poems compose a congruous and pleasing weave of allusion and reference, and never come off the rails.

A clue to the common ground which links even material and treatment as disparate as in these two sequences is to be found in 'Young Ghost', in the poem ambiguously titled 'The Finished Life'. Now that the poet's mother is dead, 'she is nothing young, and nothing old':

But takes her chances from a sleight of mind
And, castled in her unrecorded hours,
Must lend herself to what the words can find

That is, she is to be found in what the Prologue to 'Playtime in a Cold City' (one of three sequences in the most recent collection, *Borrowed Landscapes*) characterises as 'the in-betweenness of it all'. In Scupham's perspectives the broad zone of between is our mortal span as well as the world of *entre deux guerres,* and those of the family, the natural world, of *genius loci* (see the sequence 'A Habitat') and of England seen from the second half of the twentieth century. It is these areas of transaction and comparison that he has made powerfully his own, and in which he deploys a variety of touchstones in order to assay true value. No doubt the sequence offers one effective medium for doing so, with a sinuousness as supple as the cats which appear now and then throughout Scupham's richly layered work, pleasing themselves in the way felines do – but it is not the only one. Equally important are his penchant for the outer reaches of vocabulary, as much quirky or *gemütlich* as erudite, his eye for the telling detail vividly caught, his recurrent use of key words ('dust' and 'ghost' would be two) and his sheer relish. And perhaps the most vital feature of all is indicated in one of the poems in 'Dying', where he mentions one of his father's favourite quotations, which is really another transaction: 'The feast of reason, and the flow of soul' (and here I am quoting Scupham quoting his father quoting Pope quoting, or at least giving us imitations of, Horace: you see how quickly layering can become elaborate). If indeed 'ghosts are a poet's working capital', as the title poem of *Prehistories* (1975) suggests, the real return on that investment is the retrieval of the present from the past, newly enriched by it and, paradoxically, by the absences it holds. This, done with a feeling mind and a thinking heart, is the essence of Scupham's gift. In the end, the past can be re-presented, like the new version of his mother beyond her death, only in 'what the words can find'; and, as 'Figures in a Landscape, 1944' has it, with 'only a pen to turn was to is'. *Sua tela poetae.*

'? Now *local*'

A Masterclass from the Early Scupham

GREVEL LINDOP

It was Peter Scupham who introduced me to landscape. Not the outward, physical landscape, obviously, but the landscape that lies latent inside words, and that can be evoked by their proper placement. One August day in 1980 I was browsing in Haigh and Hochland – now long forgotten, then the well-known Manchester University bookshop – when I noticed a slim paperback with a beguilingly dull cover; dull, yet intriguing. The image was a grey-and-white photograph of a stubble field – parallel rows of grass cut short, bristly like a worn-out hairbrush – and behind it another stubble field, blackish rows, possibly burnt, stretching away like a piece of old corduroy. The sheer emptiness of the picture seemed to draw one in and promise something just over the horizon. Presumably I glanced inside; something must have attracted me, but I forget what. The book was *The Hinterland*, by Peter Scupham, published three years before. I bought it (amazing, now, that in 1980 one could buy a book of poems for £1.95!) and took it home. And I fell under the Scupham spell.

The spell is hard to define, as good spells naturally are. It had something to do with a casualness of tone, with an attention to the fragment. Also with lines so well-crafted that their sheer sound made you want to repeat them over and over. And other lines that completely upended the conventional rules about how a line ought to sound. One poem ('David') ended with a couplet: 'Whatever is done, undone, done, / The gathering musics run as one.' The sheer flatness of all those repeated *un* sounds could be heard as deeply uncomfortable, but was so obviously intentional that one had to pause on it, emphasise it, until it became the sound of a tolling bell, and clearly intended as such. Indeed, earlier in the poem – which seems to describe a group of garden sculptures somewhere within sound of a chime of bells – we were prepared for this: 'The bells' brotherhood gives tongue / where sallies leap to lin lan lone'. *That* was a line that, it seemed to me, descended almost into gibberish, but gibberish that conveyed its own meaning. I sensed an exuberant movement, an outburst of some kind, but wasn't familiar then with *OED*'s 'sally *sb*[2], 1: The first movement of a bell when "set" for ringing...? Now local' or its '*sb*[2] 2: The woolly grip for the hands near the lower end of a bell-rope'. As for 'lin lan lone', it set off – appropriately enough – an echo somewhere at the back of the mind, which was perhaps, as I recognised years later, Tennyson's 'the mellow lin-lan-lone of evening bells'; though I suspect that behind Tennyson there is a folk-usage that even *OED* has forgotten about.

That '? Now local' seems significant, indicating Scupham's readiness to pick up a word from dialect, or revive one almost expired. This tendency led to a huge and interesting vocabulary; so much so that for some years, and entirely thanks to Scupham, I had a rule that every poem I wrote must contain at least one word I'd never used in a poem before; a naïve enough notion, but one that usefully stretched my *vocabulary*.

Beyond the attention to language, there was a dazzling inventiveness, finding poetry in the most unlikely places. 'Answers to Correspondents' made a poem by juxtaposing, apparently with minimal intervention, extracts from the column so named in a Victorian girls' magazine:

> Paquerelle, we fall back on the language of the Aesthetics:
> Your composition is quite too utterly too too;
> Joanna, ask the cook. Gertrude, we are uncertain –
> What do you mean by 'Will my writing do?'
> Do what? Walk, talk or laugh? Maud, we believe and hope
> The liberties taken were not encouraged by you.

But most importantly there was the book's title sequence, 'The Hinterland'. This was something I'd never seen before: the last line of each sonnet became the first line of the next; this happened fourteen times, and then the repeated lines were put together to make up a fifteenth sonnet. I was fascinated by the way the repeated lines produced an effect of tension, of suspended yet insistent continuity, very different from the stability of the sonnets within a normal sequence. 'The Hinterland' was about many things – about time, about land, about the details of a household, but above all about the world wars – and not, I think, just the first, as the book's blurb suggested, for surely the Battle of Britain is being described in sonnet 12, where:

> Bandit and Angel stand
> And cool their wing-tips in a molten sun
> Of Kentish fire, their long trails wound and fanned
> Against a sky which cannot take the stain,
> The lost crews working home against the wind[.]

But the whole sequence was full of memorable lines: 'The rim of summer, when great wars begin'; 'There's a no-man's-land where skull-talk goes'; 'A spray of ghosts across the hollow square'. Its beguiling descriptions of a landscape and a dusty house in summer are permeated by the awareness of war, which will not go away, which is the hinterland of present perception, and which Scupham (a war child) would return to with something approaching a mild obsession: in 'Conscriptions: National Service '52–54'; in 'Notes from a War Diary' (both from the 1983 *Winter Quarters*, whose cover shows a pair of USAF Nissen huts) and more fully still in 1988's *The Air Show*.

The form of Scupham's interlinked sonnet sequence intrigued and impressed me so much that in due course I decided to write one of my own. 'Patchwork' took its departure from a quilt we'd been given as a wedding present: it struck me that the squareish appearance of a sonnet on the page could resemble different squares in the quilt, and to suit the title I decided to give each of the fifteen sonnets a different rhyme scheme. It was fun, and hard, and instructive. Scupham had opened a path for me, as I suspect he has done for many another poet.

But to return to landscape. There were so many exact and unexpected phrases that brought place, though rarely a specific place, into imaginative reality. 'The salt brushed pelt of trees'; 'The ferns darkening, and the lizards gone'; 'the obtuse / And ogreish language of a troubled sky'. The phrases themselves were a lesson in how to look, and how to think afterwards about what had been looked at. Two especially haunting poems, 'The

Gatehouse' from the 1980 book *Summer Palaces* and its sequel 'The Plantations' from 1986's *Out Late*, have proved especially memorable, casting a spell that hasn't faded and indeed renews itself each time I read them. In the first, Scupham listens to his son playing the piano and 'This left hand takes me down a branching line / To the slow outskirts of a market town' where, a boy again, he is taken by 'Mr Curtis' to the level-crossing-keeper's cottage ('The Gatehouse') to watch a train go past:

> Redcurrants glow, molten about the shade, //
> The cows are switched along a ragged lane...
> The Gatehouse settles back into the trees,
> Rich in its faded hens, its garden privy
> Sweet with excrement and early summer.
> New bread and sticky cake for tea. The needle
> Dances across: Line Clear to Train on Line;...
> The gate is white and cold. I swing it to,
> Then climb between the steady bars to watch...
> The lamps are wiped and lit. Then we, too, go.

Odd, yet wholly appropriate, that a passage of pastoral description should have its beauty, and its sense of persistent haunting memory, enhanced by a reference to the smell of shit; especially when it is juxtaposed so casually but meaningfully with a line about food. But such details are part of the poem's truthful way of evoking childhood.

In the later poem, 'The Plantation', Scupham revisits the scene, apparently, not in memory but in actuality, trying to find his way through the wood to where the railway line used to be:

> Ground seemed steady enough, packed with damps,
> And a small culvert pulled its low brown water
> Into green pastures – there was no restoration,
> Only leaves turning: forty seasons had confirmed them,
> To fit the sky with the same duns and ochres.

But the reality becomes more dreamlike than the memory. To his alarm, he encounters the man who now keeps the Gatehouse, and asks him for directions, but: 'His indirections to house, ruin, rubble / Could not be followed then, or perhaps ever.' And one thing is clear: 'Mr Curtis, he knew, was dead, long dead'. Reaching at last the railway track, where he had once flattened pennies 'under the engine's thunder', the poet meets a final shock. The line is in use, but unrecognisably so: peering through the leaves, he sees 'A blue diesel shaking line and outline / On its mild swerve from nowhere into nowhere.'

These poems clearly owe something to Edward Thomas, and the Romantics before him; and their unexpected and slightly enigmatic personal detail gives them an oddity, a tinge of the uncanny and disquieting which is also part of that tradition; not surprising that the first part of 'Possessions', from *Winter Quarters*, should be about M. R. James, always alert to the blend of numinous and threatening which can hang about a particular place:

> The salt groynes running black from sea and sky
> Betray his buried life down miles of sand.
> Low-tide: the beach is ebbing into dream,

> Cold bents and marram-grass hang out to dry
> On swollen dunes.

Death is never far away, but there is still value in detail: toys and jigsaw pieces, the foredge painting on a book, the 'gazebo... patched with glass and cockle-shell', the observation of 'raindrops [that] bounce and hover on the paving / In quick, unhealing rings' (this last from 'Incident Room', a calm poem about the finding of a murdered woman's body). Scupham's interplay of playful and serious, and perhaps his questioning of which is which, are matched by an interplay in his poetry of what one might call the folk and the baroque – a simultaneous enjoyment of simple and complicated, childlike and erudite. This is something strikingly rare. Shakespeare has it, and Herrick, and the early Milton of *Comus* and 'L'Allegro'; Mozart has it. Geoffrey Hill has it (and sounds at times remarkably like Scupham). But not many others. It comes, probably, only to those poets who write, however arduous their hidden labour, with real delight. These early poems of Peter Scupham's offer a masterclass – many masterclasses – in balancing the plain and the intricate, the detail of a landscape and its wide perspective.

Reading Peter Scupham

ANDREW BISWELL

I suppose I must have started reading Peter Scupham soon after the publication of his *Collected Poems* in 2002. The qualities of his writing were immediately obvious to me: I was pleased to find a poet who could make traditional forms work for him, and who roamed gleefully up and down the formal spectrum, at the same time as writing in an easily-comprehended, colloquial style. I warmed to his erudition and classicism, especially his fondness for French, German and Latin culture, which his poems communicate without fuss or formality, as if such knowledge should form part of the ordinary experience of any civilised reader or writer.

Going back to the *Collected Poems* and its successor volume recently, I've enjoyed spending time with Scupham's longer sequences, such as 'Playtime in a Cold City' in *Borrowed Landscapes* (2011), in which the poet recollects his student days in Cambridge in the 1950s. Commemorating lost times and lamenting the passing of friends who shared them, these twenty-one poems form a structure whose resonance stretches far beyond the autobiographical or the anecdotal.

Having looked into the critical reception of Scupham's poems in mainstream newspapers and journals since the 1970s, I am pleased to discover how overwhelmingly positive the reviews of his books have been. He was one of only a handful of contemporary poets to have been acclaimed by Anthony Burgess – the others being Seamus Heaney and Paul Muldoon – during his short tenure as the poetry critic of the *Spectator* (edited at that time by Alexander Chancellor) in 1977. Burgess, who was no slouch when it came to composing sonnets in novels such as *Inside Mr Enderby, ABBA ABBA* and *Byrne*, welcomed *The Hinterland* and its central sonnet sequence with the sympathetic recognition of a fellow toiler in the field of traditional verse. 'Technically,' he wrote, the sequence was 'of great interest', partly because its subject matter, the First World War, was 'the last of the wars capable of generating myth'. He judged that the collection as a whole was 'knotty, serious, with strong individual voice,' but not without occasional flashes of lightness. Burgess ended his review by quoting the 'irresistibly quotable' final stanza of 'Answers to Correspondents':

Toujours Gai, your moulting canary needs a tonic;
Xerxes, write poetry if you wish, but only read prose.
Cambridge Senior, we should not really have imagined
It would require much penetration to disclose
That such answers as we supply have been elicited
By genuine letters. You are impertinent, Rose.

Reviewing *The Hinterland* in the *Observer* on 3 July 1977, Craig Raine remarked on the 'elaborate craftsmanship' of the volume – not intended to be a compliment – and he complained about what he described as 'meaningless phrases' such as 'Wax leaves curl a dusty fragrance' and 'White flood floats dim surfaces'. Unlike Burgess, Raine was unimpressed by the technical achievement of 'The Hinterland' sequence. He commented: 'Meaning has a thin time of it [...] and you can't help feeling that doing up all the buttons absorbed most of [Scupham's] attention.' This consistently negative review marks a low point among critical responses to Scupham's poetry, but it is worth noting that Raine's objections have not been echoed by any other commentators. He remains a lone hostile voice.

The most vocal of Scupham's champions in the 1980s was Peter Porter, who reviewed several of his collections for the *Observer*. Commenting on *Winter Quarters* on 18 December 1983, Porter wrote: 'Peter Scupham often reminds me of the Oxford don who spilled boiling water on himself and wove three apposite quotations into his cries of pain.' In the poem 'Scott's Grotto', Porter identified quotations from William Blake and Dr Johnson among other 'arcane references'. He welcomed the dense texture of Scupham's poems, especially when they approached what he called 'colloquial' subject matter. He characterised the book as whole as a 'mesmerising' collection which united formal syntax with 'the firm tread of metrical regularity'.

Porter expanded on these points when he reviewed *Out Late* for the *Observer* on 31 August 1986. Praising the formality of Scupham's poetry, Porter wrote: 'He cultivates stanzas and the varied topiary of poetry with an attention appropriate to a writer so much at home in gardens, formal and domestic.' He said that the strongest poem in *Out Late* was 'Leave the Door Open' (later recorded by Scupham as the opening track on his CD of the same title), which reminded readers that 'we are frightened of more than just the dark'.

The third of Scupham's books reviewed by Porter was *The Air Show* in the *Observer* on 22 January 1989. On this occasion he pointed towards an undercurrent of menace at work below the 'ordered and rational' surface of the poems. He identified Hopkins as the presiding spirit behind 'The Loss', a 'highly original' piece within the collection. 'Most of these poems are dense,' he concluded, 'but their emotional torque is never deflected.' Porter remains the most consistent of Scupham's advocates, and his analyses of individual poems are always worth attending to.

Watching the Perseids, reviewed along with Scupham's *Selected Poems*, was hailed as 'a discreetly rewarding book' by Carol Ann Duffy in the *Guardian* on 9 May 1991. She welcomed the 'spiritual strength' of the two long sequences which address the deaths of his mother and father, and welcomed the 'decent, unembarrassed offering and receiving of love' in these poems. On balance Duffy preferred the elegies to the 'technically admirable' sonnets which are found elsewhere in the collection, but the strongest note of her review was one of praise: 'Scupham has always had a sense of how we are somehow sustained by the love left by those lives which link us to the past.'

When George Szirtes reviewed the *Collected Poems* in the *Guardian* on 14 December 2002, he speculated about the size and strength of Scupham's debts to W.H. Auden, Robert Graves, Tennyson and John Heath-Stubbs, although he was persuaded that visual artists such as Rex Whistler and Francis Bacon were also somewhere in the mix. He offered the provocative suggestion that Scupham had begun by wanting to write quotable lines and poems but now preferred to explore 'large unwritten territories'. Here, he concluded, was a major poet who deserved to be spoken about in the company of names such as Geoffrey Hill, Ted Hughes and Peter Redgrove. Among the many 'unforgettable' poems in this collection were, he said, 'The Christmas Midnight' and 'Dying' (dedicated to the poet's father, John Scupham).

Above all, a survey of Peter Scupham's critical reception reveals the extent to which his work has always been enjoyed by fellow writers. Not only is he among the most civilised of contemporary poets, but he is rightly admired for deploying forms and techniques which remind us that the multiple cultures and traditions he celebrates are (as Szirtes puts it) 'stubbornly alive'.

War Games

George Szirtes

Childhood and play, plays and theatre, theatres of stage and theatres of war, war and the stages of childhood: it is as if we walked through them by association in a single dream. Where we find the one we find the other, each giving on to the other. Here is the world, they say. Get on with it.

Peter Scupham was just six when the Second World War broke out and he spent the next six years in it. Childhood was a game of spot, hide, collect, and transform. Turn pink ham into a swastika, turn puff-pastry and lardy-cake into Goering, the whole into 'a cataract of cold regalia'. 'The soldiers are the figure in my carpet' goes the last line of 'War Games', a poem in which the child plays at soldiers while the adult remembers Henry James's short story of that name. A time bomb 'is ticking away under house and home' ('The Stain'). Children elsewhere are dying. Bombers are taking off into the sky never to return. There are 'handfuls of metal rain on a dark street' that the child will later collect.

It is worth starting with the 'And Little Wars' sequence of *The Air Show* (1988) because this – at least partly – is where imagination begins, in the childhood wardrobe of memory and play. The image of war establishes itself early as a motif to which Scupham returns time and again. In the theatre of the mind where memory, mask and miracle fuse into an image of the world, war provides many of its props and prompts. It is part of the furniture, the stage set around which action must flow.

The action has a moral dimension: it demands combatants as both heroes and a victims. It must perform as a model of life offering authentic values and transformations. War transforms as nothing else does. Like theatre, it offers metaphors and ways of behaving. It presents us with rituals, masks, comedies, disasters and the occasional miracle. Anyone who has ever seen one of the performances of Shakespeare or Chekhov produced by Peter Scupham and Margaret Steward will be aware of the power accorded to the ritual required to attain the yearned for miracle. The play takes place in woods and villas but the war goes on around and through them.

War was there in the very beginning in terms of poetry. 'A metal Poilu dies on every square' goes the final line in '*Un Peu d'Histoire*: Dordogne' from Scupham's earliest collection *The Small Containers* (1972) and is the subject of a set of poems titled 'A Wartime Childhood' in *The Snowing Globe* (also 1972), where a gas mask is addressed as 'Oh, Mickey Mouse, you ruined man' ('Gas Mask').

Other, less personal wars ghost through the *Collected Poems* of 2002. The First World War, that great war of disillusion, produces the heroic crown of sonnets, 'The Hinterland', Scupham's eulogy for the dead of the war in which the fields are peopled by '[t]he unfleshed dead, refusing to lie down'. They never lie down for long: they keep stirring and unsettling the field. The landscape is sown with their dust. Nevertheless, the poem is written at a distance, as it had to be. The war happened *there*, though the loss is felt *here*.

But then a closer version of events becomes available. Scupham's German father-in-law, Hermann Justus Braunholtz, Keeper of he Ethnographical Department at the British Museum, had been in England long before the war started and joined the British medical corps along with his three brothers. Many years after his death in 1963 the text of his wartime diaries becomes available and provides material for another, very different, sequence with a different sense of soldiering. The vision offered in 'Notes from a War Diary,' (from *Winter Quarters* (1983)), is neither elegiac nor disillusioned: it serves instead as a counterbalance to the perception of war derived from Owen, Sassoon and Rosenberg. The diaries on which the poems are based, and from which they quote, are brief, jaunty, full of a devil-may-care yet understated bravado. For Scupham this vision of war as a terse lark undercut by death is another form of theatre, a theatre that offers redemption of sorts through stoicism, defiance and vigour. To have such values expressed through a thoroughly educated German serving on the British side adds a touch of gallows humour but it also offers a way of talking.

There are various ways of describing the binaries in Peter Scupham's poetry but furnished and plain will serve. Scupham's mind is highly furnished in history and literature. It loves the apparently flimsy, the rococo, the flounce of the comically grandiose, the ability to flit around and between. It takes its references from fore-edge paintings and geology. It loves glorious nonsense and acts as the playful ghost in the rank of books. It is its own cabinet of constantly allusive curiosities. But Scupham's form of allusion is neither pedantic nor academic. It is not showing off. It is home as theatre. The plainness of yea and nay is not his natural manner: it is as bone to flesh, as flesh to dress.

Plain and furnished meet in a set of twelve poems, 'Conscriptions: National Service 1952–4' also in *Winter Quarters.* They are about Scupham,'s own time in the army and move from Braunholtz's breathless action to the duller routine of parades and exercises. The word that most frequently recurs in the sequence is bull or bulled, that is to say the polishing, to a high gloss, of army footwear, but also the target in shooting practice. Its heavy sound and associations with drivel and brusque masculinity lend a daily-grind ballast to the literary ghosts flitting in and out of the poems: Plato, Spartans, May Queens, Ducdame, Southey and much else. This is the army, Mr

Jones, says routine but the fully furnished mind is both bemused and amused by what, despite the square-bashing, is a matter of being 'Ready for Floor Games and the Little Wars' ('The Square (Blackdown Camp)'). Little wars take us back to theatre and play. But there is no sense of superiority in the sequence, no mockery. Scupham is aware that his fellow squaddies are essentially reincarnations of those sent to the fields of Flanders or the beaches of Normandy. They too are potential elegy.

*

Peter Scupham is not a war poet of course, nor does he elegise any form of jingoism; he is simply one of those to whom the sound of a bugle conjures a complex, pastoral, yet perfectly real England. The bugle is code and ritual and rituals are, after all, a central part of Scupham's imagination. Ghosts, he says somewhere, are a poet's working capital. It is ritual that summons the necessary ghosts. The sequence of poems titled 'A Midsummer Night's Dream' (from *Out Late* (1986), begins with a memory:

> I crouched there once upon that draughty landing,
> Intent upon two ghosts who once were lovers
> Rubbing fierce salts into their open wounds.
>   'Prologue', l. 11–13

The memory of a once close, now broken relationship opens the human heart of the play. The play works its common sadness into rituals. The virtues required to achieve 'amity and restoration', as the last poem in the sequence, 'Epilogue' puts it, include the disciplined, military gallantries. Things may fall apart but if the spine holds firm ghosts will furnish life rather than disrupt it.

More furniture. The furniture of theatre fascinates him. *Summer Palaces* (1980) opens with a group of poems about the magical mechanics of scenery and prop, lighting rehearsals, stage wardrobes, drop scenes and short sequences about tragedy and comedy, as well as about Twelfth Night and Three Sisters ('[...] music silvering the middle-distance / Whose bright airs tarnish as the bandsmen play. / The soldiers pass along the curving shore'). Soldiers are never far away. Theatre must register their presence.

Furniture alone is not enough. Nor are theatrical props. Off-stage, under the costume and mask, under the flesh, lie the bones. Plainness makes its demands. There are two important personal deaths that produce sequences in the *Collected Poems,* both in *Watching the Perseids*: (1990): that of Scupham's mother and father.

The sequence 'Young Ghost' celebrates his mother, Dorothy, who died in 1987. 'Dying' commemorates his father, John, who died in the year *Watching the Perseids* appeared. Only two poems separate the two sequences. Both are as much about the dying, or rather, witnessing the dying as about the lives that led up to it.

The plain speech of 'Young Ghost' has a formal delicacy that seeks to capture the fragility of the body in whose company the poet finds himself. 'Whose are these faces clinging to the gate / That seem to have been left out in too much rain' he asks in the first poem of the sequence. The diction is plainer, the allusions are kept at arm's length, the furniture is minimal. Not that it is entirely absent. 'Here is where alone // Is growing visible, spreading its mesh wide, / Easing itself always between things left and taken' it says in 'Arriving'. Both 'wide' and 'taken' find their full rhymes here in 'shaken' and 'died'. The poem is, in fact, in rhymed quatrains and rhyme haunts the whole fabric of the sequence. Rhyme is a form of furnishing.

Rhyme is not the defining feature of Scupham's poems but it does play an important role, chiefly as manners. His rhymes are likely to be precise, their courtesies supple, the fully end-stopped line tending to be employed for comic effect or as song. Even in all the unrhymed work there is a sense that rhyme is an available instrument, a music ready to be touched. In 'Young Ghost' it is a form of feather-light neatness looking to connect with something in the subject's character, a character most teasingly touched in the villanelle 'Dancing Shoes', itself a brief dance:

> 'At time's *Excuse-me*, how could you refuse
> A Quickstep on his winding gramophone?
> How long since you wore out your dancing shoes,
>
> Or his vest-pocket Kodak framed the views
> In which you never found yourself alone? '
>   'Dancing Shoes', ll. 1–5

The touch there is not typical of Scupham: it is what ornithologists call 'subsong', 'a subdued form of birdt song modified from the full territorial song and used by some birds esp. in courtship'. According to *Collins Dictionary*, 'Young Ghost' is precisely that, a subsong of courtship, harking back to mother's girlhood.

It is very different from 'Dying' which is as full of terse masculine brio as 'Notes from a War Diary', chiefly because the voice here is not the poet's but is given over to the dying father who is shown now remembering, now challenging, now declaring as the mind loses its grip on thought:

> Life's difficult. How do you know you're not me?
> You say you're Peter.
> Do you want to persist in this claim?
> You'll have a job to prove it,
> Unless your documents are in good order
>   'Who do you say you are?' ll.1–6

The tone is that of a commanding officer at the edge of Avernus.

> You know too much.
> You claim you're Peter?
> There are certain sorts of knowledge that are forbidden
> And there's only one source they can come from,
> And that's the Devil.
>
> Are you the Devil?'
>   'Who do you say you are?' ll. 21–26

There is no hint in the sequence that John Scupham was himself a military man but such raw confrontations and the terms in which they are framed suggest a life of military discipline that retains its vigour while discouraging self-pity and personal emotion. There is no rhyme here, no delicacy:

At three o'clock in the afternoon, he dies.

Causes of death:
    1a Uraemia
    1b Carcinoma duodenum
    1c Diabetes
    1d Mycardial infarct...
    '10 January 1990' ll.25–30

This is bare bones indeed. It is a way of facing death, a way to be admired. John Scupham does not require an elegy: he will provide his own non-elegiac summing-up, thank you. That his own life was fully furnished with history, politics, art and literature is made plain by references to Attlee, Morrison, Sutherland, Ayrton, G. M. Young, Browning, Wordsworth and many others. But it is the father's, not the son's furniture. It suggests a balanced, open life with a vast and stable hinterland.

The mention of a hinterland takes one back to the earliest poems, and especially to the world of *The Hinterland*. Under the elegies lie the crisp peremptory bones stripped bare by the hard processes of life.

The hardest personal death, of his son, Giles, in 2001, occasions no sequence. The cover of *Collected Poems* is by Giles, and the volume as a whole is dedicated to him, but Giles died shortly before the *Collected Poems* appeared. What followed was the plainest of plains: silence. It would be another nine years before Scupham's next and most recent book, *Borrowed Landscapes* (2011).

Despite the gorgeous ear (and Scupham has an ear as gorgeous as Geoffrey Hill's in *Tenebrae*), despite all the fully furnished and richly coloured theatre of the mind, despite the elegiac pull of the dead and ghosts of the dead, there is an army of war references throughout the oeuvre that persist in *Borrowed Landscapes*. There is 'the Captain's chalk-and-talk in the Village Hall', there are the 'Germans gathering alpenrosen' in 1913, there is the Motorised Ambulance Company of 1916–18, the 'Bosch', the 'Fritz', the Local Defence Volunteers and much else. One should understand this not merely as apparatus or, in theatrical terms, as scenery and props. This is the very nature of the play in which Scupham sees us acting our parts.

But not with a po face: there are giggles and teases throughout his work comprising a late Victorian comedy of magic lanterns and correspondence columns. Such human follies and masquerades allow for the pathos of laughter. Scupham's poetry understands the fierce salts of *Out Late* and has experienced their effect on open wounds. The wounds have to be there but the job of poetry is to see that they are dressed. Once wounds are dressed the body reappears complete in flesh and costume. Here is the picture. Colour it in. Colour is life.

Nature

PETER SCUPHAM

His eyes calm, level:
'I had a dream last night
I know now there is no such thing
as the subconscious'.

From under his bed
crept this creature,
darkening the space
between floor and door.

Its voice knew the crunch
of broken biscuits:
'I am Nature
I have come to get you'.

There he stood,
suit pressed, tie straight,
cheeks glowing pinkly
from a close shave.

I watch those eyes
fix, then cloud.
On his cluttered shelves
the books play kiss,

Locke on Education
walking out in leather
with a paperback doll:
'Zazie dans le Métro',

Under the bed
stuff creaks and mumbles,
nests between the lines
of tomorrow's obituary.

PETER SCUPHAM
for David Horovitch at 70

Hats, periwigs or firearms say
someone, it seems, has gone away,
and who are those left standing where
applause hangs scribbled on the air?
A black bag props a tilted chair;
house lights bring up the day.

Was it a ghost, that go-between,
who slipped us on from scene to scene,
who stitched the living to the dead
who turned the fire in someone's head
to flesh and blood, a dance that said
more than cold words could mean?

Off, off you lendings, and for now
back to your cupboard love. Allow
the boards to be but floorboards, all
the fear-struck room, the painted hall,
to find out moonlight, wait their call –
Come, David! Take your bow.

An Amulet of Words

KEVIN GARDNER

No amulet of words can stay
Our tender structures from decay,
Though buds unfrosted yet by Time
May flower precariously in rhyme.
('Painted Shells')

An 'amulet of words': I can think of no phrase more aptly describing the sense of wonder, of mystery, at the heart of Peter Scupham's imagination. Swelling with syntactical and phonic vigour, his poems assert the potency of literary language to forestall the certainty of decay. The printing press, though coldly mechanical, finds in moveable type an infinite source of vitality, hope and even magic: 'For words – which grew from thinginess – / have cast their spells in metal dress' ('The Old Type Tray'). Old books wait impatiently for new readers to encounter them, so to spring back to life: 'He can hear the pages fidget about and whisper, / stretch themselves out a little, breathe a sigh / through seas of ink and a mapped world of paper' ('Between the Lines'). A leaf of monastic vellum in majuscule script, though read no longer by clerics, survives in the poet's realisation of a living past: 'A slant-cut nib works on; the skin / Takes texture. God is woven close' ('Marginalia'). Words abide and poetry endures, countervailing our own demise.

Peter forges his death-defying poetry out of the revenants of the past. His poetic world is populated by ghostly presences, layers of past time interlaced with the present: 'Ghosts are a poet's working capital. / They hold their hands out from the further shore' ('Prehistories'). Weaving the past tenses of things and places with the present tense of personal and communal experience, he conceptualises a sense of time in which 'Strange, unappeasable, ancestral voices' make 'communion' with the here and now ('A Box of Ghosts'). But the past cannot be preserved in a museum, where a stuffed bird's 'nerveless limbs and pinions' are forced into 'dull parodies of motion', and where displays of humanity's historical 'flotsam' are reduced to 'Clio's rambling bargain basement'. Losing the 'casual context' of human significance, museum displays 'make submission / To the bleak dictates of monologues, monographs.' In this state, 'sealed by glass', the human element is lost; our imaginations may be kindled, but we cannot commune with the past ('Museum').

In the personal accumulation of things and relationships is meaning created. Contemplating a box of military objects and fragments hoarded during his wartime childhood, the poet infuses 'these little deaths of shot and shell' with a child's sense of wonder: 'Something enormous, with a molten core / Of huge delight'; 'Brass cartridge-cases wild as buttercups'. He recalls how he arranged them in a display of his own making, 'A reliquary cased in brass and velvet', and thereby invested them with significance. In adulthood, the poet rarely opens the box: the 'souvenirs' are 'Cold-hearted now, and most inscrutable'. Yet the box is still alive with meaning, and its treasures yearn to speak again: 'I know unguessable things are stirring there, / Troubling with their fumes and cloudiness / A past as deep and shrouded as the future' ('Souvenirs'). Time is in flux: the aging poet stretches back to his youth and innocence, while the child reaches forward to understand a baffling world of adulthood.

Here then is a paradox in Peter's poetic imagination: a poetry forged in the materiality of the past, yet woven with an intellectual submission to its ultimate inscrutability, 'and only a pen to turn was to is' ('Figures in a Landscape, 1944'). I've had the pleasure of reading Peter's poetry for many years, of immersing myself in it and writing about it, but after spending a day in his company, my appreciation for his world and his vision were immeasurably enriched. In October of 2016, I was in Cambridge for a book launch and to host a poetry reading. Peter and Margaret had graciously invited me to Norfolk, to spend a day of church-crawling and an evening at Old Hall. Here was a priceless opportunity to see the world as he does, to visit the 'parish of the dead' and hear ghosts speaking 'with riddling tongue / Of what we were, and are: / Memorial, avatar' ('Looking and Finding').

I met Peter and Margaret at the church of Ranworth St Helen, with mutual friends Ann and Anthony Thwaite. A treasure house of medieval ecclesiastical art, Ranworth is justly famous for its rood screen, but despite the holy atmosphere, the prevailing mood was jollity. I too found the humour in the images of St Agnes – partially transformed by the addition of a beard into St John the Baptist – and of St Michael and St George, who seemed to be slaying dragons merely to assert the primacy of their masculinity. At that point I felt empowered to join the indefatigable Ann for a twisting climb up eighty-nine steps to the top of the church tower, to take in splendid if dizzying views across the Broads. Later, safely back in the church, Peter drew my gaze to Ranworth's rarest treasure – an illuminated antiphoner. I thought of his passion for old books and manuscripts, and recalled his lines: 'Under the Uncials' lantern capitals, / Whose gentler reds and blues are hung / On vines of gossamer, / The blocked ink scorches on the page' ('Marginalia').

Following a delightful pub lunch with the Scuphams and Thwaites, I set off with Peter and Margaret to explore the splendours of other Norfolk churches. Our first stop was Upton St Margaret – sadly locked, but with a heaving churchyard whose poignant, whispering epitaphs called to my mind Peter's lines: 'A silence runs beneath these silences / Where the shut churches founder in the green, / And all their darkness and their brightness is / One seamless robe to lap the creature in' ('The Hinterland'). Soon we came to Acle St Edmund, with its arresting fifteenth-century font and its medieval inscription on the chancel wall – a prayer for relief from the relentless Black Death. Outside, I found myself contemplating the turreted tower of Acle church: 'The tower so clearly made of light, / The loneliness of light, from lonely money / Sighed away on a late medieval death-day. / And the pretty names: mouchettes, sound-holes, / Double-stepped battlements with pinnacles – / One of God's fairy things' ('Stone Head').

Later we came to Peter's own church, the thatch-roofed, flint-walled Burlingham St Edmund. Its chancel scene of the martyrdom of Becket is a lucky survivor of East Anglian puritanical predations, but now, alas, it survives only as a ghostly remnant, the plaster flaking slowly away. Peter's deep appreciation for this place has as much to do with its human element as its ecclesiastical charms, which include an extraordinary fifteenth-century pulpit and a preacher's hourglass. The medieval carved bench ends depict ordinary folk and animals: a local franklin; a fox running off with a goose; a spaniel, worn smooth by eight centuries of little hands stroking its back. More affecting yet are names and initials carved into chancel stalls by delinquent pupils in the seventeenth century. These human elements are, ironically, what renders this space numinous: 'From these infer the flawed, the tentative, / Are the most fitting gestures to assume? // Accept release from the burden of believing / So didactic, so complete a statement' ('Topology of Ruins').

The sacred silence became oppressive, and the autumn afternoon closed in as we stepped out into the fading sun. 'Sour brambles cling, whose nubbled reds / Light rides awash with dung and mud – / A dark look to the squandered hedge, / The daylight blunter at the edge – / October shallows into flood' ('South Cadbury'). The warmth of a homey kitchen and a pot of tea beckoned, and we soon made our way to Old Hall, the Elizabethan manor Peter and Margaret purchased in 1990 and began to restore. There I was greeted by the famed mermaids cast in plaster relief on the pediment of the imposing three-storey porch.

After a reviving pot of tea, Peter led me up two flights of creaking stairs to the gallery, to show me the greatest of Old Hall's many gems. Here are grisaille murals, dating to around 1580, of a Tudor hunt. These scenes were uncovered in 1991 and have been carefully conserved with the assistance of grant aid from English Heritage. Though the colours are sombre, the scenes are lively and vivid: 'The hunt will soon be up. / Morning trips and jingles / to walls whose bright lime / sharpens the scent, / prepares the ground' ('The Hunt'). Men on horseback pursue a deer; a dog prepares to attack a boar; and rich foliage surrounds a manor house that bears a distinct resemblance to Mermaid Manor.

The setting sun cast lengthening shadows as Peter and I made our way down a flight of stairs to his library, the shelves brimming with rare volumes and the 'tumbled bric-à-brac' ('The Small Containers') of centuries of human endeavour. Peter and I talked poetry and criticism, collect-ing books, and the rare book trade. As delectable aromas of Chicken Provençal wafted upward from the kitchen below, Peter went down to help Margaret, but not before depositing me in a deeply cushioned chair and leaving me with a generous glass of Laphroaig in my hand and the 1717 *Works of Mr Alexander Pope* in my lap, in which I took especial delight. 'A sturdy quarto, whose morocco ribs / Texture the claret dye, the wide strapwork / Of burnished ribbons, looped informally. / Endpapers calm their whirlpools into stasis; / The cobalts, whites and azures of dried oil / Chart shoals and spindrift for an unsailed sea' ('Fore-edge Painting'). In such a setting, even I might become a poet, I rather grandly imagined.

Peter and Margaret's exquisite hospitality culminated in a delicious rustic French dinner, in bottles of fine mellow wine, and in animated and sparkling conversation. That night, I slept in the Rose Room, which retains significant traces its original floral treillage wall decoration. I knocked my head only once on the lintel designed for Tudor folk less vertically enhanced than myself. That night I might have dreamed of 'ghosts talking of ghosts, / Compounded of old walls, old bones, old stories, / Watching an inch of sun slip to the West, / Playing the revenant to this house and garden / Sleepy with cats down a remembered lane / Where unaccustomed eyes look cleanly through us' ('A House of Geraniums'). It was a quiet night and a restful sleep. The ghosts were well behaved.

Though indeed 'No amulet of words can stay / Our tender structures from decay', Peter has responded to Time's 'inclemency' and the 'short, haunted, patchwork span' of life with an exceptional generosity of spirit. His poetry is equally magnanimous. Peter's greatest gift lies in humbly transmuting his extraordinary imagination and poetic vision into intricate patterns designed to help us 'Keep measure with the Infinite':

> Though Nature's laws are obdurate,
> Her sentence we can mitigate:
> The artist's work is paradox,
> A Chinese puzzle which unlocks
> To show those gifts that he was made,
> Their brightnesses transposed, repaid.'
>   ('Painted Shells')

A Brief History of the Mandeville Press

JOHN MOLE

Peter and I first met in 1970 at a poetry reading in Letchworth. I had recently returned from a year's teaching in New York and was back in St Albans while he was living in Hitchin and teaching locally at St Christopher School. We had both begun publishing our poems in various magazines and were familiar with each other's work. Over the next two years we met regularly to discuss poetry and, as it were, monitor each other's progress. It quickly became clear that we shared many poetic touchstones and were very much of one mind when it came to the contemporary poets we admired, so although I can't remember the exact moment that the idea of approach-ing some of them occurred to us, it was not long before we had decided to do so with a view to publishing small editions of their work, and for this we would need to learn the craft of letterpress printing.

So we served our apprenticeship by standing observantly beside John Myatt, a professional musician and part-time teacher at St Christopher, who also worked as a jobbing printer at his home in Hitchin. Since much of what he was asked to print was programmes, lists and brochures he was enthusiastic about becoming involved with a more creative project. As he manipulated and 'drove' his impressive Heidelberg we learned the craft by proxy. This was in 1972 and, as neophyte publishers, we had decided to invite our poets to offer a poem for a series of single poem pamphlets, accompanied by an illustration, much as Faber and Faber had done with their *Ariel Poems*. My wife, Mary Norman, along with her – and

Peter's – artist friends and colleagues, contributed most of the illustrations while a few of the poets found some of the illustrators themselves. We published eighteen of these pamphlets under the imprint of The Cellar Press, printed handsomely by John and collated, folded, and stitched (never stapled) by Peter, his wife Carola and myself as a little cottage industry in Peter's study at Taylor's Hill. Among the poets were Norman Nicholson, Anthony Thwaite, John Fuller, Freda Downie, Neil Powell and David Day. Sales were initially through personal contacts as the word spread, helped by the fact that a number of these were themselves associated with magazines and presses such as Harry Chambers' magazine *Phoenix*, John Fuller's Sycamore Press, John Cotton's Priapus Press and the Keepsake Press which the journalist Roy Lewis started as a cure for insomnia.

By 1975 we felt ready to start out on our own, Peter having received £250 from his father, earmarked for type and a press. With trays of Baskerville (our favoured typeface) and Ehrhardt, a small Adana handpress, and a selection of frames, rollers, leads and quoins, we got to work as The Mandeville Press in Peter's basement. Our editorial principles remained those we had already established of approaching poets we felt had been overlooked or undervalued and publishing them alongside familiar 'names'. We used the best quality laid paper and card that we could find, and continued to produce frontispiece illustrations, some being lino cuts and others processed line blocks. In several cases the title pages were hand-coloured. Peter was rightly proud of the fact that we operated on a no loss, no gain, no pay basis, understood and approved by our poets, and when eventually we closed down after he had moved to Norfolk in 1990 all drafts, correspondence and related material were donated to The British Library. My own role throughout was mainly editorial and typesetting. Machine work was Peter's expertise as we moved from the Adana via a larger treadle press to the substantial, mechanised Vicobold, a press used by jobbing printers in the 1930s and found for us by our friend Roger Burford Mason who had also learned the printer's craft from John Myatt and, at the same time as we began at Mandeville, started his own Dodman Press.

Our first two pamphlets were Andrew Waterman's *Last Fruit* and *Night Music* by Freda Downie. In Waterman's case we had seen and admired poems by him in *The New Humanist*, for which the poetry editor was George Hartley who had also run The Marvell Press. Hartley was best known as the publisher of Philip Larkin's first full collection and was about to 'resurrect' his press to publish Waterman's own first collection, *Living Room*, but there was room for a pamphlet as well and, with Waterman's agreement and support, Mandeville was underway. Freda Downie's poems first came to my attention, through John Cotton, and her pamphlet was her first substantial appearance in print, though she was soon taken up by Secker and Warburg whose poetry editor was Anthony Thwaite.

By now Peter and I were publishing our own poetry regularly, me with Secker and Warburg and Peter with OUP, reviewing for various journals and, in my case, presenting poetry programmes on the BBC, including *Poetry Now* and *Time for Verse*. All this made us part of a poetry community, in touch with many of the poets who would seek us out to publish their work or, in the case of those who were more established and whom we particularly admired, we would ourselves approach. The latter included Anthony Hecht, published in this country by OUP, R. S. Thomas, C. H. Sisson, and E. J. (Joy) Scovell – also taken up after her long silence as a poet – by Secker and Warburg and about whom I made a programme for Radio 3. In Joy's case we became good friends, and her Mandeville pamphlet *Listening to Collared Doves* is one of which I am particularly proud to have been the publisher, just as I know Peter is of Hecht's *A Love for Four Voices: Homage to Franz Joseph Haydn* and our edition of the *Selected Poems* of Michael Rivière. In addition to these are so many other titles there is not room to mention, but it is possible to see most of them on the website: The Poetry of The Mandeville Press at Ash Rare Books (www. ashrare.com)

In addition to single poet pamphlets, we printed anthologies, notably *A Mandeville Fifteen, Home Truths* and the appropriately-named *Mandeville's Travellers* as well as several envelopes of *Dragon Cards*, all of them omnia gathera, bringing together what by now we felt to be our special community of poets. Each Christmas we produced a small pamphlet of three of our own poems, as give-aways to subscribers, illustrated by my wife, but that was the sole significant departure from our policy of only publishing the work of others.

Two incidents stand out to illustrate how Peter and I were both encouraged and occasionally disappointed by the responses we received, as editors, from the poets we had reviewed and sought out for Mandeville. Both incidents ended productively. At a time when he felt somewhat overlooked, though I hadn't realised this, I wrote enthusiastically in the *TLS* about a collection by Patric Dickinson, and thus began a personal friendship and our publishing four small collections of his later work. He was soon to be dropped from the Chatto and Windus list, and we, in effect, became his only publisher. The other experience provides a perfect example of Peter's rigorous diplomacy and editorial panache. We were about to start work on a pamphlet by Geoffrey Grigson, a writer we both admired and who was initially well disposed towards us as the publisher of Freda Downie and Joy Scovell, both of whom he rated highly, but he took exception to my review of his latest collection in *The New Statesman*. In a mainly favourable review I had regretted the inclusion of some bad-tempered squibs, and this was enough to make him write to Peter, withdrawing his poems. Peter wrote straight back: 'Surely the hatchet man of English Literature will not quarrel with an honest review'. This must have struck a nerve in a poet who was himself fond of quoting Coleridge's 'praise of the unworthy is robbery of the deserving', and by return of post came his reply: 'Keep the poems. Come to dinner.' To his regret this was an invitation Peter didn't take up, not least as the cook would almost certainly have been Jane or Sophie!

In a short BBC film about the press, *A Dragon's Print*, made midway through our progress, Peter spoke eloquently about the continuity of letterpress printing and how it connected us with a tradition going back to Caxton. In the same programme he quoted John Berryman when asked what our print run was (usually 250–400 copies approx.):

'I only have six readers or thereabouts, but they're awful bright'. Of course, our pamphlets had many more readers than that but they remained part of a growing family of individuals that owed much to the tradition they belonged to. W. H. Auden once claimed that art is our chief means of breaking bread with the dead. To which I would add that publishing the work of contemporary poets one admires is a means of breaking bread with the living.

For me it has been a privilege to work with Peter and, under his guidance, to be a part of that tradition. Our respect for each other as poets, and the fact that we share a similar taste in writers and artists, has been the basis of an enduring friendship, and here in admiration, fond recollection and forward-looking celebration of his eighty-fifth birthday is a poem by the junior partner in the firm of Scupham and Mole, printers and publishers:

THE VICOBOLD
  for *Peter Scupham*

The slap and clank
Of start-up, ink

Applied, not slab
But thick enough, a dab

Of oil from your old tin
Long-beaked can

On the big wheel's
Axle. What else?

Tighten the chase,
Hammer and press

One last time, bed
Loose slugs, unsettled

Or uneven lines,
Check all four quoins

Then pass the poem
Over to the hum

Of readiness, insert,
Adjust, make straight

And line by line
Admire the good work done,

Stand back, lean in
For the wheel's lugubrious spin

To gather speed
As each laid sheet

Is printed, stet,
Unchangeably displayed.

Invitation to View

PETER SCUPHAM

Pity you didn't know us in our day –
We might have found you sitting by the lime
in sleepy summer, or in scented May
at lunch with Peter looking for a rhyme
he'd kicked into the long grass by the pond
and Margaret tickling some old cat. Yes, fond

of desultory stuff as life went by
with frogs and flowers and idiotic talk
under trees shuffling green about the sky.
We're sorry that you couldn't break your walk,
unlatch the gate and find the front door wide
on chequered shade and bric-a-brac, inside

find rooms life found itself too short to dust
and cobwebs that went back an age or two,
spot a Ravilious plate and Shakespeare's bust –
Old brochures say just what old brochures do:
'*A house of books and pictures*'. Cakes and tea?
A pleasant might-have-been – but let it be.

We'll watch you puzzling at us from the lawn
until the faces hidden by our names
turn into whispers, rustles, all forlorn
as maidens, crumpled cows and played-out games.
Don't tell us who you are – *we* needn't know.
The dark will tell you when it's time to go.

The *Mermaid* Catalogues

PETER DAVIDSON

Peter Scupham and Margaret Steward's *Mermaid Books* is a very wonderful and very strange enterprise: it is a most effective niche bookseller for topography, antiquarian books, and literature, and at the same time it is a wild poetic enterprise, so much opposed to the commercial genius of this age as to have a flavour of revolution or surrealism. The enterprise has no internet presence whatsoever. All business is done by means of catalogues which are themselves minor but beguiling works of art. They take the form of nicely printed pamphlets, their covers adorned with a mosaic of puzzle quotations. Many of their pages are not devoted to selling things at all, but to varied gratuitous delights and diversions: Christmas competitions with generous prizes of books and prints, occasional poems of Peter's father's or his own, a page of inter-war visual puzzles that has taken his eye. Books are described in wonderful detail, regardless of how much they cost: as much elegant writing and top-class bile is lavished on selling a book priced at £5 as on the description of the most expensive antiquarian items. Business is conducted by telephone, briskly and cheerfully. I am always surprised and heartened by how quickly the books sell, even if I ring on the day when the catalogue arrives. Very often when the bill comes, there is an unsolicited discount in view of the cost of the postage.

Apart from their elegance, surrealism and accuracy, the catalogues are honest to a fault. The smallest defects become occasions for a celebration of candour between friends, which is also inevitably a sustained parody of the slippery pretensions of the carriage-trade antiquarian book dealers. No other bookseller would be as anxious for the customer to know that there is a 'slight indentation on the front board as if a caterpillar had died there'. Memorably, one of these observations is followed by the enchanting sentence, 'you wouldn't have noticed if I hadn't told you that it was there'. Sometimes, the reader is all-but-defied to buy an item, 'Oh this would make a pleasing addition to the shelves of someone better-dressed than me.' If anyone plucked up their courage to ring up and offer for that particular book, I wonder how they opened the conversation. The hardest sell which I can ever recollect being employed was a plea that the old cat Goodman needed to be fed, so that it would be appreciated (especially by the cat Goodman) if someone would take a particular item off the firm's hands. There are surprising and plangent discounts:

> 123. Well here we go again. This is quite a shocking state of affairs.... For the fourth time of asking can I persuade an unsuspecting Romantic to take The Complete Works of the Opium Eater. Sixteen neat octavos... Opium, Essays, Lake Poets, Politics, Portraits, Philosophy, Tales, Murders, etc etc Adam & Charles Black, the 1844 reprint. Now offered at the alarming price of £59.

Occasionally poets unknown are offered with the suggestion that the reader might like to experiment and venture into new territory:

> 35. Wrey Gardiner The Dark Thorn. Dw. 'This book is about me' – very forties – Chapters headed 'The Poet, the Dancer and the Dream' and 'The Spider, the Web and the Wind.' Google him! I can't resist a further quotation, at random, the start of a paragraph: 'The madman's thunder is the doom of love. But art, that strange, eternal worm of life goes on'... Give me more, give me more. Grey Walls, 1946. £5

There are unequivocal and howling bargains (Peter said in conversation that he couldn't be a bookseller if his friends and customers didn't get a 'thumping' bargain now and then):

> So, allowing for what I allow for, turning round three times backwards and invoking the God who looks after Decrepit Poets turned Amateur Booksellers, I offer you my copy [of Ravilious's illustrated *Consequences*] for ... £295.00

An interwar high-bohemian association copy is offered enhanced by the vendor's inability to read Nina Hamnet's atrocious handwriting, followed by an evil parody of the 'prestige by association' line of argument found in the glossiest antiquarian catalogues:

> 55. Nina Hamnet, 'Queen of Bohemia' Laughing torso... In an amazing scrawl the title page seems to read: *To the better looking Ela Mupiatt from Nina*. It may well be another name but the lady's handwriting is wild... So, touch the ink directed by the hand that caressed Modigliani, Brzeska, Roger Fry, Old Uncle Tom Cobley and all. Constable, 1932. £45.

Sometimes, personal anecdote – fragments from the autobiography which I for one hope that Peter will start writing very soon indeed – takes over from the prosaic business of selling a book:

> 30. Never Such Innocence: A New Anthology of Great War Verse. Edited by Martin Stephens and inscribed as a gift by him.... Martin Stephens *'has written twelve books and is now the headmaster of the Perse School for Boys Cambridge.' (Well, lucky old Perse. My Headmaster there was known as Old Gob, and I had recurrent childhood dreams of him stalking me, gowned and mortar-boarded, in some vast pre-supermarket grocery store, while I dodged, throwing tinned fruit and canned beans at him.)* £10.

Sometimes, a touch of undergraduate sark breaks in, hard up against lurking poetry:

> 12. Stowe Temples of Delight: Stowe Landscape Gardens, by John Martin Robinson (*Librarian to the Duke of Norfolk, just as I am still Librarian to Margaret and the cats Goodman, Tom, and Hatty.*) The evolution of the garden and its temples etc described in context. As new in its dw. Monochrome and colour plates – I always find the colour a bit much, having been brought up in black-and-white. George Philip/National Trust, 1990. £6

Often the wares in the catalogue are assessed with an exemplary frankness:

> 119. Restif de la Bretonne Monsieur Nicolas or the Human Heart Unveiled: the Intimate Memoirs of Restif de la Bretonne... 'The 'human heart' which is unveiled seems to

have been situated between the memoirist's thighs, which is anatomically unusual...'

Here is a wonderfully unworried bibliographical shrug, closely followed by reflections on time, change and decay:

21. Byron The Letters and Journals... There was a slim supplementary volume later, but that snark is a boojum and cannot be found, as Richard Holmes says '[...] in raciness, self-portraiture, scandal, intelligence and sheer devilish charm, one of the great flowerings of English Romantic prose... it will surely endure as long as Englishmen remain literate and proud.' Oh dear, wasn't that till yesterday? John Murray, 1973-1982. £85

After reading a few of the catalogues almost any customer begins to feel that they have joined a welcoming and well-read circle of friends, held together by shared enthusiasms for Peacock, for nineteenth-century topography, for ghost stories, for beaten-up but wonderful seventeenth-century folios, for provincial watercolour painters around the turn of the nineteenth century, for the English illustrators of the mid-twentieth century. They begin to know some of the names which recur as authors of the consistently accomplished entries for the restricted-writing competitions. And they begin to realise that there are some circles and authors which at least one of the proprietors of Mermaid Books does not especially love: Bloomsbury as a whole and Virginia Woolf in particular come under sustained attack. D. H. Lawrence is compared unfavourably to Arthur Ransome (and quite right too). Ted and Sylvia have no fans in South Burlingham and tend to appear at bargain prices: 'I do not like these poems [Hughes] but that doesn't mean you won't either'; 'the book claims to display A MYRIAD NEW INSIGHTS [into Plath] Oh dear. £8.' Contemporary poetry written down to children gets short shrift, (I devoutly hope that 'Ayesha took my bookbag / and dumped it in the loo' *is* a parodic invention) as do all agents of enforcement, dumbing-down, the new conformity, and – perennially – *health and safety*, which is characterised most gravely as the enemy which would prevent any future occurrence ('if not duffers won't drown') of Swallows and Amazons. The painter Stanley Spencer receives a deadly, genuinely unforgettable side-swipe as 'the thinking man's Beryl Cook'.

Held together by these running jokes, shared enthusiasms and drawn in by the sheer welcoming civility of the whole enterprise, it is a pleasure to belong to this community of readers and wits. The experience is far removed from anything which would currently be identified as a commercial relationship – it is rather a sense of belonging to a most agreeable shared culture. On the one hand it is a little like the community of readers brought together by devotion to a fine, unshowy writer, whose writings define a particular world – Sylvia Townsend Warner and John Meade Falkner come to mind. On the other it is like being admitted to a circle which shares a memory of lives and letters, almost like the circle of seventeenth-century readers who shared the recollections and relished the anecdotes contained in John Aubrey's wonderful, open-ended, unfinished, unfinishable *Brief Lives*.

I asked Peter and Margaret about their community of readers. (We were in a memorably plain Norfolk crossroads pub at the end of the summer, surrounded by damp harvest fields and big trees.) They said at once that Mermaid Books had formed a community of friends, indeed that they had started the enterprise in the winter of 1992, when they had moved to their house in Norfolk, fearing isolation in the sticks amidst the fields of beet, with the specific aim of gathering such a circle of connected correspondents. I asked them who makes up that circle. Both ventured an immediate sense that their readers are not young – 'I mean I think of X____ as young and she's forty-seven' – but that they are well-read, unpretentious people in a variety of occupations, 'perhaps most of them are academics, but not the sort of academics who like universities as most of them have become. I think they are *rogue* academics, but they appreciate a book "in the dress of its own time". They're people who know what they're buying, all of them are good at one thing or another, but' – an expression to relish and remember – 'no one puts on too much dog about what they're doing.'

And that is the public to which Mermaid Books offers glorious old soldiers in folio, Regency picturesque, tales of terror, illustrated Batsfords, little verse volumes of the 1940s and '50s, runs of journals, every sort of thing that can delight a modest and well instructed mind, living in the England of the present but with half an eye on the past. Only Mermaid Books could conjure a whole gothic novel from a name written in a book and offer tactfully that the customer might prefer *not* to buy the copy with that daunting association:

Two copies of The Father Brown Stories are on offer: 'One of these volumes, *and only one*, was a gift from the Countess of Unthank. You could ask specifically not to have that one, if it worries you. £8

Peter the Teacher

JANE GRIFFITHS

I first knew Peter as a teacher, though he would say that what he did wasn't teaching, and in the strictest sense there may be some truth in that. What he did was talk, sitting at the head or on the edge of a long table in one of the even longer echoey upstairs classrooms, or almost invisible in a cocoon of silk scarves, green Barbour and pipe smoke in Margaret's tiny room above the theatre. It would start with something particular – in *Tess of the D'Urbervilles*, the paragraph where Tess kisses Angel's shadow, or where she slips her letter under the door – and spin swiftly into a reading that took in the whole of the book, Hardy, fate and the life of the English countryside. It wasn't a monologue; the questions were fast and frequent, and even hesitant or wildly off-the-mark responses were woven into the commentary, which became a fantastic kind of collaboration. Somewhere I still have a cassette of a class I got a friend to record for me when I was in bed with flu. It's not easy to make out the words, except for one sudden exclamation, very much in the foreground, 'Swapna, are you *taping* this?', but what does carry clearly is the laughter. And also Peter's speech cadences: the BBC-microphone-defying swoop and clip which don't quite come across in formal recordings of his readings, which for all their skill are slightly flatter, and without the quick upward 'Hah!' of response to a remark that surprised or delighted him. It was wonderful teaching; it also very clearly wasn't work. Even people who were doing English A level *faute de mieux*, with no particular interest in the subject, seemed to be having fun with it. For someone who had been at a school in Holland where literature didn't exist, and where pupils sat two-by-two in benches till the age of eighteen or even twenty, learning the grammar of six different languages by rote and being tested weekly on the facts (and nothing but the facts) dictated to them, Peter's non-teaching was a revelation. It's no coincidence that he first introduced me to the word *sprezzatura* – though that surely can't have been in relation to *Tess*. In my mind it's written – in Peter's surprisingly small, neat caps – across the top of a photocopied set of notes on Chaucer that includes a line drawing of his 'verray parfit gentil knight' cantering from right to left at the foot of the page, lance tilted against jobsworths, purveyors of high moral seriousness and Dutch grammar school teachers – but that can't be quite right either.

A second revelation was discovering Peter's poetry precisely at the time when I was rediscovering England. Coming to Hertfordshire from a particularly subdued Dutch new town that contained just three designs of house neatly laid out on grey brick roads with four-foot-high trees at regulation intervals, even Letchworth Garden City seemed gloriously untamed. Trees were climbable and lavishly showed the seasons; pavements were lifted by their roots; houses were detached and had more rooms than logic dictated; newsagents smelt richly miscellaneous (tobacco, sherbet, wet paper); railway embankments were a scramble of nettles and buddleia. I wanted words for all of this, and found them partly in MacNeice and partly in Peter's writing, particularly in *Out Late*, which was then just published. I took it out one night in the school library; it must have been early on in my first term, as I was very aware I'd never read a poem before – or, other than *Flower Fairies of the Garden* and *When We Were Six*, even seen one on the page. What was it, I wondered, that a poem could do that prose couldn't? I carefully read 'Cat's Cradle' and 'Ragtime', and – without understanding them – realised they were a kind of protective spell, a kind of incantation. Then I read 'Borderland' and saw, through it, the verges and the edgelands I'd been noticing on trips to Cambridge and London, and began to see how words could match a place – or, better than matching it, make articulate the seeing of it. And this, of course, is still more pronounced in *The Hinterland*, which I must have read soon after, and which became a touchstone. Though Peter may be horrified, in my mind it fused not only with MacNeice, but also (differently) with *The Four Quartets* ('Burnt Norton' in particular), with John Farleigh's wood engravings of London in the Blitz and with Woolf's London: not so much that of *Mrs Dalloway*, but the dustier one of *The Years* and of *Jacob's Room* in which two girls, hatless, stride triumphantly across Waterloo Bridge (which itself had got mixed somehow with the London of Charles Williams' *All Hallows Eve*). I suppose this conflation was a less conscious, less competent version of the kind of discovery Auden describes a young poet making: 'If an undergraduate announces to his tutor one morning that Gertrude Stein is the greatest writer who ever lived... he is really only saying something like this: "I don't know what to write yet or how, but yesterday while reading Gertrude Stein I thought I saw a clue".' What they seemed to share, and what I wanted to capture, was an aliveness to the real presence and shimmering impermanence of English country and city, and an ability to make visible the act of observing them through words with bare etymological roots or through white lines cut into dark wood. Their influence was horribly apparent in the first poem I ever wrote, which Peter was directly as well as indirectly responsible for; when I tentatively showed him a short story I'd written, he said that while it wasn't a very good story, it might make a good poem – and although the idea of writing poetry so terrified me that I hid under the bed to rework it, it came out well enough to be the first thing I published. Incidentally, thinking of responsibility, he also told me to tear up my application to Cambridge and to apply to Oxford instead.

All of that, though, is by the way. Still more alive than the images of Peter teaching are the ones of his house in Hitchin, a red-brick Victorian cottage that managed to be simultaneously small and extensively rambling, with barely two rooms on the same level. Walls creaked in sympathy with the floorboards whenever someone moved. Upstairs was the ten-foot-square west wing: seventeenth-century folios, a gas fire, a tiny sofa and two chairs, and something like an altarpiece of gilt Chinamen taking up the whole of one wall. Also rag rugs, light-catching short-stemmed red glasses for Martini, taken neat, and a large, ornate wooden wastepaper basket, which proved to be strikingly robust: sometime around Christmas one year when indoor fireworks threatened to set the room alight, George with great presence of mind swept them into the basket and carried them out, blazing like a particularly ornate Olympic torch.

Below the west wing was a piano (Peter's wife's and son's) and below that was the cellar and the two printing presses that did the work of the Mandeville Press: a Vicobold that had previously been used to produce a local paper, and the little foot-operated treadle press Pearl. The Vicobold was electric, or semi-electric: to start it you simultaneously pulled down on the fly-wheel with your right hand while swinging your left up to the ceiling to flick on the switch – an odd acrobatic manoeuvre as if you were torn between leaping for the stars and scooping up change from the gutter. Its rumble went through the whole house, but the sound of Pearl was the gentle rhythmic smoothing of a steam iron, audible only from the top of the stairs. Along the back wall and the side wall of the cellar were the type trays: Ehrhardt, mostly, and Bembo, and Baskerville, as well as some beautifully swashbuckling Caslon display type. There was a table crowded with type set up in racks, ready to be moved to the chase and tapped down with a wooden mallet. There was a smell of white spirit, predominantly, but also centuries of cellar dust and damp and something white-spirit-related, but thicker and more lavish, which was the ink: tubs of it, the consistency of treacle, in black, dark blue, turquoise and sepia, to be spread out on a slab and buttered onto the presses with a bone-handled knife that had clearly been pinched from the kitchen. This, and a dock-tailed white and black and ginger cat called the Flying Dumpling, who was somehow always slightly underfoot, the sound of Roger playing the piano, and the house shaking – all bar the cellar – when Peter came down the stairs in a single bounding skid, or skidding bound, from top to bottom, hands on the banisters but feet clear of the treads. As I remember it, the first thing I typeset were the poems by the third of Peter and Carola's four children, Giles, for his book *The Good Voyage*. This may not be entirely accurate. But certainly I spent hours there that added up to days, weeks, even months, setting line after line, helping to proof the poems, pulling out the wrong 'uns: the rogue Bembo b that had crept into an Ehrhardt tray, and of course the endlessly reversible p's and q's.

This should seem a very long time ago. Even OUP was probably still using moveable type then. But in fact it feels entirely immediate: the type pricking the thumbs, the sense of physically creating a poem on the page, something permanent from a single piece of handwritten or typewritten ephemera. And the sense that this was something that people had done for centuries: written, and turned writing into print. Not that anyone was self-consciously perpetuating the traditions, but simply that they were what was being done. Or as no one would have said: 'History is now, and England'. Or sitting in the west wing, easing open the sash just a crack, looking out through the creeper to the scrub and trees across the lane, scabbing the blistering black paint on the sill while reciting, gaps and all:

Leaves pressing home their small advantages
Beyond the sill, beyond the frayed sash-cords

This summer when the shagged elms tower and die

August, September, hang their weights upon
The rim of summer, when great wars begin.

That, and a glorious surface insouciance.

Cat Ice

PETER SCUPHAM

Wake on a blue morning,
find a sky you could fall through,
greet your childhood

and those long slides
from the shouting playground
into a happiness

whose slivers break
from the crazed surface
as you do your cat-dance

over eastern tinklings
while the cold
deepens, deepens,

and the night tells you
how thick ice offers
as much as you can bear.

Peter Scupham, Teacher

PETER BLEGVAD

Peter taught English at the school I was lucky to attend as a teenager. I'd never loved going to school before, and I haven't since. It was an unusual place – co-educational, vegetarian, pacifist (founded by Quaker-Theosophists), permissive and 'progressive'. It was also an unusual time, the mid- to late sixties, a time of political and creative ferment. There was a heady sense of promise in the air which classes, conversations, amateur theatrics and occasional soirées with Peter nourished.

Peter is justly celebrated as a poet, but I would like to pay homage here to his genius as a teacher. He made his passion for literature – for the life of the mind – highly contagious, successfully communicating it to many dozens of us. Years later, inspired by his example, I worked as a teacher myself, doing what I could to pass the virus on in turn.

In 1969, aged seventeen, I was very much under Peter's spell. I was keen on the Beats, but Peter enlarged my scope. Yeats was the key. Peter really brought Yeats to life in his classes. I began to acquire those handsome Macmillan hardbacks, the poetry, the essays, the autobiographies, the mythologies, and within a few terms I was happily saturated. I swapped my hippie motley for a tie and jacket, affected an Irish brogue, and began to imitate the cadences of *Per Amica Silentia Lunae*[1] in my essays. My pal Ross Campbell and I even went to Sligo with bicycles, to the Yeats Summer School, where we tried to raise Yeats' spirit with a Ouija board. As Scupham said to my father on one of the school parents' days, 'Yeats has reached out of the grave and touched your son.'

Not long afterwards my father heard from the mayor of Roquebrune Village, in the Alpes Maritimes above Menton, what is by now the well-known story of how Yeats, some of him at least, may still be lying in a communal grave there. The poet had died and been given a hasty burial in the village just before the war. After it, Ireland sent a ship to retrieve his remains that they might be reinterred according to his commands in 'Under Ben Bulben'. The French were too embarrassed to admit it to the Irish delegation, but the local gravediggers had been helpless to identify what was Yeats and what was not. There was a ceremonial handing over of a casket containing a skull and some bones, but there's no telling whose they were. It may be that a French peasant's brain-pan now lies in the churchyard under bare Ben Bulben's head.

It seemed wonderful to me when, four decades later, Peter unearthed another surprising story about Yeats, this one concerning the great man's 'Steinach operation' for sexual rejuvenation which Yeats called 'one of the greatest events, if not the supreme event, of my life'.

Without prudery or prurience, this delightful memoir by Avies Mary Platt vividly evokes the mature poet and the streets and salons of pre-war London. It was published in the *LRB*.

Peter had a saint's tolerance for the flummery and flim-flam of youth. He seemed, and still seems, youthful (*sans* flim-flam) himself. He taught naturally, by example. The subject he taught was exoterically literature, but to me it always felt like the set books were a front for a clandestine syllabus which was the whole ball of wax, limitless, imaginative life itself.

Out of *anima mundi* a vision swims of Peter in black polo neck, crouched on the seat of a chair at the head of his class (gosh, don't they all look gorgeous! Peter Larmour! Rolli Murray!!) in the BBC documentary *Tyger Tyger* filmed in 1968. His eyes wide shut the better to see his thought, he's analysing Blake. He makes thinking an adventure, and participation in it something to relish. His apparent interest in our (not always very interesting) efforts kindles self-respect, curiosity and courage. Humanity, even.

I'm temporarily eternally grateful. Cheers, Peter! Here's to you, and to your fellow unacknowledged legislators of the race: the poets *and* the teachers.

NOTE

1 In *Mythologies*, W. B. Yeats, the emerald green hardback edition which Macmillan put out in 1962 uniform with *Autobiographies*, and *Essays and Introductions*. No wrapper; a little faded. Hash burns on the end-papers. Inscribed 'Blegvad '69'.

From the Classroom

CATHERINE ALTPERE

Thursday was the best day at St Chris. Spaghetti, *Top of the Pops* and *The Man from U.N.C.L.E*, viewed in the standing-room-only hut which doubled during the day as our English classroom. I can't be sure, but I like to think that the joy of Thursday evenings was augmented by a daytime English lesson, presided over by Peter, perched on his desk, one leg dangling as he peeled open the petals of English literature in general and poetry in particular.

During these lessons we were beguiled by his unassuming rapport with us. We respected him because he was a teacher (a respect not universally bestowed) and because he treated us exactly as what we were: nearly adults waiting only to be shown how to find and absorb knowledge. The flow of discussion was two-way; he seemed genuinely interested in hearing our thoughts as well as imparting his own.

Cornily, I could say that Peter *opened doors*, showed us what lay behind them, and then left us to decide whether or not to pass through to the other side. I certainly walked through the Thomas Hardy door: I can still feel the tingle of reading his poems, gently prised apart by Peter. That is perhaps why I felt a shock of recognition when, in maturity, I came across the poems of R.S. Thomas, which plucked the same chords within me. And of course Blake we will never forget.

I was only at St Chris for two years. I have few anecdotes to recall. I do remember acutely the realisation in Peter's classes that school did not have to be time-marking and punishment-based, and there could be male figures in our lives who were entirely benign, recognising, respecting and nurturing our embryonic individuality. He *knew* we hadn't been born bad, only curious.

Peter left a double imprint on my life: academic and personal. He was close to us in age but able to be a mentor. I suspect he never set out to be one, knowing now that he preferred to remain a poet first and teacher second (perhaps that was his secret).

And when we finally drove out of Arundale's gates for the last time, we each received a final gift in the shape of a postcard from Peter, commending us on our A level and S level results. A parting hurrah, which was so like him.

---

3 Riders to the Sea

For Sydney Harrod

PETER SCUPHAM

Swan Vestas: a scrumpled coffin
surfaces in a forgotten drawer:
'Stones from Yeats's Grave'.

The curtains time has gathered
ease a little for the Irish light
to dance its watery veils for us

free-wheeling now, after sixty years,
still riding westward, stowed gear
weighing no more than a handful of dust,

old money light in our pockets,
showered with gifts and amazements:
colour-washed houses floating by,

our bent heads filled with poems,
a girl, a grey house, the fuschia's blood-gouts,
dreams unpunctured, bones unbroken.

Our flaming meths head-overs into the night
from a tent pitched on a stony hill;
an old woman keens to her spinning wheel.

Galway, Connemara, Sligo –
'In Drumcliffe churchyard Yeats is laid' –
Bending down in awkward reverence

I steal chippings from the grey shroud
hiding that suspicious jigsaw
packed off home from Roquebrune,

watch two cold-eyed cyclists pass me by,
on the long way back, one with a matchbox:
'Stones from my grave'.

Night Thoughts

PETER SCUPHAM

1. Glimmerings

Listen to the voices that ride the air,
shaking Orion in his long stride:
the broken morse of drifting owls,
the growl of wind in clung leaves;

find yourself lost for words
which might decode these messages
where trees, hunched over glimmerings,
tell small tales of pain and hunger.

Tremble when the dead brush by you,
weave a spell over your cold hands;
glimpse a passing tongue-tied angel,
wings feathered by a secret love.

2. The winter farmhouse

builds itself out of deepest dark.
Under a pelt if thatch and frost
chamfered bone shivers in the wind,
shivers in the eastern wind.

We shrink into otherness; our fingers whiten.
The house is our nest of apprehension,
a cavern of ash and sighs where rats tap-dance

as Daisy, Dapple, patched out of moonlight,
Strike flown sparks from tumbled cobbles,
whinny in the break and tangle of our dream.

We had not know the inside was so out,
The droves of night so full of watching,
The out so in, swung doors at sentry-go

As the dead with owl-faces and bleak eyes
busy with milk-pails, whips and ribbons
cross sill and threshold in a dry-leaf hush.

The cold, such cold
Where cats creep out of their garden-graves
To keen in the wind,
To keen in the eastern wind.

3. Darker Still

Yes, they say, how the days draw in,
how all our summers gutter down
until the light can hardly lift itself
to find life crouching in its nest of fur,
the late fruit shrivelled, the charred wick
twisting away from the ghost of flame.

Darker still, where a dead house
puts bricks of broken cloud together,
and children you can no longer name
share loneliness with twigs and birds,
the dry abrasions of a missing gate
awkwardly swung between then and now.

Step into the night beyond the kitchen door,
let rooms decked with heat and laughter
greet the cold, astonished air,
as your breath feathers you out and further
than those bleak reaches hope must traverse
under the disposition of a star

BEST POEM

Chris Preddle

LESS VIRGIL

He would settle by Mag Brook, himself
his barque laid up on the bank like a forearm leaning.
The ship's cat, gone thin as a hem of a sail,
        he brought to the earth, its for-me-alone
inhuming. Let this diminutive hill of Troy
be all the west, he thought, and all ages,
        all persons; let Mary quite contrary
to this geography sit grudging on Europe's edge.
It was in May. The trees of Mag Hill were in leaf.
Cattle came down to Mag Brook like the coming of life.

He met the wise Sappho in her circle
of the mind. I live, she said, at the very hem
or selvedge of the isles of Greece, their dulse and seakale,
        already, like you, after Homer,
but I look to the east. Asia like silk, Sardis
like a purple sandal lie there, and a woman like the moon
        who once was mine. They leave us sad
and are therefore with us. By 'in the underworld' I mean
in me. I am much peopled. Envy the cows
paddling here, they have no gods to accuse.

A shade spoke, his habit and his mood
black. In Byzantium once I was the Emperor's
Lord Chief of the Wardrobe, whom the Lord's unmade
        to the monk Gregory. The eastern Impious
thicker than sins possessed our Christian City,
my thousand-year New Rome. Such a fall
        of Europe there was, we no more see it
Europe. From now on western ages fail
as a measure of us. Here or there, all's one.
The monk like an icon suffered, passive in his belief, or sullen.

The winter came. Mag Brook
froze. It snowed, falling in generations, and deepened
on the halls of the dead. A skater came, Rebecca
        skating as if on the Boston Frog Pond,
skimmering upriver. She heard the ice creak
as her childhood advanced, no less than Amy ice-
        fallen in Concord. This English creek
would be a partial idyll, a pastoral compromise.
The twentieth century was over. Winter cattle
breathed. Those wars were over, this peace local and curtailed.

Plum blossom came, the friend
of winter. Li Qingzhao was there. She wrote,
I send this verse or letter from the far end
of time, its Silver River. Far out
in the Eastern Sea separated, for him I sever
a branch of red blossom. The petals let go
anxieties all round the meiping vase.
I cannot tell if my mood will set or go,
or my hard fortunes. Child of misfortune, unpin
your clouds of hair, lie down with all that has happened
to you.

May again. Berthe Morisot
painted a young woman in green sunlight
on the grass, with a green parasol. Berthe was morose.
That girl is beautiful – so let Sensuous
be anxious as myself. But she made the muslin frock
of white sunlight. A person has only the past
to step from. What else is mine I make for,
but it turns from me, like a model the artist puts
in back view. Those painted girls of hers were meant
to oppose outside time what the times put women to.

He had settled by Mag Brook, less
Virgil the guide, more one that shades would visit
as if Mag Brook was their riverbank of loss.
There's no heaven or hell to deserve,
no judgment of souls, they said; Avernus undone,
we are indifferently ourselves. Rebecca's horse
grazed on the grass where they sat mundane
as a picnic. They had found no Great Because
or Higher Mind. What is real, unseen, unself
is apprehended here now, come life fall, sun fail.

BEST TRANSLATION

James Womack

translation from the Spanish of Manuel Vilas's 'Macbeth'

This morning I got on the ferry that runs to La Gomera
from Santa Cruz de Tenerife; I sat at the deck
bar and started on the Campari and the olives,
and after a while I was completely hammered; a Scottish woman
– scruffy and heavily made-up, around 40, fat inches of cleavage,
showing off her beautiful dark balanced breasts –
sat down to drink with me; she studied Spanish
at Madrid University, she said, and stuck out her tongue
as she did so; 'Where is Scotland?' I asked,
to which she replied, 'And where's your cock?'
And we switched from Campari to gin,
and after a while I spoke to this Scottish woman:
an inspired screed in Spanish, which she did not understand at all:

Blessed is everything that lies beneath the water,
from the shipwreck to the rhinestone necklace
that fell into the sea in an act of loving carelessness.

The book of my life lies also beneath the waves,
kept there by some rusty enchantment;
there, with the fish and coral, the seaweed and darkness.

The Scot laughed and took off her shorts
and was left wearing just her pants as though they were
a bikini, come on, take off your pants I said, let's leave the deck,
take them off, and she took them off, and in a corner of the boat,
in a little room full of overalls and an empty
bucket, we screwed like two drunks without scruples,
but with the good fortune and skill to get stuck into one another,
and afterwards, I took her earrings and threw them in the sea,
and she took my wallet and said you're a sad sack of shit,
those earrings were made of gold and worth ten dicks like yours,
and she took from my wallet the ten banknotes I'd been keeping
to be able to eat alone on the island, drink gin in some bar on the beach.

The kingdom of God is decorated with the gold
all the best men have brought Him,
I smoked a lot that night and was coughing; I went from dive
to dive, and at dawn there was only warm beer left;
you look like a renegade saint, or else a beggar, one of my listeners said.

Distant and shrivelled, all heroes abandoned the heaven and the earth:
their distance makes my life sad; their neglect is my abandonment.
I grew up with them, a child waiting at a balcony over a river,
or swimming in the sea on July evenings,
and I heard them come and they did not come.
I heard them speak to me and they did not speak;
I heard them love me, and they forgot about me.

The sea takes my vulgar gift, those gold earrings,
in honour of the centuries that it has been alone,
and is pleased that I remembered about her for once.
Life has rotted away,
I cannot always be in love,
and now I desire nothing.

The night filled with stars, the white whale,
the tenth century BC, a hut plonked in the middle of the world,
a river, a language with no way of being set down, fruits,
vegetables, a couple of goats, a wounded hare, a fire,
a cave, a lambskin, a stone-tipped spear;
the sea like a shield, like the bare flesh of every sin,
and the gods, petty, invented,
the forest, snow, the fire; the sea is pure terror,
gross terror, the faces of the dead, death itself,
the dolmen, the granite,
the sense that God is coming.

Black lens of the ocean, crypt of salt water far below me,
the photograph of a distant past; there was nothing,
and nothing wishes to dwell in me,
and the sea pulls back and the dawn comes
and I go back to the hotel where I am staying.
The child vanished; the heroes sang and were never heard,
the sea strode on to a great silence,
and I got drunk
and spent the whole afternoon asleep.

And I should expect nothing from all the gifts that come with old age,
such as honour, and love, and tact and obedience,
and the whole grand army of my friends.

Judy Brown

STEEPED

We are swimming through strong brown.
All light has turned to tea, a mild infusion.
Warm grey curls off the paintwork.
Our actual ankles are ankle-deep in soft shadow.

The windows are curtains of dry rain
which drop like dirty waterfalls from their frames.
Each object is outlined with a cushion of shadow.
The mothers-to-be are swollen with babies

made of shadow: they don't allow talking.
They spit moths of dust into their teacups.
Oak trees are bouncing on trampolines of shadow.
Even outside, the same rules apply.

The mothers-to-be pat their must-filled bumps.
The floor is a skin of lion-light and mink-shade.
When the test proved positive, the dentists poured
the mercury from their teeth and stopped them with shadow.

I am the barren girl off to one side.
My chest is so flat, it captures no shadow.
The unstoppable grey falls on me nonetheless.
I delight in the fireworks of my monthly bleed.

While it lasts the neighbourhood dogs cannot settle
in their beds of straw and serge,
and the pigeon-grey landladies bang on the pipes
in case something coloured might be flowing.

Stewart Sanderson

LOVE'S LABOURS WON

Unlike the vanished *Hamlet*, this
loss would have been a comedy:
five funny acts, to take the piss
    out of that monster, love –
an ancient vice, like poetry,
    which no one is above.

Pinched from a dog-eared chronicle
picked off the barrows at St. Paul's,
the plot remains untraceable
    though if compelled, I'd guess
that it involved strains, dying falls
    and someone saying yes.

The scene is equally obscure:
a blank utopia no art
of reconstruction can restore;
    a placeless mystery
from which we'll never pluck the heart –
    such is love's victory.

In this void the protagonists
are struck dumb, their soliloquies
consumed by time's entropic mists
    towards whose censorship
all our assumed identities
    inevitably slip.

I picture them: the boy, the girl
played by a boy, the clever clown
who sang and sometimes rolled a pearl
    of rare wit on his tongue –
the troubled head under a crown,
    the duke no longer young.

Two thousand or three thousand lines
of prose and blank verse, pared away
till in the end all that remains
    is three words to remind
people about this missing play
    substantial as the wind.

For all the miles of text his hand
set down, a single speech survives
and six scrawled signatures, like sand-
    grains cast up by the sea:
a clutch of desiccated leaves
    to prove there was a tree.

Not everything he wrote was great.
Even for him, there were off days
when no words could interrogate
    this world which took his son
and, given two *Love's Labour's* plays,
    gave back *Love's Labour's Won*.

Rachel Spence

BIRD OF SORROW
(Medea's Song)
after St Augustine and Emily Dickinson

I

She remembers islands. An archipelago shaped
like a meniscus. Grids that refuse language

Some idea of happiness

II

Her task is to unstitch time, lay it on the beach
in bolts of raw, unpicked cotton

the women singing
the hobbled syntax of exile

Her gaze rakes
the horizon   She is seeking the
books
packed in leaky crates
                                    vulnerable as turtles
making a run for the sea

III

She remembers doves. Kings leaping
into the childless blue. A time when
the circle was the perfect expression
of justice

She has bitten her nest
out of the rock.   Gone deep
in border country, untenanted ground
A land where long-eyed women sew
lengthwise and crossways

Do not
trespass. Do not step on the cracks

Soon, she will reach
The blue peninsula

Her chicks will levitate

Crystal Anderson

REAL WOMEN

Microcosm of bones, ligament networks,
human structures stomping down
laminated lanes in some big city not
in a grisly horror film
reveal but in spotlights to fragile applause.

In these places, human hangers preview not
bodies but styled ideas,
architectural impossibilities,
impractical as the thin
women bearing the weight of this industry.

Models are fleeting, fabric laden oxen;
each woman painted, arranged
by gauche couturiers, those artless experts
who misunderstand the breast's
geometry, the frequencies of hips, thighs.

Live mannequins, their skin opaque but cobweb-
on-skeleton obvious
as to how each strutting person is puzzled
together while transmitting
cultured cloth, lines and tchotchke to and fro.

A life of paring the fat to fit into
less, make bigger the name that
takes the credit. The fault lies not in woman's
intrinsic frame, no matter
how small, paid for. These brittle women cry, too,

staining sleeves with salt you and I cannot buy,
afford as I take up too
much room, my curves in profound conversation
with Tesco. It understands
my mediocrity, my commonplace tears.

The real woman's form is positivity,
red dress charity affair,
waves and troughs celebrated on occasion.
Then nimble fingers return,
crafting for tall rectangles that we say is

not real. Women now hated by women
for being thin, wanted for being
thin, face forgettable even in the brief
moments they are young, useful;
always one more go-see away from done. Separated off
from our pack, bred for this
carapace art that wears them
down like living on coffee and cigarettes,
the designs overworking their
just-as-real femme physique. This is not their fault.

Andrew Wynn Owen

The Fisherman

Slow morning. Fish were taking their sweet time.
Sunrise surprised me, as it often can,
      With impish motey streaks.
Bethsaida blurred, receding, home of tomb
And temple. Air was energetic, clean.
      With choppy strokes
      Past heron, swallows,
    Softly we skiffed across
    Each undulating crease.
A greener depth replaced the glistening shallows.

Peter was leaning out to cast his net
While I, daydreaming, watched saltwater's ruptured
      Mirror. Remembrances
Spiralled. Mosaic of fractals. Passion's knot
Revolving. Tell me, have you been enraptured
      By moments, mess,
      The weathervane
    Of who and why we are?
    It is a source of awe
I've always felt. It ripens on the vine.

When in Achaea, I saw triumphal arches,
Rough gateways that the Romans built to mark
      Dominion here and there.
Their aqueducts loom in the farthest reaches,
Such is their industry, their lust to make –
      In distant Tyre,
      Phoenician Acre,
    And down the restless coast
    Where hundreds like us cast
Quick lines and chant. The usual. Beaches echo.

But when I turned and saw him, all things changed.
The rumoured mercy of this riddled world
      Shone clear. A sudden lift,
Sun crinkled through the branches. Birdsong chimed
With water's slosh. Dispersing, clouds ran wild.
      Unruly light,
      Having no heed
    Of death's deranging bite,
    Enveloped sea and boat.
No halo framed that love-extolling head

Yet tender fury tumbled from its nod,
As if amphorae and sarcophagus
      Were nothing in his scheme.
That gesture said the maker had no need
For power, how living's caustic struggle goes.
      Sea quaked. Did some
      Vast bird swoop over?
    Then all was crystal still
    And sunlight filled our sail.
I had the feeling this could last forever.

So many things we see but do not notice:
Crisp bracken, insect wings, the minuscule
      Courageous sapling shoots.

Balance is nestled by the stalks of nettles,
A dock-leaf's balm. The rearing mountain's call
      To chase new heights
      Can soothe old feuds
    And, though we honour towers,
    Flatlands are glories too,
Tousled or tussocky, bud-crowded fields.

Once, rambling by the beach, he seized my arm,
A look like nothing earthly in his eyes,
      And whispered, 'We are one,
Dear brother, with the same unswerving aim.
The plan is real and Satan's cruellest ice
      Can't hurt. Life's throne
      Persists, and all
    Is as it's meant to be.
    The boat, the sky, the bay –
Love is our lamp and every soul the oil.'

What was his purpose, truly? You have seen.
The stone is rolled away, and here we stand.
      Don't fear the wilderness:
Dry wind, moon chill, heat shivers – each a sign
Voracious heaven sent to leave us stunned.
      Voluminous
      Reality
    Advances in our cause
    And here are all the clues:
Love makes a bond no discord can untie.

God is a name for saying what we guess
Deep laws that underwrite our world are doing.
      Believe me when I say
I thought that truth would always be disguised
Until I saw sure proof of this undying
      Mystery: the sea
      Buoyed up his feet
    And, unexpected marvel,
    The liquid held like marble.
When miracles occur, why should we fight?

It is not finished, no, and it may never.
Some stories have beginnings but no end.
      I cannot now forget
How fierce he was, unwearying renewer.
That certainty, that moving stillness, and
      The gentle gait
      Which, when I look
    At any rocking keel,
    Is conjured. I recall
The day that Yeshua walked across a lake.

Iain Galbraith

translates from the German
Peter Waterhouse's 'Umgang mit Abständen'

DEALINGS WITH GAPS

Why did we occupy the gaps? The two ends
are unknown. The unscrambled mid-point calls:
me. Thus begin our happy dealings with gaps. Will there
be failure? O, we have already failed. Waking
up in the morning we are used to saying to ourselves: Hello
failed middling me. Today
is the next great Project Failure. Welcome.
With silver eyes (might as well shut that silver eye
already), with lips opened long before each spoken word
(they too could be clapped down early on), with fingers, ears, navel
etc. (all on the cusp of happiness – even the navel
lives in ecstatic readiness – so one should rightly say: O you navel): May I
be urged (by whom?) into the least known moment of the day, and may this
be called the day of the unknown navel: Good morning. Are all gaps
unchanged? Yes, all gaps are unchanged and in their examples lie.
You often hear the cry: Please clap out the gaps in good time, navel
etc.: Please find the best form of ecstasy. One
might almost wish to become a navel: Bounded form at
the centre. So the question is: Are we a navel?
No. Can we at least have dealings
with the navel? No, the navel is intractable.
We have dealings with gaps. Are such dealings
pleasurable?
Yes.
No.

Yvonne Reddick

translates from the French
Maurice Chappaz's 'Wind in the Spruce Trunks'

INQUIRY INVESTIGATING THE PRESIDENTS OF THIS AND THAT

Those fat-necked pimps with the red flea of the Legion of Horror in their
buttonholes are gambling the country away at cards. A fist thumps the table.
    – Monte Rosa! – Take Mont Gris! – Rotten trafficking. Not my fault. –
Trump! Two TVs, five MPs. – Seven entrepreneurs. – Payoff, trumps! – A cheat?
How so? Notary X. Five scythes: three aces! – A useless road! – Unnecessary
pollution. – Backhander! Brrroo, brrroooo... (Like great spotted woodpeckers,
those black-winged scroungers.)
    A fist thumps the table.
    There goes a swallow!
    Each downs his pint of souls.
– Successful libel. Bravo, board of The Daily Drool. Victory at the elections. –
Justice is with us! – The clergy's on our side! – Blue sky swindling. – Double
murder. – Muttonhead! – Lamebrain! – Here's to grease! – Here's to grace! –The
S. A. Forgers are genuinely bankrupt – I'll pass on the bill to the Holy Spirit. –
I'll pass. I'm cleaned out.
    A heel stomps on the table.
– The meadows, the mountains! – The safe! The safe – I'll jump on the safe!
    They smother the green baize with their arses the way the pestle
    crushes grapes in a vat. A country caught between brimstone and
    mignonettes.
– Squashed rats, good sirs!

Simon Smith

adapts from the French
after Charles Baudelaire's 'The Cygnet'
(for Dorothy Lehane)

I
Andromache
my thoughts are with you

from a little trickle
poor & sad mirror of Ages ago
echo to your unbearable loss

now the sour Stour busted with your tears
shocking my teeming memory
into action –

from the close
dog's leg crossing Beaconsfield Road
then down the back alley

– recalled for me the new Carrousel –

old Paris is no more
sadly the shape of a city
switches to the quick of a heartbeat

as in a vision
I see improvised work camps

a jumble – a jungle in heaps
of rough-cut columns & capitals

– undergrowth overgrowing huge blocks
stone discoloured with verdigris
& all that

tangle of tat glitters from shop windows

right there a zoo spread out
right there one morning

at the chilly zero hour
a cold & clear sky

as Work rising from sleep
as the road workers
break silence with their din

a cygnet lost to its mother
its webbed feet flapping
along the dry road

dragging his grey wings
across the roughened surface
beside the dried up drain

the poor thing beak wide

desperately thrashing its wings
in the muck
with a heart full

of need for his natural state
& element
hissed

'o water when will you rain down again
when will your thunder rip through Heaven'

I see that troubled bird
foreign & fatal myth

sometimes towards the sky
like Man in Ovid's tales

towards an ironic and punishing blue sky

raises his starving head
with a twist of the neck
to shout down God

II
Paris changes
but my sadness
will not budge

tower blocks cranes
prefab concrete façade
all flipped to myth

& my memory weighed down more than
stone

& so next to the Louvre
I am frozen by the image –

I recall my majestic bird
& his thrashing wings

with the exiles
ridiculous & Sublime

gnawed at by unending recollection
& then you

Andromache
tipped from the hero's embrace
a defiled chattel

in the hands of pompous Pyrrhus
Hector's widow wife of Helenus
Isis bride slave of Daesh

on BBC News 24 the emaciated woman
of colour – sick
from her odyssey

her bloodshot eyes staring vainly
through the murk

for the palms of Africa
not there

I recall all of them lost
who can never ever
reclaim what they've lost

those who drink their own thirst
in their own tears
like Romulus & Remus at the breast

& think of all children starved & shriveled like flowers

Eve Grubin

*translates from the twelfth-century Hebrew
Yehuda Halevi's 'You Knew Who I Was'*

You knew who I was before making me.

Now, a kernel of your spirit lies inside, protecting.

If you pushed me, could I stand?
If you blocked me, could I move forward?

What can I say when my thought is in your hand?

What can I do if you don't help?

I beg you. Please answer. Cloak me.

Please stir me.
Wake me to bless your name.

*

here
in the dark wood
where I'm exiled with my mind

an old memory rings the bells

& I think of all the mariners lost on a desert island
of all the prisoners of all the desolate –
& of all the others

Karen Leeder

*translates from the German
Ulrike Almut Sandig, 'Das Märchen vom Schlauraffenland'*

TALE OF THE LAND OF MILK AND HONEY

Good evening, Deutschland, turn the fog lights on

we're after telling it like it is, being on cue:

those who want in must chomp their way through
a cake that's not found anywhere in Grimm;

those who want out are gone in two shakes, quicker
than the time it takes to think of a four-syllable word.

Just say three times: MilkandHoney, MilkandHoney.
We've lost our way in your shopping malls

can't tell them apart any more. In Höxter

a fat girl buys an angel of clay and asks

at the till: what does hope mean? In Steinheim

Hakan drinks his coffee strong, last night he dreamed

again he swam across a honey-cake-Mediterranean
only to be beached in the end on the streets

the brown-silt sands of the Land of Milk and Honey.
In Jena after a three-year trial a priest receives

a hefty fine, for steering at a police car
to avoid hitting the line of demonstrators.

'My homeland is not only the cities and villages...'
it's also the doorman before them. I dreamed

he looks like Kaya Yanar and asks for the code word:
tell me the land where the donkeys have silver noses.

Say it three times over: you're not getting in,
you're not getting in, you're –

Paying its Way

Evan Kindley, *Poet-Critics and the Administration of Culture* (Harvard University Press) £27.95

Reviewed by KARL O'HANLON

Evan Kindley's succinct book *Poet-Critics and the Administration of Culture* presents a timely and necessary addition to the ongoing conversation in modernist studies surrounding what one of the pioneers in this sub-field, Mark McGurl, describes as modernism's 'fall into institutionality' (p. 409). This scholarship has origins back in Lawrence Rainey's groundbreaking study *Institutions of Modernism*, which sought to wrench modernism out of a traditional critical narrative of its claims for the aesthetic autonomy of 'high' art, re-contextualising it within a cultural and consumerist economy. Whereas Rainey's work focused on the wealthy benefactors who became patrons of modernism, and McGurl picks up the story in the 1950s with the emergence of the creative writing programme and the infiltration of the academy by writers, Kindley seeks to account for the transitional period, after the Wall Street Crash of 1929 and the Second World War had financially crippled the aristocratic patron class that supported modernism. His anteleological approach has much in common with revisionist historiography in resisting a determinist account of what may seem from our vantage point the inevitability of literature ensconcing itself within academia: 'our awareness of where [writers] finally came to settle should not obscure our knowledge of their itinerary' (p. 10); nevertheless, at times the briskness of this study serves to flatten history's 'mesh of nuance, complexity, and contradiction' (Foster, xvii).

The introduction maps the terrain, with a declaration that 'this is a book about justification', the ways in which poet-critics – a hyphenated identity that emerges in the very crucible of the period under examination – sought to navigate from being what Edith Stein caustically referred to as 'village explainers' from one particular village, a moneyed elite, to another – administrative bodies of the state (including non-governmental outliers such as philanthropic bodies). Kindley distinguishes between their respective value systems; in the early patronage stage, it is primarily aesthetic (a good that he defines as the 'best that has been thought and said'). He asserts that a Kierkegaardian binary of aesthetics/ethics animates American high modernism, giving way to the ethical stance in the democratic and liberal energies released by opposing Nazism and later, Communism, during the forties, a project that was not only consonant with the aims of the US government, but which was 'in fact impossible to complete without it'. The aristocratic and liberal-democratic phases of modernism in turn usher in an enormous expansion and 'improbable syn-thesis' of the two in the post-war 'technocratic' phase – the rise of the American research university and the growth of the philanthropic sector, a situation that is by and large the dominant paradigm today. Values are simply a matter of expertise, and the experts in question, Kindley argues, are the poet-critics who flocked to academia and charitable foundations in the middle of the century (pp. 12–13).

The first two chapters focus on the aesthetic/aristocratic phase: T. S. Eliot is pitched as a promoter of the figure of the poet-critic even as he is quintessentially anxious about the role. Kindley examines a 1920 essay 'A Brief Treatise on the Criticism of Poetry', in which Eliot avers that although the poet-critic is the most perfect type of critic, since his passions are cauterised in creation rather than criticism, it is precisely that superiority that militates against the poet-critic diverting their energies into criticism of inferior books (p. 29). Kindley channels this pessimistic critical doctrine into a reading of Eliot's 'Gerontion' as a poem 'about criticism and the dangers it poses to poetry', an enervated meditation on the 'thousand small deliberations' the critic makes in order to 'protract the profit' of the aesthetic encounter (pp. 30–35). The second chapter focuses on Marianne Moore; Kindley coins the phrase 'antagonism towards agonism' to describe Moore's avoidance of polemic, reading it against the grain of the aggressive stances taken up by Pound and other modernists (a reading that risks reinscribing the gender binaries he sets out to criticise). He performs close readings of Moore's 'Critics and Connoisseurs', 'Picking and Choosing', and 'When I Buy Pictures', arguing that Moore disdains the intellectual 'humbug' of criticism to side with connoisseurship and consumerism as less antagonistic and dishonest modes of taste-making, situating both within her patronage by Schofield Thayer, co-owner of *The Dial*, and Moore's appointment as managing editor in 1925.

The third chapter considers the 'precarious institutional arrangements of the 1920s' (p. 55), before modernism was enshrined in the canon by the professors, and its influence was arbitrated by student bodies (a suggestive term that Kindley resists marshalling into an explicit queer reading). W. H. Auden's early poetry is read as both a parody of public school oratory and its Marxist dialectical understanding of residual nineteenth-century liberalism as the Janus face of fascism). Kindley rounds the chapter off with an analysis of 'Six Odes', as both an ecstatic celebration of the student body (and their bodies), and anxieties about the pedagogical inculcation of perdurable and worthy values (p. 70).

In these early chapters the case studies can feel like vignettes: in the Auden chapter, for instance, counterevidence (the crucial role of professors at universities such as Vanderbilt and Chicago, and university-affiliated magazines such as *The Fugitive* in gaining a foothold for modernism within the academy in the early twenties) is in short supply, while the Moore chapter would have benefited from more thorough research; Kindley does not cite Victoria Bazin's scrupulously crucial work on Moore as editor, let alone provide original research into

The Dial/Thayer papers as to Moore's actual editing processes, nor does he reference such significant statements on the link between creation and criticism as her 1921 *Dial* review of Eliot's *The Sacred Wood*.

Chapters one to three are in some ways ancillary to the original research presented in the final two chapters. In the fourth chapter, Kindley focuses on Franklin Delano Roosevelt's invitation to Archibald MacLeish to become Librarian of Congress; Judge Felix Frankfurter writes in recommendation of MacLeish as uniting qualities of the 'hard-headed lawyer with the sympathetic imagination of the poet' (qtd p. 74). Drawing on Greg Barnhisel's 2015 study *Cold War Modernists*, Kindley traces the gradual conversion of MacLeish from defender of the autonomy of art to a chief proponent of civic modernism, a recasting of modernism as an instrument of cultural diplomacy and 'a bulwark of liberalism, individualism, and even capitalism' (p. 84). The remainder of the chapter is a fascinating examination of the interaction between African American poets and the Federal Writers' Project, examining the complexity of that involvement with nuance and style. Mining unpublished source material located at Howard University, Kindley focuses on the poet-critic Sterling A. Brown, examining what he dubs Brown's 'ethnographic lyric' – a mode of poetry that marries sociology, an interest in African American vernacular, and the dramatic monologue, and an enactment of the difficulties of the middle-class black intellectual's distance from the black labouring class and the concomitant temptation, which Brown thought was to be resisted, to lose the distinctiveness of dialect and forms of life, a charge he levelled at Harlem Renaissance luminaries (pp. 88–95). Brown's involvement with the FWP and Slave Narrative Collection, Kindley argues, transcended the primary impulse of economic stimulus and relief, whereby such anthropological materials were appropriated by New Deal liberal cultural renewal (p. 97). The chapter finishes with a fascinating discussion of the clashes between the responsibility of African American intellectuals to their folk subjects, and the segregated, racially-stratified protocols of administrative labour, with white supervisors co-opting the work of their black colleagues once the field work was completed (p. 102). Kindley offers a satirical memorandum by Brown to a colleague as an example of 'the poetry of bureaucracy' (p. 107).

The final chapter is similarly rich in archival research, focusing on R.P. Blackmur's role as an adviser to the Rockerfeller Foundation. Kindley relays Blackmur's canvassing of fellow writers to determine eight or less worthy recipients of the Foundation's financial support from among the now-much-diminished cultural clout of the little magazines to rejuvenate their influence. The responses are illuminating: William Carlos Williams rails against the grinding of editorial axes, little magazines like 'small imitations of some Soviet-like direction implicit in their editorial policies' (qtd p. 119); Auden: 'to be quite frank, I can't read more than one or two contributions in any of the magazines you mention' (qtd p. 121); Wallace Stevens: 'Poetry [sic]... would require something like $1,000,000.00 to carry on... Everyone would expect poets to buy the drinks' (qtd p. 123). Stevens, Kindley

notes, recognises that by allying itself with charitable organisations, poetry is having to make itself 'an object of perpetual critique' in terms of justification (p. 125).

Poet-Critics and the Administration of Culture is an uneven book; it is especially compelling in these later chapters and the presentation of completely original research, while overall the study's breadth of focus is under-served by the relative ground that Kindley has to cover in what is a short book. The marriage of formalist criticism and a sociological study of bureaucratic reformulations of culture in mid-century America is admirable, especially on those occasions when the readings of poems moves beyond allegory or thematic paraphrase to subtle analysis of the interactions of the bureaucratic contexts and the form of the poems, as in his deft reading of Brown's 'ethnographic lyric'.

SELECT BIBLIOGRAPHY

Greg Barnhisel, *Cold War Modernists: Art, Literature And American Cultural Diplomacy* (Columbia University Press, 2015)

Victoria Bazin, 'Hysterical Virgins and Little Magazines: Marianne Moore's Editorship of *The Dial*', *The Journal of Modern Periodical Studies*, 4.1 (2013), pp. 55–75

Roy Foster, *The Irish Story: Telling Tales and Making It Up in Ireland* (Oxford University Press, 2002)

Mark McGurl, *The Program Era: Postwar Fiction and the Rise of Creative Writing* (Harvard University Press, 2009)

Marianne Moore, 'The Sacred Wood', review of T. S. Eliot, *The Sacred Wood* (1920), *The Dial*, 70.3 (March 1921), pp. 336–39

Lawrence Rainey, *Institutions of Modernism: Literary Elites and Public Culture* (Yale University Press, 1998)

Poets will be poets

John Greening, *Threading A Dream: A Poet on the Nile* (Gatehouse Press) £10

Reviewed by ANDREW HADFIELD

From 1979–81, the last years of Anwar Sadat's rule in Egypt, and before his first collection was published, John Greening and his wife lived in Egypt as teachers working for Voluntary Service Overseas. Thirty-five years later he has written a memoir, a series of observations and vignettes, interspersed with poetry from his many volumes. Greening has developed a fascination with Egyptian life and culture over many years and he looks back to explore his relationship with the country, its ancient civilisation and modern culture.

Greening is often a disarming and engaging guide. He tries to explain how difficult it is to realise that one is actually standing next to the pyramids and how to make sense of an overwhelming tourist experience which might be better realised on the page, rather as Wordsworth wished he had left Mont Blanc unseen. Tourists really need to stand for hours contemplating the mystery and majesty of them but that is far from easy when surrounded by beggars, vendors and tourist guides. Of course, sometimes guides are indispensable. On a trip to the Nubian Damn one tells the Greenings that this masterpiece of engineering and symbol of Egyptian modernity has its own dark secrets:

> The High Damn was like the war, you were expected to die... One night in 1964, two thousand men died when a stray dynamite detonated... I was there next morning in the same position ... The lorries had taken the bodies away, the boxes were made and the bodies were sent with a thousand pounds and a handshake back to evicted Nubian families... Nothing was said. No one knew how many.

Greening writes well about the Egypt he experienced at the end of the 1970s, with its mixture of religious culture and the relatively recent arrival of Western culture. He neatly contrasts his own restlessness and sense of impermanence with the ancient civilisation which still determined the nature of Egyptian life. He recounts the panic of losing their small kitten, Mitzu, who was discovered after two days lodged in the tyre of a parked car, alongside reflections of the well-attested enthusiasm for cats in ancient Egypt. Other reflections are more serendipitous and curious. After the poet has published some works on his (disappointing) encounter with Tutankhamun's tomb his father reveals that he travelled to Iceland in the Second World War on the *Champollion*. Not only was the ship named after the linguist who deciphered hieroglyphs using the Rosetta Stone, but it was the ship which carried Howard Carter to Egypt when he discovered the tomb. There is also a harrowing account of being marooned on a tourist boat in the middle of Lake Nasser as complacency and irritation turn to panic before everyone is rescued.

While I enjoyed *Threading A Dream* a great deal, I was sometimes a bit irritated by Greening's desire to take himself rather too seriously as a man of words who exists in the world of poets. He is far more engaging and informative when he allows his more curious and modest persona to take over and communicate openly with the reader as he makes sense of a wide range of experiences acquired over many years. The book is best read, I think, as a quirky collection of miscellaneous observations of different types, which is surely how it was designed. There are poems, images by the author's daughter, mixed with a variety of reflections which combine the historical, the personal and the whimsical: only a truly cynical or overly sceptical reader could fail to share the author's obvious enjoyment of his past.

The Exquisite Face

Solmaz Sharif, *Look* (Graywolf) $16.00; Pascale Petit, *Mama Amazonica* (Bloodaxe) £9.95

Reviewed by MARY JEAN CHAN

As a 2016 National Book Award finalist, Solmaz Sharif's *Look* will be familiar to admirers of contemporary American poetry as an extraordinary book painstakingly wrought from the ruins of the Iran–Iraq war (1980–1988). As such, Sharif's debut collection is aptly fragmentary, its formally experimental poems littered with terms mined from the United States Department of Defense *Dictionary of Military and Associated Terms*. As an American poet of Iranian descent, Sharif offers a profound perspec-

tive on how American foreign policy must necessarily be interrogated through the lens of its own violent lexicon – the way 'LOOK' refers to 'a period during which a mine circuit is receptive of an influence' – even as the speaker confronts a war-mongering Republican: 'You would put up with TORTURE, *you mean* and he proclaimed: *Yes*;', then offers a heart-wrenching aside: 'whereas I thought if he would LOOK at my exquisite face / or my father's, he would reconsider;'. *Look* highlights the casualties of imperialism, the innumerable ways in which, for most, 'there is no part of your life that has not been somehow violently decided for you by a narrative that was established before you were even born' ('An Interview with Solmaz Sharif', *The Paris Review*).

The opening poem, 'Look', is one of the collection's most thought-provoking, its 'whereas' statements allowing the speaker to marry disparate realities that are often unbearable for us to associate: the callous ease with which fighter jets routinely conflate a 'child' for a 'dog', or track a human's body heat in order to locate a 'PIN-POINT TARGET', which Sharif poignantly defines as 'one lit desk lamp / and a nightgown walking past the window':

> Whereas years after they LOOK down from their jets
> and declare my mother's Abadan block PROBABLY
> DESTROYED, we walked by the villas, the faces
> of buildings torn off into dioramas, and recorded it
> on a handheld camcorder:
>
> Whereas it could take as long as 16 seconds between
> the trigger pulled in Las Vegas and the Hellfire missile
> Landing in Mazar-e-Sharif, after which they will ask
> *Did we hit a child? No. A dog.* they will answer themselves;
> [...]
> Whereas my lover made my heat rise, rise so that if heat
> sensors were trained on me, they could read
> my THERMAL SHADOW through the roof and through
> the wardrobe;
> [...]
> Whereas I cannot control my own heat and it can take
> as long as 16 seconds between the trigger, the Hellfire
> missile, and *A dog.* they will answer themselves;
> [...]
> Let it matter what we call a thing.
> Let it be the exquisite face for at least 16 seconds.
> Let me LOOK at you.
> Let me LOOK at you in a light that takes years to get here.

As the 2017 Poetry Book Society Autumn Choice, Pascale Petit's *Mama Amazonica* lyrically fuses the traumas stemming from her mother's experiences as a survivor of rape and sexual abuse with the horrors of species extinction in the Peruvian Amazon. Often, the mother figure is rendered as plant, animal or insect, the human flickering within:

> She's drawing the night-flying scarabs
> into the crucible of her mind.
>
> Over and over they land
> and burrow into her lace.
>
> By dawn she closes her petals.
>   ('Mama Amazonica')

Petit navigates the corridors of mental health through her deft use of metaphor, conveying at once the tribulations of mental illness and the excruciating impact it has on the speaker who is 'trying to sew her [mother] / back together, / to make a patchwork / of gold dusk / and ghost vines' ('Jaguar Girl'). Given the dazzling imagery which pervades *Mama Amazonica*, the poems which pare back their use of language are particularly effective:

> *Comfort your mother*
> Dr Pryce says.
>
> My mama is perched
> on top of the wardrobe

growling. She's holding
her spider monkey teddy
in her six-inch talons

> the way she used to hold my hand
> when we crossed the boulevard
>
> and I let go
>
> because being hit by cars
> felt so much safer.
>   ('Her Harpy Eagle Claws')

The allure of this poem lies in its ability to convey the devastating anguish which underpins the speaker's understanding of her mother's 'paranoia' – a wildness which no medicine appears able to tame. We are invited to consider the profound impact this has on a growing child, her mother's hands morphing into 'six-inch talons', menacing and lethal. The abrupt statement 'and I let go' appears to mirror the speaker's decision to abandon her mother, as exemplified by the poem's momentary disintegration from couplets into a single, solitary line. The speaker fears her mother's many states of 'psychosis', which inadvertently pose a threat to her daughter's sense of safety and selfhood. As an adult, the speaker 'enter[s] the hospital like a fawn who must be sacrificed', the visceral encounter between mother and child evoking memories of her mother's capacity for self-harm:

> Dr Pryce says I set fire to myself last night but I say
> the flames are jaguar tails and my cigarette burns are spots.
>   ('Waterlily-Jaguar')

While the collection does not offer any clear sense of redemption, its tensile strength brings to mind W. H. Auden's elegiac line on W. B. Yeats: 'Mad Ireland hurt you into poetry'. Petit too appears to write productively from a place of hurt, her wounds transmuted into art: 'your broken mama / laid out like a long-table / for the rest of your life to feast on.'

Pas de Politics

A Monkey at the Window: Selected Poems, Al-Saddiq Al-Raddi, translated by Sarah Maguire and Mark Ford (Bloodaxe) £12

Reviewed by N. J. STALLARD

Al-Saddiq Al-Raddi's *A Monkey at the Window* is an unusual collection of selected poems, as the selection process excludes one of the Sudanese writer's most popular forms – his political poetry.

Unlike the censorship in his native Sudan, which ranked 174 out of 180 countries on the Press Freedom Index 2016, the exclusion is not due to Al-Saddiq Al-Raddi's political ideas. In her introduction to *A Monkey at the Window*, Sarah Maguire, who co-translated the collection with Mark Ford, writes how the 'avowedly political poetry' is 'not translated here since the density of its contextual references makes it all but impenetrable to outsiders.' The poet's words are so entwined with Sudan's histories and collective memories that the poems are resistant to the act of translation itself.

Known as one of the leading African poets writing in Arabic, Al-Saddiq Al-Raddi is an important figure in Sudanese and Arabic poetry. Born in Omdurman, Khartoum in 1969, he was a published poet by the age of fifteen. In 2012 he was sacked from his position as cultural editor of *Al-Sudani* newspaper and subsequently exiled. In an interview with *The Guardian* in 2006, the poet was reluctant to promote his role as an activist and pointed to the work of underground writers in Sudan instead. 'There are poets who are political activists and members of underground organisations,' he said, 'and there are poets like myself who do not participate actively in underground organisations, but who have strong political views and a strong vision which has sometimes landed them in trouble.'

A Monkey at the Window is therefore a strange creature – a slim collection of thirty-one poems, with the original Arabic poem and its English translation neatly presented side by side, like the reflection of trees on a still lake. Sudan's vast array of cultures and millennia of history are expertly filtered through Al-Saddiq Al-Raddi's vivid and deft lyrical mode. Love poems and tender childhood self-portraits sit alongside more complex meditations on Sudanese history and the role of language and the writer, such as the sequences 'Poem on the Nile' and 'Weaving a World'.

The latter poem, co-translated by Mark Ford and Hafiz Kheir, is a good example of the collection's agile translation:

How beautifully you offered
me the moon, as I caressed
away your tears, and you, alight
with love, thrust
at my vitals with a kitchen knife.
Was I here   or there?
How one we were!

The collection also includes a series of commissioned poems from a residency at the Petrie Museum of Egyptian Archaeology in London, inspired by the museum's collection of Sudanese artefacts, such as the grave goods from the isolated burial of a woman on the east bank of the Nile and a crouching frog carved from limestone:

When I first saw him alone, lost in thought,
poised behind glass,
I recalled how his sperm had once spawned from the suck of
    motherly mud
to snatch prey with spit

Throughout Al-Saddiq Al-Raddi's poetry, the past is an unresolved state. History is cyclical and restless – the centres never hold. The figure of the poet searches for a Sufi-like transcendence but also for accountability among the broken cities. Whether in ancient Meroe or contemporary Khartoum, Al-Saddiq Al-Raddi asks what will survive, what will be recorded or who will be blamed? As the short poem 'Record' abruptly ends:

Memories of cities - fall
Expectations - fall
Histories of forgery - fall

Believing in the invisible

Nothing Is Lost
Selected Poems

Jordi Doce
Translated by Lawrence Schimel

Jordi Doce, *Nothing is Lost: Selected Poems*, trans. Lawrence Schimel (Shearsman); Ron Winkler, *Fragmented Waters*, trans. Jake Schneider (Shearsman)

Reviewed by IAN SEED

Jordi Doce's *Nothing is Lost* brings together poems selected from six collections published in Spanish between 1990 and 2011. This is the first translation in book form of Doce's work into English, and Lawrence Schimel has done such a good job that for the most part readers will forget they are reading poems that were written in another language. It should also be pointed out that the spirit of Doce's poems is perhaps as much English as anything else. In his 'Author's Note', Jordi states that many of these poems were written during his stay in England from 1991 to 2000, and acknowledges a debt to English poetry, which he has studied and translated. Although they are 'determinedly rooted in the Spanish literary tradition', he goes onto say that 'poetry is born in part out of a contrary dialogue with one's own heritage, and English literature has given me a much-needed vantage point from which to examine and re-evaluate my own Spanish tradition' (p. 115).

Doce's work is threaded through with the kind of agnostic faith that the theologian Paul Tillich described as 'ultimate concern'. In a manner reminiscent of different figures such as Blake, Rilke and Eliot, Doce seeks to penetrate to the heart of the meaning of our existence. Ever present is a sense of astonishment, as, for example, in 'Succession' (p. 45), a prose poem dedicated to his daughter, Paula:

Is birth the victory? Victory over what? From the faithful certainty of your body, my question watches you questioning me. You have not conquered death. Death is not the nothingness before life. The miraculous is this: you come from the nameless, from non-existence. You were inconceivable. Now, conceived, you are the clearest face of existence [...] At what moment did you cease to be us? [...] We'd like [...] certainty that converses and confirms us in time's home.

There is an aching for a sense of aliveness, or for a state of innocence before intellect and language came between us and the world as it is, for a time 'when the mere existence / of things / imprinted on one's eyes / cleanly' ('Ancient Flight', p. 86). Everyday observations lead to a glimpse of the transcendent. What we see will point beyond itself if we allow ourselves to be open:

I've followed, from up above,
from beside the careless trembling of the curtains,
the flight of this sparrow, so intimate,
making the air wider,
unravelling a sky
between the parterre and the swings
[...]

two wings leave behind their wake,
force me to believe in the invisible
   ('Sparrow', p. 84)

Jordi clearly believes that it is the task of the poet to investigate the ways in which the physical can reveal the metaphysical, yet knows that language, however artful, can never replicate reality, always beyond our reach:

Not even if you paint it
to scale, or in relief,
with exacting mimetic detail,
the beak in its place,
feathers as prescribed by the manual,
not even then will that little fowl
take off in flight
   ('Warning', p. 36)

Rather, as Doce puts it, we need to 'make a hollow in air' (ibid.), to create a kind of Heideggerian space in order to feel something of the presence of being. Language will never be adequate to the task. Nevertheless, it is a gift that we humans have, and it imposes on us a duty to attempt to give a meaning to the world we live in, however much existence may be governed by chance. Indeed, it is in the opportunities offered by chance that we will discover the stories of our lives, and be able to affirm all that they have to offer.

Ron Winkler's *Fragments of Water* is a collection of poems which could also be described as life-affirming, but here the affirmation comes through a delicious playfulness of language, full of unexpected twists and turns, continually shifting registers of tone, and a witty use of puns and neologisms. As Jake Schneider points out in his 'Translator's Note', a 'word, in a Ron Winkler poem, is a double agent' (p. 85). To convey the effect of the original German, Schneider has had to invent a few words of his own in English, a task no translator would envy, but which Schneider manages with great skill and delightful effect, for example 'evangelephant ears', 'breathalizably' and 'bonnet-bee software'. Winkler has published four collections in German. *Fragments of Water* is the first to be translated into English, and has left this reviewer hungry for more.

As with the work of John Ashbery (we are all now of course in a post-Ashbery age), one has the feeling of a chorus of many different, often deliberately dissonant voices meeting, separating and coming together again. Nevertheless, the poems tend to be grouped around themes, such as observations of animals and nature, the nature of language and its relationship to reality, and the way technology can shape our perceptions (confusing reality with virtual reality). Above all, Winkler makes great use of the imagery of water and the way it permeates so much of what is within and beyond our field of vision.

There is never any straightforward prose sense to these poems, but they are instantly engaging and ring true with their playful, fragmented lyricism, at times reminiscent of Gertrude Stein's *Tender Buttons*:

apron was a border as porous as twilight.

we could sense kisses behind it like mute crickets

though that quiet cream hardly trickled
    ('little house on the Saale', p. 9).

As with the work of British poet Jeremy Over, impossible things seem as if they might just be possible if we surrender to a sleight-of-hand in our perceptions, for example in these haiku-like observations from the poem 'maritime visit diagnostic' (p. 13):

by all accounts, the colors of the sea
seem overexcitable.

yet the water strikes you as rather thin.

there's a competition between things: two windswept pines
rivaling for aesthetic inclines.

the tide inexhaustible – you could say
it was making payments on a larger debt.

the wind stroking the sea like an enthusiastic father.

The compact nature of the language – it is impossible to find a wasted word in this book – combined with the richness and arresting qualities of the imagery, creates an enchanting pastoral or ecological poetry, with links to modernist predecessors such as Wallace Steven's 'Thirteen Ways of Looking at a Blackbird'. Winkler's poems highlight the interconnectedness of the 'natural' and 'artificial', of language and reality, of the empirical and transcendent. Perhaps language is ultimately the only tool we have to make sense of the world 'out there', but we can have great fun with this in our attempt to do so. Who, after all, could resist the following?

so these cows, right, were parading
around like absurd typewriters.
for that matter they weren't cows at all.
more like black-and-white moments caught in pixels.
and no typewriter could muck up
a meadow. whatever. what mattered
was the blink-of-an-eye-ness of a thing.
together with airy psyche, right [...]
 here
the meadow and there the contorted messages
of their horns. eyes
like uninhabited planets. cows, right,
as agreed upon, cows –
at the end of their biography.
    ('x-referential field portrait', p. 82)

Some of the work in *Fragmented Waters* can be read as satire of other genres, for example sentimental verse, the realist novel, or the travel journal. However, for the most part it springs from a wider European tradition of nonsense literature, which offers us, as Chesterton once stated, 'an escape into a world in which things are not fixed horribly in an eternal appropriateness'. We are all the more fortunate for that.

Thrift

Rae Armantrout, *Party: New and Selected Poems 2001–2015* (Wesleyan University Press) $28

Reviewed by IAN POPLE

Rae Armantrout's vatic, spare poems have, for some time, been amongst the most lauded from the L-A-N-G-U-A-G-E poets of North America. The blurb accompanying this volume describes the poems as, variously, 'refined', 'visionary', and 'potent, compact meditations'. And much of that is true. The poems very seldom run longer than one side of the page, and, even at that length may contain two or three sub-sections, each comprising not more than six or seven lines; each section separated by a short, horizontal line on the page. The titles are often only a single word, and there is an amusing irony in the fact that 'What We Can Say' is, at four words, the longest title in the book.

There is a kind of centripetal quality in all this brevity. In a poem such as, 'Life's Work', that inward pull is quite literally present. The 'I' that begins each line feels very deliberately the 'empirical' Rae Armantrout, even where the tensions emerge from contradiction, 'Did I say I was a creature/ of habit? // I meant the opposite. // I meant behaviour / is a pile of clothes // I might or might not wear.' The sparse syntax and the short lines freight the poem so that the reader moves slowly down the page, at the same time as Armantrout draws the reader into her world, with the pun on 'habit'.

That sense of the centripetal combined with the short titles and the very short lines creates immense pressure within the poems. This pressure is, perhaps, where Armantrout scores as a L-A-N-G-U-A-G-E poet. Although each poem moves the reader very quickly amongst 'things', there is a chance for those 'things' to resonate, so that the poems have a music in both the language and in the disposition of the ideas. 'Versed' begins with this short section: 'The self-monitoring function / of each cell / "writ large," // personified – / a person.' And the next section, states, 'The "Issues of the Day" / are mulled steadily / by surrogates.' The movement of the poem starts with this science 'statement', which is not a statement as the grammar is not that of a sentence. The next section then suggests that the 'monitoring' of the first section, has become the 'mulling' of the second, but this time the monitoring is not 'self-monitoring' but it is 'mulling' by 'surrogates'. The 'message', if we dare call it that, of the poem, moves from the self, to someone who stands instead that self. Then in the next section, the fragmented grammar pushes that message into an exploration of metaphor, which is both on the surface of the text but also a critique of the text, 'Metaphor forms / a crust / beneath which / the crevasse / of each experience'. Though what the crevasse actually 'does' we do not find out; even in the rest of the poem. The poems heft the language, and foreground that hefting, but they do not leave the reader bereft of a kind of semantic purchase. If Armantrout 'teases' the reader, she does so in ways which are playful rather than baffling.

And, for all her allegiance to radical poetics, Armantrout is not afraid to make political points, as in the poem 'Voices', the final section of which concludes: 'Men in uniforms / are clubbing onlookers. // I've been informed / this is all for show. // Those are not real / audience members.' This is a viperish irony, and its skilled, careful construction and deployment is a testament to the expertise on show throughout this satisfying volume.

Brevity, eternity

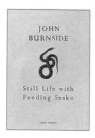

John Burnside, *Still Life with Feeding Snake* (Cape); Roy Fisher, *Slakki; New and Neglected Poems* (Bloodaxe)

Reviewed by JOHN MUCKLE

These two poets, a generation apart, seem an oddly assorted pairing. But both – the younger a Catholic, the older resolutely secular – grapple with the thinginess of things, and the tragedy in human stories, and try to make something larger of it; to construct something upon which to rejoice, in T. S. Eliot's phrase from 'Ash Wednesday'. For Burnside this impulse is religiously motivated; for Fisher the necessity springs from circumstance. He came (so he thought) from a land of ashes.

John Burnside's poetry bristles with narrative and drama, is alive with vivid observations and turns of vocabulary, much of it supplied by the ready-made empyrean of his inherited faith, here often crystallised around the figure of his mother, as 'script and ideal', a Stevensian idea of order. He is an allegorical writer, a storyteller, and it is on this level, despite his passing beauties of language – the level of narratives and how we read them – that meaning springs from his deftly managed syntax. He understands delay, closure, and how to withhold both of these things in order to scratch his reader's itch for them. 'The Beauties of Nature and the Wonders of the World We Live In' sets the story of Saul's blindness and recovery against another story of a man, blind from birth, who regains his sight only to be disappointed by the actuality of the visible world compared to his imagining of it. He has slowly to learn how to accept and appreciate the look of things, just as Saul has to learn to be patient before God restores his sight, to live with separation and doubt.

His storybook title sets up an expectation of homily, which Burnside in the end satisfies, whilst declaring himself to be on the side of those who must wait in frustration and face disappointment: a hard lesson on accepting the ineluctable will of old poker face. The Book of Job springs to mind. His title poem is another compressed narrative, drawing readers eager for the temptation of Eve, this time about a painter who is reluctant to tear himself away from his *wabi-sabi* art-making when called upon to do so by his wife to witness a snake swallowing a bird under their house. His reluctance to do so, his perfunctory glance, he decides finally, makes him no less a predator than the innocently feeding snake. And he looks for his partner to ask her forgiveness. Without her tenderness and patience he couldn't be an artist. If this summary sounds banal, it's excellent in the telling; but there does tend to be a pat answer being delivered by a wise priest.

Christian mysteries aside, Burnside is also attracted by the heroism and misadventures of the Russian cosmonauts, perhaps as a modern, secular version of the Prometheus myth, and the lost crew of the *Soyuz 3* space station recur in childhood dream-images commemorating a lost world-view and a lost brother. And yet the poetry is often built out of the momentary, the half-understood and early painful memories – which keep it human and moving even as we wait for it all to be reconfigured by God, wrestling with our doubts, or just living unresolved in the mundane. But this fine book contains at least a passing allusion to that most alluded to Williams 'thingy' poem, the one about nicking the plums, in:

> I am the boy who stole the sodium
> and dropped a single drain
> into the fish tank.
>
> Forgive me; but I never thought of this
> as malice,
>
> only another instance of that idiom
> where anything intact is set aside
> as inadmissible.
> ('Self-Portrait as Blue Baby', p. 18)

Haunted by a sort of inquisitive destructiveness, and pointless suffering, Burnside is continually looking around for grounds for belief.

Roy Fisher – early, whimsical; later, wry – was a completely secular writer, and was never a Marxist either. He had no grand narratives to bounce around. In an afterword expressing a likeable blend of modesty and arrogance he tells us how these 1950s and '60s poems came to be neglected. They were offcuts from his Fulcrum Press *Collected Poems* (1968), judiciously excised by his editor Stuart Montgomery and thereafter forgotten by later publishers. Fisher presents himself as careless of his own work, always rather stupidly running into dead ends, but pursued by editors and bibliographers: a condition he takes for granted, flattering as it is, but somewhat galling to any writer who hasn't been continually hounded into print. What made him so good? Fisher himself would be the last person to ask, but he seems to know.

Fisher describes himself as 'ineducable in philosophy, in observation passable', and casual readers of this book might agree, but it is partly the lack of an identifiable

From the Archive

Issue 140, July–August 2001

TOGARA MUZANENHAMO

From a contribution of fourteen
poems, alongside 'Hawker
(Johannesburg)' and 'Winter'.
Fellow contributors to this issue
include John Ashberry, Yehuda
Halevi, Lawrence Sail, Jeffrey
Wainwright and Matthew Welton.

MAN IN THE BOWLER HAT
for Anna

I am now the dislocated stranger
Stationed somewhere in your thoughts,
Dreams, or on the mundane streets you walk:

My back turned, face concealed or obliterated.
Although I am everywhere you fail to notice –
Bunched amongst myself and alone.

I can never speak but only ever stand;
A whole legion of myself, an entire place
Of a faceless face – obstructed or draped [...]

---

logos or particularly vivid descriptive powers that sup-
plies one of his poetry's enabling constraints. What else
is there, after all, except the physical world and ideas
about it? Works like *The Ship's Orchestra* and *The Cut Pages*
were constructed according to a sort of proceduralism,
and Fisher usually substitutes accounts of his aesthetic
decision making (I cut up the pages) for any account of
what he was trying to say, of his ideas in any wider sense.
Intellectual content, or the lack of it, is somehow taken
for granted, remains elusive. He tends to present himself
as a forgetful, ham-fisted bricoleur, mixing up who knows
what inefficacious medicine or preservative:

    Varnish and milk
    in equal measures. No ideas
    but in mixtures, suspensions,
    conglomerates, slags
    in variety. Apply time, note
    when the milk outstinks the varnish
        ('Bench', p. 20)

To read these final and rescued poems is to encounter
once again this paradoxical quality of Roy Fisher's writ-
ing. He demurs, he persists. He describes, presents. He
refuses to celebrate anything particularly, or to commit
himself to much more than continuing to stick things
together. Poets are generally expected to be celebrants of
something, as Burnside is in his poems about his moth-
er, but we would be hard put to find much of that in
Fisher, more of an allegedly plain man's account of how
things are, leavened by a show of playfulness of spirit,
for example in the way his father, in the unsanitary
French trenches, enjoyed 'the pleasure of making the
sharp flashes of his heliograph / go skittering over the
filth for miles' ('Signs and Signals', p. 13).

Early Fisher as salvaged here reveals an archly whim-
sical and skilled magazine poet playing about with
dilemmas of late romanticism about the bright artifici-
ality of art and the greyness of reality. Fisher is deter-
mined not to be dragged down by reality. Aestheticism,
a piss-take of the folksy ballad (about a knitting compe-
tition), a poem about an sleeping frog and a ferret
drowned by a prince's tears, which sounds as though he
had just read Edmund Wilson's *Axel's Castle*, an amusing
erotic fantasy about nuns ('A Gift of Cream') from 1955,
and an uneasy attempt to write about dustmen that
decides after all to leave them in their dusty world ('Divi-
sion of Labour'). This final section is bracketed by the
much stronger poems 'Double Morning' and 'A Vision
of Four Musicians' (1955, 1952), the former exploring these
tensions more satisfactorily as a dream of 'unknown
freedom and appetite' is left behind for 'an ashen world'
still haunted by thousands of war dead. Dreams offer
them back 'denuded of identity and pain'.

The sixties work here is leaner; there's a beat-inflected
jazz poem, and a take on Williams' variable foot which
has his triadic metre being to do with an old man walking
upstairs; but is it brief, glancingly ambiguous encounters
that have made their way back most tellingly from the
cutting room floor; a few poems stand out to sound the
Fisherian agnostic urban elegiac note – here with a touch
of Mallarme about it – that integrates these impulses,
and was the making of him:

NIGHT WALKERS

Darkness hisses at the town block's end.
Salt-glaze of sleet
Pocks fingers, coldly grits the walks
Sprung flat, like table-knives.

There's a smashed box of wind in every street,
And lamps, for startled hours,
Wistfully guard
Behind their glistening panes shaken with blows
The blanched gold cheeks
Of those we seek for miles sardonically.

Beside the sea

Thomas A Clark, *Farm by the Shore*
(Carcanet) £9.99

Reviewed by GERRY MCGRATH

Imagine if, instead of a poetry collection, the book we were given to read was a history of height. How long would it be before the feelings of anticipation and excitement we felt at being taken to the high altitudes were replaced by the familiar airsick slide to habituation? Reality in Thomas Clark's uncontrived new collection is, by small miracles, quite different. Set amongst the cheek-by-jowl landscapes of a lowland farm and a shoreline on the Fife coast in east Scotland where he has lived for more than four decades, Clark's poetry shares with the reader a vision of optimistic change that is disarmingly ambitious, modestly and unerringly sustained. That it does so while avoiding the pitfalls of an exiguous naturalistic flatlining that has claimed one or two others installs him as a poet of astute observational skills and no mean ability. His writing possesses, arguably has always had, a rare quality, a rinsed freshness that is entirely its own.

Refreshingly Clark takes issue even with the description of his poetry as 'work', preferring instead a commitment towards establishing a 'phenomena of poetry'. Such care and commitment without the pre-Reformatory zeal is a welcome addition. On the evidence of this book (and the last two) he is well on his way.

The lightness of touch in the treatment of poetic self is exquisite, reminiscent in its clarity and rigour of recent poetry from Belgium and Holland (De Coninck, Kopland, Van Hee, Gerlach, Van Vliet). The narrative excels, the shifts in mood and theme are beautifully and deftly handled; like daylight itself. Formally the collection is extremely tight, shaped by considerations of discourse and a real sense of textual as well as textural playfulness that verges on the childlike. Lyrically the book is faultless, you get a real sense of an individual poem's phrasing, its movement, contour and flow, as well as its place within the whole. Reading Clark, it can seem as if a mountain's weight may be felt in its shadow.

Farm by the Shore is a terrific book, not a formidable one. It is of its time. Thomas Clark has been writing and publishing poetry for well over forty years and the pedigree shows. This reader hopes the judges are listening over dinner:

> much that is light
> outshines itself
> dazed in a grace
> that comes to it
> as unimpeded movement
> it throws a thought
> and catches it
> farther on.

SOME CONTRIBUTORS

Anthony Rudolf is the author of *European Hours: Collected Poems* (2017) and lead editor of *Yves Bonnefoy: Poems* (2017). He is currently working on prose texts about Paula Rego, Kitaj and other painters.

Neil Powell's most recent books are *Benjamin Britten: A Life for Music* (Hutchinson, 2013) and *Was and Is: Collected Poems* (Carcanet, 2017).

Angela Leighton has published four volumes of poetry, most recently *Spills* (Carcanet 2016). A pamphlet, *Five Poems* (2018), has just been published by Clutag Press.

Ian Seed's translation of Pierre Reverdy's *Le Voleur de Talan* is published by Wakefield. His article 'Nonsense and Wonder: An Exploration of the Prose Poems of Jeremy Over' is due out in 2018 in the critical anthology *British Prose Poetry: Poems Without Lines* from Palgrave Macmillan.

Gerry McGrath has published two poetry collections, both with Carcanet. A third, *Self-portrait as a horse*, is projected for publication in 2019.

Ian Pople's *from The Evidence* is published by Melos Press.

N.J. Stallard is a writer and editor. Her work has been published in *The Guardian*, *The Atlantic*, *Ambit* and *Tank magazine*. She is currently studying poetry at the University of Manchester.

Mary Jean Chan is a co-editor at *Oxford Poetry*. She was shortlisted for the 2017 Forward Prize for Best Single Poem, and has been recently nominated for the 2018 Hawker Prize for Southeast Asian Poetry.

Vahni Capildeo's books include *Venus as a Bear* (Carcanet, 2018) and *Measures of Expatriation* (Forward Prizes Best Collection). She is the Douglas Caster Cultural Fellow at the University of Leeds.

Ned Denny's collection *Unearthly Toys* was published by Carcanet in February 2018. The three books of his version of the *Divine Comedy* (*Blaze*, *Bathe*, *Bliss*) will be published as a single volume, also with Carcanet, titled simply *B*, in 2020.

Grevel Lindop's most recent books are *Luna Park* from Carcanet and *Charles Williams: The Third Inkling* from Oxford University Press. He lives in Manchester and his website is at www.grevel.co.uk.

Kevin Gardner is professor and chair of English at Baylor University. He is the editor of *Building Jerusalem: Elegies on Parish Churches* (Bloomsbury Continuum).

George Szirtes's *Reel* (2004) won the T. S. Eliot Prize, for which he has been twice shortlisted since. His latest is *Mapping the Delta* (Bloodaxe 2016).

Lawrence Sail's *Waking Dreams: New & selected Poems* (Bloodaxe Books, 2010) was a Poetry Book Society Special Commendation. His most recent collection, *The Quick* (also Bloodaxe), came out in 2015 and a new one, *Guises*, is due from Bloodaxe next year. He is a Fellow of the Royal Society of Literature.

Rachel Mann is a parish priest and Visiting Fellow in English, Manchester Met University. Her latest book is *Fierce Imaginings: The Great War, Ritual, Memory & God*. She is a contributor to *New Poetries VII*.

Jamie Osborn founded Cambridge Student PEN and his translations of Iraqi refugee poems have appeared in *Modern Poetry in Translation* and elsewhere. His poems are forthcoming in *New Poetries VII*.

Peter Blegvad is a writer, illustrator, songwriter, broadcaster and teacher (retired). His latest album is *Go Figure* (2017). His comic strip, *The Book of Leviathan*, is published by Sort Of Books (in English) and is also available in French and Chinese.

Vahni Capildeo's books include *Venus as a Bear* (Carcanet, 2018) and *Measures of Expatriation* (Forward Prizes Best Collection). She is the Douglas Caster Cultural Fellow at the University of Leeds.

Jane Stevenson has taught at the Universities of Cambridge, Sheffield, Warwick and Aberdeen, and is now Senior Research Fellow at Campion Hall, Oxford. Publications include six novels and a variety of academic work, most recently *Baroque Between the Wars* (Oxford University Press, 2018).

John Mole's most recent collection is *Gestures and Counterpoints* (Shoestring Press). A writer for children as well as adults, his poetry for both is represented on the Poetry Archive. He has received the Gregory, Cholmondeley and Signal Awards, and plays regularly as a jazz clarinettist.

Anthony Thwaite's most recent collections have been *Collected Poems* (2007), *Late Poems* (2010) and *Going Out* (2015). He was born in 1930, has taught in universities in Japan, Libya, the United States and England, and has also worked as a literary editor.

Patricia Postgate was born in 1914 in Liverpool, where her father Thomas Eric Peet was an Egyptologist at the university. She accompanied him to his excavations at Amarna in 1921 at the age of seven. She read French and German at Oxford and married Ormond Postgate in Jerusalem in 1940. After the war like him she taught in Malvern and Winchester, dying in 2003.

Andrew Biswell is Professor of Modern Literature at Manchester Metropolitan University and a general editor of the Irwell Edition of the *Works of Anthony Burgess* (Manchester University Press).

Jane Griffiths is a Fellow and Tutor in English at Wadham College, Oxford. Her most recent collection of poems, *Silent in Finisterre*, is published by Bloodaxe Books.

Robert Wells's *Collected Poems and Translations* was published by Carcanet in 2009. A pamphlet, *A Last Look*, was published by Mica Press in 2016.

Peter Scupham was born in Liverpool. He was Head of English at St Christopher School, Letchworth. Together with his wife Margaret Steward he has restored a derelict Elizabethan Manor house in Norfolk, where they put on plays. With John Mole he founded the Mandeville Press, a small press using traditional letterpress methods of printing. The press produced hand-set editions of work by Geoffrey Grigson, Anthony Hecht, John Fuller and many others. Its archive is now in the British Library. Currently he runs a catalogue book business with his wife, specialising in English Literature. His poetry collections include *Borrowed Landscapes* (2011), *Collected Poems* (2003), *Night Watch* (1999), *Watching the Perseids* (1990) and *The Snowing Globe* (1972).

award-winning and shortlisted poetry collections
from

CARCANET

SINÉAD MORRISSEY *On Balance*

winner of the Forward Prize for Poetry (Best Collection)
shortlisted for the Costa Book Awards

CAROLINE BIRD *In These Days of Prohibition*
ROBERT MINHINNICK *Diary of the Last Man*
TARA BERGIN *The Tragic Death of Eleanor Marx*

shortlisted for the T.S. Eliot Prize

available at carcanet.co.uk and in all good book shops

LITTLE ISLAND PRESS
Publishing Services

TYPESETTING

EDITORIAL

PRODUCTION

DESIGN

A British
Book Design &
Production Award
Winner 2017

info@littleislandpress.co.uk

—————— COLOPHON ——————

Editors
Michael Schmidt (General)
Luke Allan (Deputy)
Andrew Latimer (Production)

Editorial address
The Editors at the address on
the right. Manuscripts cannot
be returned unless accompa-
nied by a stamped addressed
envelope or international reply
coupon.

Trade distributors
NBN International
10 Thornbury Road
Plymouth PL6 7PP, UK
orders@nbninternational.com

Design
Luke Allan
Typeset by Little Island Press
in Arnhem Pro.

Represented by
Compass IPS Ltd
Great West House
Great West Road, Brentford
TW8 9DF, UK
sales@compass-ips.london

Copyright
© 2017 Poetry Nation Review
All rights reserved
ISBN 978-1-78410-146-6
ISSN 0144-7076

Subscriptions (6 issues)
INDIVIDUALS (print and digital):
    £39.50; abroad £49.00
INSTITUTIONS (print only): £56.00;
    abroad £70.00
INSTITUTIONS (digital):
    subscriptions from Exact Editions
    (https://shop.exacteditions.com/
    gb/pn-review)
to: *PN Review*, Alliance House
30 Cross Street, Manchester
M2 7AQ, UK

Supported by